W9-CDV-771

THE
COMIC BOOK
STORY OF
Baseball

THE
COMIC BOOK
STORY OF

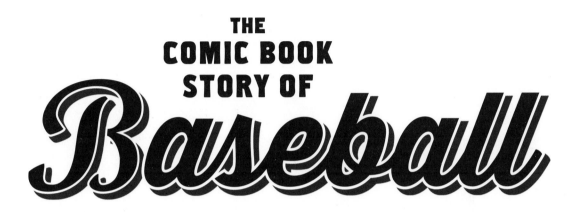

THE HEROES, HUSTLERS, AND
HISTORY-MAKING SWINGS
(AND MISSES) OF AMERICA'S
NATIONAL PASTIME

ALEX IRVINE
ART BY **TOMM COKER** AND **C.P. SMITH**

TEN SPEED PRESS
California | New York

BAT-AND-BALL GAMES ARE MENTIONED IN SOURCES FROM *HUNDREDS OF YEARS* BEFORE DOUBLEDAY IS SUPPOSED TO HAVE TAKEN OVER ELIHU PHINNEY'S COW PASTURE. EVEN *JANE AUSTEN* MENTIONS "BASE BALL" IN ONE OF HER NOVELS.

OVERRUNNETH NOT THE BAG, PRUDENCE!

PURITAN SETTLERS PLAYED *STOOLBALL*, A GAME SO OLD IT'S MENTIONED IN THE *DOMESDAY BOOK.**

*AN ELEVENTH-CENTURY SURVEY OF ENGLISH TOWNS AND POPULATIONS.

THROUGHOUT THE EIGHTEENTH CENTURY, THERE ARE MENTIONS OF *"BASE" AND "BASE-BALL"* IN VARIOUS ENGLISH SOURCES. EVEN REVOLUTIONARY WAR SOLDIERS PLAYED "BASE" WHILE TRAINING AT *VALLEY FORGE.* THEN THERE ARE *ROUNDERS, TOWN BALL,* AND SO ON.

IN 1806, EXPLORERS *LEWIS AND CLARK* HAD SOME SPARE TIME ON THEIR TRIP TO THE PACIFIC COAST, AND THEY USED IT TO TEACH THE LOCAL NEZ PERCE INDIANS *"THE GAME OF BASE."*

THERE WAS ALSO A GAME KNOWN AS *OLD CAT,* OR *ONE-OLD-CAT,* APPARENTLY AMERICAN IN ORIGIN, THAT WOULD LATER BE CLAIMED AS EVIDENCE OF BASEBALL'S AMERICAN ORIGIN. (MORE ABOUT THAT TO COME.)

BY THE EARLY 1800S, CRICKET CLUBS WERE ESTABLISHED IN THE EASTERN UNITED STATES, AND, IN PARALLEL, CAME THE FIRST ORGANIZED BASEBALL GAMES.

AT THE SAME TIME, IRONICALLY, *COOPERSTOWN, NEW YORK*--THE FUTURE HOME OF THE NATIONAL BASEBALL HALL OF FAME AND MODERN BASEBALL'S MYTHICAL EDEN--*BANNED THE PLAYING OF BASEBALL* IN THE STREETS. VIOLATORS WERE FINED ONE DOLLAR.

A DOLLAR!?

IN 1839, NEW YORK CITY FOLLOWED SUIT, BUT THE CITY ALREADY HAD AT LEAST TWO ACTIVE BASEBALL CLUBS. ONE OF THEM, LATER KNOWN AS THE *KNICKERBOCKER BASE BALL CLUB,* WROTE DOWN ITS VERSION OF THE RULES UNDER THE GUIDANCE OF A BANK CLERK BY THE NAME OF ALEXANDER CARTWRIGHT.

IF *ANYONE* CAN BE SAID TO HAVE INVENTED THE GAME AS WE KNOW IT, CARTWRIGHT IS THE GUY.

The Knickerbocker Rules

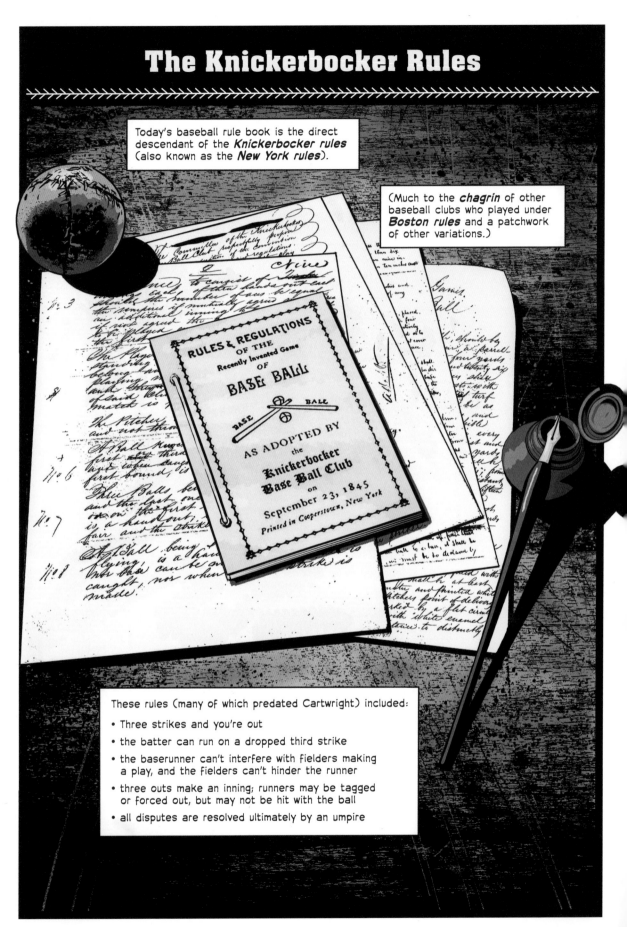

Today's baseball rule book is the direct descendant of the *Knickerbocker rules* (also known as the *New York rules*).

(Much to the *chagrin* of other baseball clubs who played under *Boston rules* and a patchwork of other variations.)

RULES & REGULATIONS
OF THE
Recently Invented Game
OF
BASE BALL

AS ADOPTED BY
the
Knickerbocker
Base Ball Club
on
September 23, 1845

Printed in Cooperstown, New York

These rules (many of which predated Cartwright) included:

- Three strikes and you're out
- the batter can run on a dropped third strike
- the baserunner can't interfere with fielders making a play, and the fielders can't hinder the runner
- three outs make an inning; runners may be tagged or forced out, but may not be hit with the ball
- all disputes are resolved ultimately by an umpire

ANOTHER INNOVATION OF THE KNICKERBOCKER RULES WAS THE STANDARDIZATION OF *FOUL TERRITORY*--ESSENTIALLY THE AREA OUTSIDE THE LINES RUNNING FROM HOME PLATE TO FIRST AND THIRD BASES. THIS GAVE THE BASEBALL FIELD ITS *SHAPE*... AND ALSO GAVE *SPECTATORS* A PLACE TO GATHER.

BY THE 1850S, THE KNICKERBOCKER RULES HAD BECOME *STANDARD*. EVEN BEFORE THAT, AROUND THE TIME THE RULES WERE LAID DOWN, *WALT WHITMAN* WAS ALREADY ENOUGH OF A BASEBALL FAN TO WRITE:

I SEE GREAT THINGS IN BASEBALL. IT'S *OUR* GAME, THE *AMERICAN* GAME.

THE RIVALRY BETWEEN THE *BOSTON* AND *NEW YORK* VERSIONS OF THE RULES WOULD GO ON FOR A WHILE (PREFIGURING THE INTENSE BOSTON-NEW YORK RIVALRY THAT *STILL* ENERGIZES CONTEMPORARY BASEBALL)...

...BUT THE *KNICKERBOCKER* RULES WOULD TRIUMPH.

EVEN SO, ORGANIZED BASEBALL WAS *STILL* PLAYED PRIMARILY IN THE NORTHEAST. IT WOULDN'T SPREAD THROUGH THE REST OF THE COUNTRY UNTIL....

TERRA INCOGNITA

BASEBALL PLAYED HERE

THE CIVIL WAR

NOW, LET'S GET BACK TO ABNER DOUBLEDAY, WHO HAD *NOTHING* TO DO WITH THE INVENTION OF BASEBALL, BUT DID *FIRE THE NORTH'S FIRST SHOT* IN THE CIVIL WAR WHEN HE RETURNED FIRE FROM A BESIEGED FORT SUMTER.

FIRE!

DOUBLEDAY MAKES *NO REFERENCE TO BASEBALL* IN ANY OF HIS CIVIL WAR PAPERS, BUT PLENTY OF OTHER SOLDIERS DID.

THE GAME SPREAD AMONG UNION SOLDIERS AT FIRST--A LEGENDARY GAME ON HILTON HEAD ISLAND IN 1862 REPORTEDLY SAW *FORTY THOUSAND SPECTATORS*--AND THEN TO THE CONFEDERATES BY MEANS OF *PRISONER-OF-WAR CAMPS.*

BY THE END OF THE WAR, THE GAME HAD SPREAD WHEREVER SOLDIERS HAD FOUGHT. IT WAS ALREADY BEING REFERRED TO AS THE *"NATIONAL PASTIME."*

IN THE AFTERMATH OF THE WAR, *BASEBALL* WAS ONE OF THE THINGS THAT BEGAN TO KNIT THE COUNTRY BACK TOGETHER.

IT WAS NOT THE LAST TIME THAT BASEBALL WOULD SERVE THIS FUNCTION, AS YOU WILL SEE IN THE PAGES AHEAD.

AS THE GAME SPREAD, *AFRICAN AMERICANS AND WOMEN* PLAYED, TOO. VASSAR COLLEGE (A WOMEN'S COLLEGE UNTIL 1969) STARTED A BASEBALL TEAM IN 1866.

IN 1875, THE FIRST PROFESSIONAL GAME *BETWEEN WOMEN'S TEAMS* WAS PLAYED IN SPRINGFIELD, ILLINOIS.

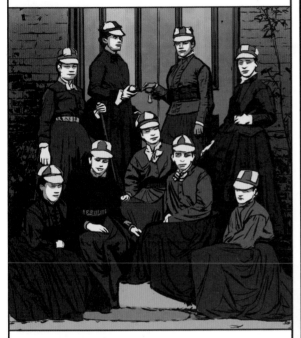

THE FIRST ORGANIZED BLACK TEAM WAS THE PYTHIAN BASEBALL CLUB OF PHILADELPHIA, CHARTERED IN 1867.

THE PYTHIANS PLAYED IN WHAT IS PROBABLY THE *FIRST GAME BETWEEN ORGANIZED BLACK AND WHITE TEAMS*--AGAINST THE PHILADELPHIA OLYMPICS IN 1869.

IN ADDITION TO BEING A SUPERB INFIELDER, THE PYTHIANS' FOUNDER *OCTAVIUS V. CATTO* WAS ALSO A CIVIL WAR *VETERAN* AND EARLY CIVIL RIGHTS *ACTIVIST.*

HE WAS *MURDERED* ON ELECTION DAY 1871 WHILE ORGANIZING AFRICAN AMERICAN VOTERS.

The First Curveball

The inventor of the *curveball* is widely assumed to be William Arthur "Candy" Cummings, who reportedly began throwing it in *1867*, while with the Brooklyn Excelsiors. The pitch not only confounded hitters but also catchers, who at the time positioned themselves twenty feet or so behind the batter. It wasn't until Cummings was paired up with a new catcher in 1870 with the Brooklyn Stars that he could throw the pitch in a game. That catcher was *Nat Hicks*, who singlehandedly revolutionized the position by getting into his crouch *directly behind the hitter* so he could receive Cummings's curve. Catchers have played that way ever since, making Nat Hicks one of the unsung revolutionaries of the game.

Fred Goldsmith, another candidate for inventor of the curveball, demonstrated the pitch for legendary sportswriter and baseball historian *Henry Chadwick* on August 16, 1870--when Goldsmith was just *fourteen years old!* Despite this recorded demonstration, Chadwick later supported Cummings's claim to inventing the pitch.

AT THIS POINT, IN THE 1860s, BASEBALL CLUBS WERE STILL *TECHNICALLY AMATEUR*, BUT PLAYERS HAD BEEN PAID *UNDER THE TABLE* SINCE THE FIRST ORGANIZED LEAGUES EMERGED.

THEN, IN 1869, THE INEVITABLE HAPPENED: THE *CINCINNATI RED STOCKINGS* BECAME THE FIRST *ALL-PROFESSIONAL* BASEBALL TEAM.

HERE, KID. JUST BETWEEN YOU AND ME. FOR THAT *THING* YOU DID.

THE RED STOCKINGS FINISHED 1869 *UNDEFEATED*, WITH A RECORD OF EITHER 54–0 OR 70–0 DEPENDING ON HOW YOU COUNT EXHIBITIONS.

OWNERS HIRED PLAYERS FOR OTHER JOBS AT INFLATED WAGES... OR *"REIMBURSED"* PLAYERS FOR *"EXPENSES."*

WHAT'S HE PAYING YOU? I'LL BEAT IT BY *TEN DOLLARS* A GAME.

THE UNITED STATES OF AMERICA WAS *GROWING UP*, AND *BASEBALL* GREW RIGHT ALONG WITH IT. LEAGUES ALSO BECAME ASSOCIATED WITH *GAMBLING INTERESTS*. THIS WORRIED OWNERS, WHO SAW A NEED FOR A SINGLE ORGANIZATION WITH *REAL AUTHORITY* OVER ITS MEMBERS.

IN OTHER WORDS, A *FULLY PROFESSIONAL* LEAGUE.

SMALL LEAGUES PROLIFERATED, AND TEAMS QUICKLY *MASTERED THE ART* OF STEALING EACH OTHER'S PLAYERS.

WE MUST GET *GAMBLING* OUT OF OUR GAME.

AND STOP THIS *MOVEMENT OF PLAYERS.* THE *BUGS** NEED TO KNOW THEIR FAVORITES WILL STAY PUT.

WE NEED *ONE* LEAGUE--WITH ENFORCEABLE *RULES*.

THEN WE'LL MAKE SOME *REAL MONEY.*

*"BUGS" AND "CRANKS" WERE TWO EARLY TERMS FOR FANS. THE WORD "FAN" DID NOT COME INTO COMMON USE UNTIL THE 1880s.

Baseball on Tour: Golden Spike

The driving of the *golden spike* at Promontory Summit, Utah, on May 10, 1869, marked the ceremonial completion of the Transcontinental Railroad, which *linked America's Atlantic and Pacific coasts* for the first time.

Western migration was already spreading baseball *beyond the Mississippi*, too. The first recorded game in San Francisco occurred in 1851, and by the mid-1860s there was an established baseball scene there and in Sacramento.

The Cincinnati Red Stockings took advantage of the *Transcontinental Railroad* to embark on a western tour that included eight games in California and two in Nebraska. Between September 25 and October 12, they outscored their opposition by a collective 526–53.

THE NATIONAL LEAGUE

IN 1876, OWNERS OF SEVERAL PROMINENT BALL CLUBS--LED BY CHICAGO WHITE STOCKINGS OWNER WILLIAM HULBERT--GOT TOGETHER AND FORMED THE NATIONAL LEAGUE (NL) OF PROFESSIONAL BASEBALL CLUBS.

ITS CHARTER MEMBERS WERE:

BOSTON RED STOCKINGS

CHICAGO WHITE STOCKINGS

CINCINNATI RED STOCKINGS

HARTFORD DARK BLUES

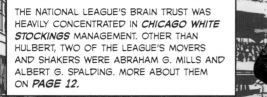
LOUISVILLE GRAYS

NEW YORK MUTUALS

PHILADELPHIA ATHLETICS

ST. LOUIS BROWN STOCKINGS

THE NATIONAL LEAGUE'S BRAIN TRUST WAS HEAVILY CONCENTRATED IN *CHICAGO WHITE STOCKINGS* MANAGEMENT. OTHER THAN HULBERT, TWO OF THE LEAGUE'S MOVERS AND SHAKERS WERE ABRAHAM G. MILLS AND ALBERT G. SPALDING. MORE ABOUT THEM ON *PAGE 12*.

THE NATIONAL LEAGUE'S EARLY YEARS WERE TURBULENT, AS THEY *BATTLED FOR SUPREMACY* AGAINST OTHER LEAGUES AND SAW SEVERAL OF THEIR CHARTER MEMBERS *FOLD* FOR FINANCIAL REASONS

NORTHWESTERN LEAGUE (1883 - 1887)

PLAYER'S LEAGUE (1890 - 1890)

UNION ASSOCIATION (1884 - 1884)

AMERICAN ASSOCIATION (1882 - 1891)

HOWEVER, BY 1890, THE NATIONAL LEAGUE HAD ESTABLISHED ITSELF AS AMERICA'S *PREEMINENT* PROFESSIONAL BASEBALL LEAGUE.

THE RIVAL AMERICAN ASSOCIATION PROVED HARDEST TO GET RID OF. ITS TEAMS SOLD *ALCOHOL* AT THEIR GAMES AND KEPT TICKET PRICES LOW TO ATTRACT *BLUE-COLLAR* FANS.

Who's Who in the National League

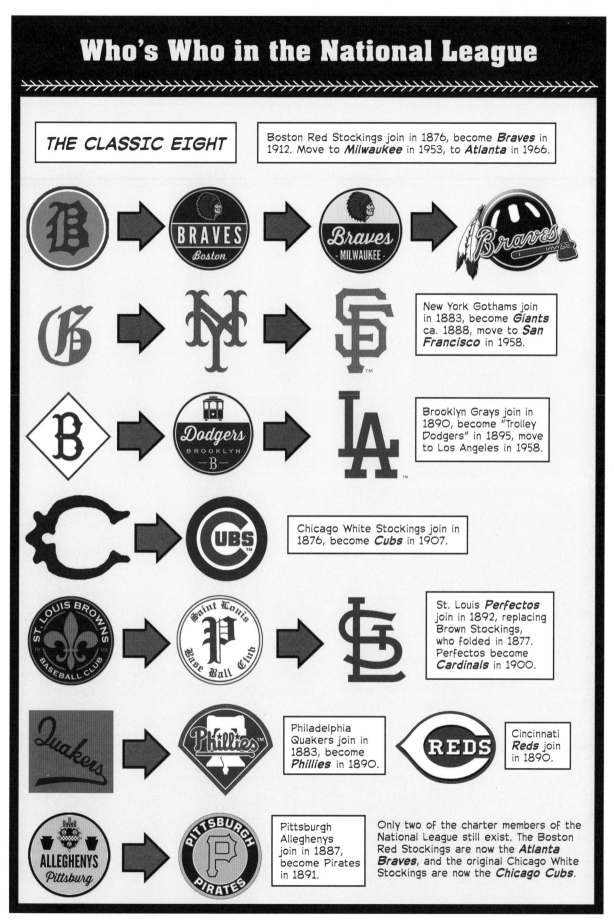

THE CLASSIC EIGHT

Boston Red Stockings join in 1876, become *Braves* in 1912. Move to *Milwaukee* in 1953, to *Atlanta* in 1966.

New York Gothams join in 1883, become *Giants* ca. 1888, move to *San Francisco* in 1958.

Brooklyn Grays join in 1890, become "Trolley Dodgers" in 1895, move to Los Angeles in 1958.

Chicago White Stockings join in 1876, become *Cubs* in 1907.

St. Louis *Perfectos* join in 1892, replacing Brown Stockings, who folded in 1877. Perfectos become *Cardinals* in 1900.

Philadelphia Quakers join in 1883, become *Phillies* in 1890.

Cincinnati *Reds* join in 1890.

Pittsburgh Alleghenys join in 1887, become Pirates in 1891.

Only two of the charter members of the National League still exist. The Boston Red Stockings are now the *Atlanta Braves*, and the original Chicago White Stockings are now the *Chicago Cubs*.

HULBERT DIED IN 1882, LEAVING MILLS AND SPALDING IN CHARGE OF THE NATIONAL LEAGUE'S FORTUNES. MILLS HAD BEEN ONE OF THE PLAYERS IN THAT *FAMOUS HILTON HEAD GAME* DURING THE CIVIL WAR, AND ALWAYS SAID THAT HE TOOK A BAT AND BALL WITH HIM *WHEREVER HE WENT* DURING CAMPAIGNS.

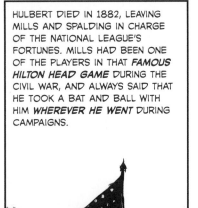

SPALDING HAD BEEN TOO YOUNG TO SERVE IN THE WAR. IN THE 1870S, HE WAS A *HOTSHOT PITCHER* WHO FOLLOWED THE MONEY FROM CHICAGO TO BOSTON.

AS HE GOT OLDER AND MOVED INTO A MANAGEMENT ROLE, HE CAME HOME TO CHICAGO AND WAS INSTRUMENTAL IN THE CREATION OF THE *NATIONAL LEAGUE*--WHILE STILL PLAYING.

SPALDING WAS ALSO A *PIONEER* IN THE DESIGN OF *BASEBALL GLOVES* (AND IN ENDORSEMENT DEALS).

SPALDING FOUNDED A SPORTING-GOODS COMPANY TO SUPPLY TEAMS, AND WORE ONE OF HIS OWN GLOVES DURING PLAY.

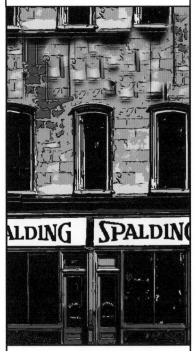

THE COMPANY, *SPALDING SPORTING GOODS*, SURVIVES TO THIS DAY.

AMONG SPALDING'S OTHER INNOVATIONS WAS THE CONCEPT OF *SPRING TRAINING*. IN 1886, HE TOOK THE WHITE STOCKINGS TO *HOT SPRINGS, ARKANSAS*, WHICH SOON BECAME A POPULAR SPRING-TRAINING SPOT FOR OTHER TEAMS AS WELL.

HE ALSO PUBLISHED THE FIRST OFFICIAL BASEBALL RULE BOOK--WHICH STATED THAT ONLY *SPALDING BALLS* COULD BE USED.

SPALDING'S OWNERSHIP MASTERSTROKE OCCURRED IN THE OFF-SEASON OF 1883, WHEN HE MET WITH THE HONCHOS OF THE NORTHWESTERN LEAGUE AND THE AMERICAN ASSOCIATION. DUBBED THE *"HARMONY CONFERENCE,"* THIS GATHERING PRODUCED ONE OF THE MOST HATED BITS OF RULE-MAKING IN THE HISTORY OF AMERICAN PROFESSIONAL SPORTS: THE *RESERVE CLAUSE*.

IT WASN'T LONG BEFORE THE NORTHWESTERN LEAGUE AND THE AMERICAN ASSOCIATION WENT *BELLY-UP*, BECAUSE THEY COULD NO LONGER POACH PLAYERS FROM NATIONAL LEAGUE CLUBS.

NORTHWESTERN LEAGUE

AMERICAN ASSOCIATION

Glove Work

Some other players were already wearing gloves by the time Spalding took the mound with one sometime in 1877; however, the practice wasn't universal. Glove-wearing players were often *mocked*. Spalding helped change that, by the force of his star power. Remember, he was a great pitcher, *probably the best* of the 1870s. It also helped that by 1877 he had started his own sporting-goods company. Stars of the day such as *Michael Joseph "King" Kelly* endorsed Spalding gloves, and so did Spalding himself, in advertising for his own company.

1860   1880   1900   1920

1940   1950   1970   2016

By the 1890s, nearly every player wore gloves. In 1895, new rules were published (in Spalding's own baseball magazine, of course) *standardizing* their dimensions. The next innovation would come in 1920, when St. Louis pitcher Bill Doak patented the *leather-strap design* that gave the glove its "pocket," as we know it. By this time, A. G. Spalding's sporting-goods company was worth several million dollars. He was as good at *marketing* as he was at *pitching*.

The Reserve Clause

The reserve clause held that each team could *"reserve"* eleven players every season, preventing those players from playing anywhere else and *stripping them of any negotiating power* they might have. Players were essentially at the mercy of club ownership. Generations of baseball greats tried to challenge the reserve clause, but it survived every challenge until 1975, when St. Louis outfielder Curt Flood took his case all the way to the Supreme Court and *baseball free agency* (see page 128) was born.

1888

BASEBALL THEN SWUNG FULLY INTO ITS FIRST *GOLDEN AGE.* THERE WAS RELATIVE STABILITY, A LITTLE BIT OF *MONEY* FOR THE PLAYERS (AND A *LOT* FOR THE OWNERS). AS AMERICA ASSUMED A MORE PROMINENT ROLE IN WORLD AFFAIRS, BASEBALL OWNERS SAW A CHANCE TO DO A LITTLE *MARKET EXPANSION.*

THIS LED TO BASEBALL'S FIRST *INTERNATIONAL TOUR* IN 1888.

LED BY STAR PLAYERS, INCLUDING ADRIAN CONSTANTINE "CAP" ANSON, THE TOUR MADE STOPS IN *HAWAII AND ASIA,* BEFORE A GAME WAS PLAYED IN THE SHADOW OF THE *PYRAMIDS OF EGYPT.*

THEN THE TOUR CONTINUED ON TO EUROPE. ITS PURPOSE WAS TO *SPREAD AMERICAN IDEALS* VIA THE EXAMPLE OF BASEBALL. THE RESULTS WERE DECIDEDLY *MIXED.*

THE *LANCASHIRE EVENING POST* SPOKE FOR MANY BRITONS WHEN IT CHARACTERIZED BASEBALL...

...AS MUCH OUT OF PLACE IN ENGLAND AS A *NURSERY FROLIC IN THE HOUSE OF COMMONS.*

BUT THE TOUR DID LEAVE SOMETHING OF A MARK. THE *NATIONAL BASEBALL LEAGUE OF GREAT BRITAIN AND IRELAND* WAS ESTABLISHED THE NEXT YEAR. ONE OF ITS EARLY CHAMPIONS WAS DERBY COUNTY.

EVEN AFTER THE BASEBALL TEAM FOLDED, ITS STADIUM--KNOWN AS THE *BASEBALL GROUND*--REMAINED HOME TO ENGLISH SOCCER TEAM *DERBY COUNTY,* WHICH PLAYED THERE FROM 1895 UNTIL THE STADIUM'S DEMOLITION IN 2003.

Cap Anson, Moses Fleetwood Walker, and the Color Line

Adrian Constantine "Cap" Anson, generally credited as the first man to collect *three thousand hits*, is also regarded as the person most responsible for the *establishment of baseball's color line*. Notorious for refusing to take the field against a team featuring black players, he caused a number of owners to first pull their black players out of games against Anson's White Stockings and then stop signing blacks entirely. He was hardly the only person at fault for the color line, but his *star power and influence* provided cover for other less-public racists to achieve their goal of all-white baseball.

No official rule ever spelled out that African Americans were prohibited from playing major league ball. The practice persisted because of a *"gentlemen's" agreement*, and a desire on the part of the owners to avoid anything that might bring *controversy* to the game. They also didn't want black fans in the stands, because many of their white patrons wouldn't attend events with *mixed* audiences.

The last black player in the original incarnation of the National League was *Moses Fleetwood Walker*. He was released from the Toledo Blue Stockings along with his brother Welday late in the 1884 season––after Anson had refused to play against Toledo, before being informed that if he sat out he would forfeit Chicago's share of the gate receipts. Walker moved to the International League's Newark Little Stars for the 1887 season, during which time that league's owners *voted to stop signing black players* to minor league deals. Two years later, Anson *again* refused to play against Walker, this time in a minor league exhibition against the Syracuse Stars. The Stars relented and kept Walker out of the game. By the end of 1889, a *handshake agreement* was in place keeping the National League and American Association (soon to become the American League) segregated. Baseball's color line would *remain unbroken* until 1947.

In an interesting historical footnote, the first professional black baseball player, *Bud Fowler* (born John Jackson), was a native of Cooperstown, New York. So the site of baseball's Hall of Fame can *legitimately* claim that particular first, even though its claim to be the birthplace of baseball is, shall we say, *contested.*

BY THE 1890S, A *RECOGNIZABLY MODERN* FORM OF BASEBALL HAD ESTABLISHED ITSELF. PITCHERS WERE NOW ALLOWED TO THROW THE BALL HARD INSTEAD OF TOSSING IT FOR THE BATTER TO HIT. FOUR BALLS EQUALED A WALK. BALLS CAUGHT ON A SINGLE BOUNCE WERE NO LONGER AN AUTOMATIC OUT.

THE GAME GREW *FASTER AND MORE ATHLETIC* THAN IT HAD BEEN IN ALEXANDER CARTWRIGHT'S DAY.

EVEN THOUGH THE NATIONAL LEAGUE HAD A STRANGLEHOLD ON PROFESSIONAL BALL, THE GAME *SPREAD AT EVERY LEVEL.* BASEBALL WAS INCREASINGLY SEEN AS A *PASTORAL, INVIGORATING COUNTERBALANCE TO A HELTER-SKELTER, OVERWORKED AMERICA.*

WOMEN PLAYED BASEBALL IN GREATER NUMBERS, TOO. TEAMS OF BLOOMER GIRLS CRISSCROSSED THE NATION, PLAYING LOCAL SEMIPRO TEAMS.

MEN WOULD OFTEN PUT ON *WIGS AND BLOOMERS* TO TOUR WITH THESE BLOOMER GIRL TEAMS. SOME NOTABLE *BASEBALL CROSS-DRESSERS* WERE FUTURE HALL OF FAMERS ROGERS HORNSBY AND HOWARD ELLSWORTH "SMOKEY JOE" WOOD.

ONE OF THE 1890S' NOTABLE CHANGES WAS THE MOVE OF THE PITCHER'S MOUND BACK TO ITS CURRENT DISTANCE OF *60 FEET, 6 INCHES* FROM HOME PLATE IN 1893. THIS CHANGE WAS IN LARGE PART DUE TO A NEW BREED OF HARD-THROWING PITCHERS, INCLUDING DENTON TRUE "CY" YOUNG, WHO THREW SO HARD HIS FAVORITE CATCHER OFTEN PUT A *PIECE OF STEAK* INSIDE HIS GLOVE TO CUSHION THE IMPACT OF YOUNG'S FASTBALL.

THE CHANGE RESULTED IN ONE OF THE *GREAT OFFENSIVE EXPLOSIONS* IN BASEBALL HISTORY. IN THE 1894 SEASON, SIX PLAYERS HIT OVER .400. THE BOSTON *BEANEATERS'** HUGH DUFFY PUT TOGETHER A SEASON FOR THE AGES, HITTING .440 AND LEADING THE LEAGUE IN HITS, DOUBLES, HOME RUNS, TOTAL BASES, AND RUNS BATTED IN (RBIS).

HEY, CY, LET'S GO TO THE CHANGE-UP A LITTLE MORE.

*LATER THE BOSTON BRAVES, AND NOW THE ATLANTA BRAVES.

IT WAS ALSO IN 1894 THAT BAT MANUFACTURER *HILLERICH & BRADSBY* APPLIED FOR A TRADEMARK ON THE TERM *LOUISVILLE SLUGGER*.

OVERALL, THE 1890S WERE THE TIME OF BASEBALL'S FIRST GENERATION OF HEROES. IT WAS A *NATIONAL GAME* NOW, AND ITS BEST PLAYERS WERE NATIONALLY KNOWN, DRAWING CROWDS WHEREVER THEY PLAYED.

AS A. G. SPALDING HAD ENVISIONED, BASEBALL WAS BECOMING *BIG BUSINESS*. AND WITH ONE LEAGUE IN A POSITION OF UNCHALLENGED DOMINANCE, IT WAS ONLY NATURAL THAT A CHALLENGER WOULD COME ALONG...

Softball

Not long after the invention of baseball--so the story goes--a group of Ivy League alumni were in a Chicago yacht club listening to the results of the 1887 Harvard-Yale football game (a 17-8 win for the Elis) on the radio. One of the alums threw a boxing glove at another, someone took a swing at it with a stick, and a *new game* was born. Known variously as *indoor-outdoor, kitten ball, pumpkin ball, and mush ball*, the game quickly took hold in workplaces across the Midwest. That was because it could be played indoors by workers on break. It also became popular among *women* almost immediately. And, as a competitive sport, it is now known primarily as a women's game. The name "softball" was coined in 1930 and quickly became standard, as did the larger, softer ball we know in the game today.

Rule Changes, 1877-95

The following timeline shows how much the game changed between the founding of the National League in 1876 and the beginning of the modern era in 1901.

1879 Nine balls is a walk.

1880 Eight balls is a walk.
Baserunner is out if hit by a batted ball.

1883 Foul balls caught on one bounce are no longer outs.

1884 Six balls is a walk.
Pitchers could deliver the ball overhand and stride during their motion.

1885 One side of the bat could be flat.

1887 Five balls is a walk.
Batters can no longer call for high or low pitches.
Batter is awarded first base when hit by a pitch.

1889 Four balls is a walk.
Sacrifice bunts are recognized.

1893 Pitcher's mound is moved to 60 feet, 6 inches.
Pitchers must have one foot on pitching slab.
Bats must be round and made of hardwood.

1894 Foul bunts are strikes.

1895 Bat size is standardized.
A held foul tip is a strike.

Infield fly rule (see Glossary) adopted.

THE *DEMISE OF THE AMERICAN ASSOCIATION* IN THE EARLY 1890S LEFT THE NATIONAL LEAGUE IN A POSITION OF *UNCHALLENGED DOMINANCE...*

...UNTIL BYRON BANCROFT "BAN" JOHNSON ANNOUNCED THE FORMATION OF THE *AMERICAN LEAGUE OF PROFESSIONAL BASEBALL CLUBS* BEGINNING WITH THE 1901 SEASON.

BORROWING A PAGE FROM SPALDING'S BOOK, JOHNSON MARKETED THE AMERICAN LEAGUE AS A *FAMILY-FRIENDLY ALTERNATIVE* TO THE ROWDY NATIONAL LEAGUE.

AT FIRST, THE NATIONAL LEAGUE DID EVERYTHING IT COULD TO *DESTROY* ITS UPSTART RIVAL.

BUT THE AMERICAN LEAGUE OFFERED *BETTER SALARIES* AND A *CLEANER GAME.* (JOHNSON MADE SURE PLAYERS RESPECTED THE UMPIRES.) *FANS FLOCKED TO THE NEW LEAGUE.*

EVENTUALLY OWNERS CALLED A TRUCE AND AGREED THAT THE A.L. WOULD GET A TEAM IN NEW YORK. THE BALTIMORE ORIOLES THUS BECAME THE NEW YORK HIGHLANDERS, AND LATER...*THE YANKEES.*

THE OWNERS OF BOTH LEAGUES ALSO REALIZED THAT A *SEASON-ENDING CHAMPIONSHIP** WOULD BE A HUGE DRAW FOR FANS.

MAY THE *BEST LEAGUE* WIN.

IN 1903, THE *FIRST WORLD SERIES* WAS PLAYED. FITTINGLY, *CY YOUNG* THREW THE FIRST PITCH OF GAME 1 FOR THE BOSTON AMERICANS.

THE AMERICANS WON THAT FIRST SERIES, AND THREE MORE BY 1918...BEFORE THE CURSE OF THE BAMBINO SET IN (SEE PAGE 135).

*THE NATIONAL LEAGUE AND AMERICAN ASSOCIATION (AA) HAD PLAYED END-OF-SEASON SERIES A FEW TIMES IN THE 1880S.

Who's Who in the American League

THE AMERICAN LEAGUE'S CHARTER MEMBERS

Like the charter members of the National League, the American League's founding clubs have done a lot of moving and renaming over the years. *Only the Detroit Tigers* are still playing in the same city and under the same name as they were in 1901.

1902: Milwaukee Brewers become the *St. Louis Browns.*

1902: The Cleveland *Bluebirds* become the Clevleland Broncos. In 1903, the *Broncos* became the Naps. In 1915, the *Naps* are renamed the Indians in honor of *Louis Sockalexis.*

1903: The Baltimore Orioles move to New York and are renamed the New York *Highlanders.* In 1913, the Highlanders become the *Yankees.*

1904: The Chicago White Stockings become the *White Sox.*

1908: The Boston Americans become the *Red Sox.*

1954: The St Louis Browns move to *Baltimore* and become the new *Orioles.*

The PhillADELPHIA Athletic move to *Kansas City.* Then in 1968 they move again, to *Oakland, California,* keeping the *Athletics* name.

THE VICTORY OF THE *UPSTART* AMERICAN LEAGUE TEAM WAS A SHOT IN THE ARM FOR BASEBALL. *NEW COMPETITION* MEANT NEW FAN INTEREST.

THERE WERE NOW *INTRACITY RIVALRIES* IN NEW YORK, BOSTON, PHILADELPHIA, CHICAGO, AND ST. LOUIS...

...AND *NEW CITIES MEANT NEW AUDIENCES* FOR GREAT PLAYERS. THE GAME GREW BY LEAPS AND BOUNDS AFTER 1903.

IN 1894, THE NEW YORK GIANTS DREW *387,000* FANS TO THEIR HOME PARK, THE POLO GROUNDS. BY 1908, THAT NUMBER HAD EXPLODED TO *910,000*.

THOSE GREATS INCLUDED CY YOUNG, WHO ON MAY 5, 1904, THREW THE FIRST MODERN *PERFECT GAME**-- AGAINST FELLOW PITCHING GREAT RUBE WADDELL.

WADDELL HAD CHALLENGED YOUNG TO FACE HIM, AND WHEN HE MADE THE GAME'S FINAL OUT, YOUNG SHOUTED:

HOW DO YOU LIKE THAT, YOU *HAYSEED?*

*SEE GLOSSARY

THERE'S NO RECORD OF WHAT WADDELL SAID IN RETURN.

OVER IN PITTSBURGH, *HONUS WAGNER* WAS IN THE PROCESS OF WINNING *SEVEN OF NINE* BATTING TITLES BETWEEN 1903 AND 1911, ESTABLISHING HIMSELF AS ONE OF THE *TOP PLAYERS* EVER TO PLAY THE GAME.

THE NEW YORK GIANTS WOULD HAVE MET THE BOSTON AMERICANS IN THE 1904 WORLD SERIES, BUT GIANTS' OWNER JOHN BRUSH *REFUSED* TO PLAY THE REIGNING CHAMPS.

THE GIANTS ARE ALREADY WORLD CHAMPIONS. WE WON THE ONLY REAL MAJOR LEAGUE.

THE NEXT YEAR WITH PEACE RESTORED, WADDELL'S ATHLETICS LOST TO THE NEW YORK GIANTS.

BUT WHILE NEW YORK CELEBRATED, AN OLD DISPUTE FLARED UP *OFF THE FIELD*. IT WAS TIME FOR BASEBALL TO DECIDE ON THE *STORY OF ITS ORIGIN*.

Baseball's Great Eccentrics: Rube Waddell

Baseball has a long and treasured history of *misfits and weirdos*, and one of the first to achieve truly legendary status in that regard was *George Edward "Rube" Waddell*. In an era when pitchers mostly *pitched to contact*--trying to get hitters to put the ball in play to fielders--Waddell racked up *back-to-back three-hundred-strikeout seasons*--a feat that would not be repeated until Sandy Koufax did it in 1965 and 1966. Waddell's strikeout prowess was such that in exhibition games he would often *wave the other players off the field* so they could watch him strike out the side.

But his *personality* made him stand out even more than his pitching. He left the mound during games to go fishing or to *chase fire trucks*. Opposing fans could wave *puppies* at him from the stands and distract him from the game.

There is perhaps no better way to sum it up than sportswriter *Lee Allen's rundown* of Waddell's life in 1903. Waddell began the year "sleeping in a firehouse at Camden, New Jersey, and ended it tending bar in a *saloon* in Wheeling, West Virginia. In between those events, he *won 22 games* for the Philadelphia Athletics; *toured the nation* in a melodrama called *The Stain of Guilt*; courted, *married*, and became separated from May Wynne Skinner of Lynn, Massachusetts; saved a woman from *drowning*; accidentally shot a friend through the hand; and was *bitten by a lion*.

The managers of the major leagues *gave up* on Waddell in 1910, and he kicked around the minors until he contracted pneumonia while helping residents of Hickman, Kentucky, escape a flood in the spring of 1912. He died two years later.

THE COOPERSTOWN MYTH

BASEBALL HAS HAD ITS SHARE OF GREAT WRITERS. HENRY CHADWICK WAS ONE OF THE FIRST.

HE WAS ALSO THE MAN WHO GOT ALBERT SPALDING RILED UP ENOUGH TO TRY TO PROVE THAT BASEBALL WAS A PURELY AMERICAN GAME.

IN 1903, CHADWICK PUBLISHED AN ARTICLE IN *SPALDING'S OWN MAGAZINE* CLAIMING THAT BASEBALL WAS DESCENDED FROM THE BRITISH GAME OF *ROUNDERS*.

BASEBALL? A *BRITISH* GAME!?

PROVOKED BY CHADWICK'S ARTICLE, SPALDING FORMED A COMMISSION OF BASEBALL'S *MOVERS AND SHAKERS*, LED BY HIS OLD PAL ABRAHAM MILLS, TO *SETTLE THE QUESTION* OF THE GAME'S ORIGIN.

OUR GOOD OLD *AMERICAN* GAME OF BASEBALL MUST HAVE AN *AMERICAN* DAD!*

*SO SPALDING WROTE IN A LETTER TO SPORTSWRITER TIM MURNANE IN 1905.

THE COMMISSION WANTED BASEBALL TO BE AN AMERICAN GAME, AN EXPRESSION OF AMERICAN IDEALS. *NONE* OF THEM HAD ANY PATIENCE FOR THE IDEA THAT IT WAS AN *IMMIGRANT* GAME.

THE MILLS COMMISSION MET FROM 1905 TO 1907, AND *SYSTEMATICALLY IGNORED* ALL EVIDENCE THAT POINTED TO BASEBALL'S *EVOLUTION* FROM OTHER BAT-AND-BALL GAMES.

YOU'RE NOT WELCOME HERE.

INSTEAD, THE COMMISSION SEIZED ON A LETTER FROM A MINING ENGINEER IN DENVER, *ABNER GRAVES*, WHO ALLEGED THAT HE HAD *SEEN* A TEENAGED ABNER DOUBLEDAY LAY DOWN THE RULES OF BASEBALL IN COOPERSTOWN, NEW YORK, IN 1839.

THAT WAS *EXACTLY* WHAT MILLS AND THE COMMISSION WERE LOOKING FOR. THEY SEIZED ON GRAVES'S LETTER, IGNORING A NUMBER OF *PERTINENT PROBLEMS* WITH THE STORY.

ONE: ABNER DOUBLEDAY WAS AT *WEST POINT* AS A CADET IN 1839.

TWO: GRAVES RECALLED THE EVENT WITH *REMARKABLE DETAIL* GIVEN THE FACT THAT HE WAS *FIVE YEARS OLD* AT THE TIME.

THREE: DOUBLEDAY *NEVER MENTIONED* INVENTING BASEBALL IN ANY OF HIS PAPERS OR CORRESPONDENCE.

NONE OF THAT MATTERED. THE MILLS COMMISSION HAD THE *AMERICAN DAD* THEY WERE LOOKING FOR, AND THEY WENT WITH THE STORY.

ABNER DOUBLEDAY INVENTED BASEBALL!

THE REPORT DID NOT MENTION ABNER GRAVES, WHO LATER *KILLED HIS WIFE* AND DIED IN AN ASYLUM.

ANOTHER *STRANGE ANGLE* ON THE DOUBLEDAY MYTH IS THAT DOUBLEDAY--LIKE MILLS'S PAL *ALBERT SPALDING*--WAS A DEVOTEE OF MADAME HELENA BLAVATSKY'S OCCULT *THEOSOPHICAL SOCIETY*. PERHAPS THE MADAME HERSELF HAD AN INSIGHT.

YES, I SEE... COOPERSTOWN... A *COW PASTURE*...

DOUBLEDAY, HAVING *DIED IN 1893*, WASN'T AROUND TO SET THE RECORD STRAIGHT, SO THE MILLS REPORT BECAME THE *OFFICIAL STORY OF BASEBALL'S AMERICAN ORIGINS*...AND LED TO THE LOCATION OF THE NATIONAL BASEBALL HALL OF FAME IN COOPERSTOWN.

HENRY CHADWICK DIED A FEW MONTHS AFTER THE REPORT WAS ISSUED.

1906 CHICAGO CUBS

WHILE THE MILLS COMMISSION WORKED ON ITS STORY, THE TALK *ON THE FIELD* DURING 1906 WAS ALL ABOUT THE CHICAGO CUBS.

THEIR 1906 TEAM IS CONSIDERED ONE OF THE BEST EVER, WINNING AN ASTONISHING *116* GAMES. NO OTHER TEAM HAS MATCHED THEIR SEASON-WINNING PERCENTAGE.*

*THE 2001 SEATTLE MARINERS ALSO WON 116 GAMES, BUT IN A 162-GAME SEASON. THE 1906 CUBS PLAYED ONLY 152 GAMES.

THE *HEART OF THE TEAM* CONSISTED OF THE LEGENDARY INFIELD COMBINATION OF JOSEPH (JOE) BERT TINKER, JOHN (JOHNNY) JOSEPH EVERS, AND FRANK LEROY CHANCE. ALL THREE WERE *FUTURE HALL OF FAMERS.*

"TINKER TO EVERS TO CHANCE" BECAME A BYWORD FOR EXCELLENCE IN TURNING *DOUBLE PLAYS*--WHEN FIELDERS RELAY THROWS TO GET TWO BASERUNNERS OUT ON A SINGLE BATTED BALL.

THE CUBS' BEST PITCHER, *MORDECAI "THREE FINGER" BROWN*, WAS ANOTHER FUTURE HALL OF FAMER. IN 1906, HE POSTED AN *EARNED RUN AVERAGE* (ERA)(SEE GLOSSARY) OF 1.04, WHICH STILL STANDS AS THE NATIONAL LEAGUE RECORD.

BROWN'S PITCHING HAND, DISFIGURED IN A FARM ACCIDENT WHEN HE WAS A CHILD, GAVE HIM A DEVASTATING CURVEBALL. AFTER RETIRING FROM BIG LEAGUE BALL, HE WOULD GO ON TO MANAGE A BLOOMER GIRL TEAM AND ONE OF THE FAMOUS HOUSE OF DAVID BARNSTORMING TEAMS. (MORE ABOUT THEM LATER.)

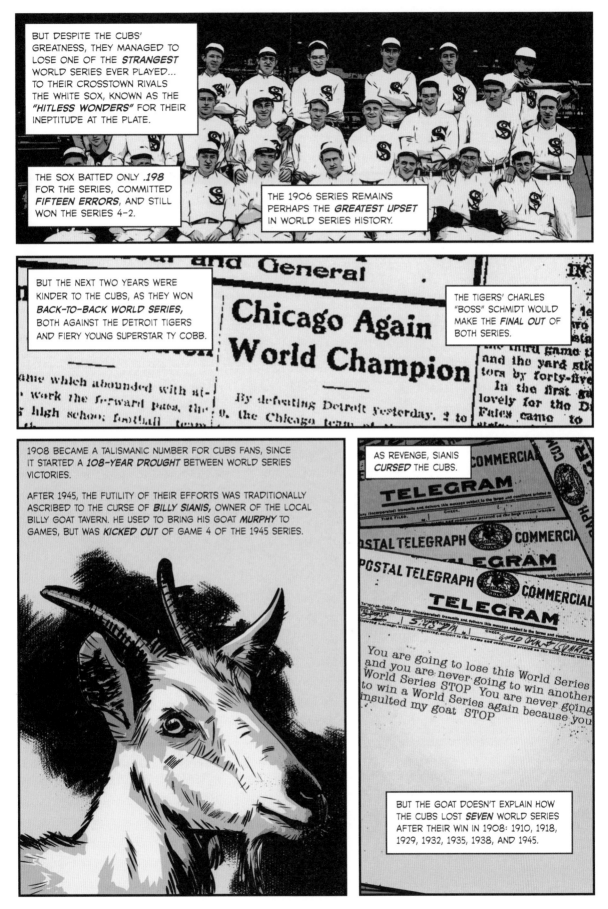

BUT DESPITE THE CUBS' GREATNESS, THEY MANAGED TO LOSE ONE OF THE *STRANGEST* WORLD SERIES EVER PLAYED... TO THEIR CROSSTOWN RIVALS THE WHITE SOX, KNOWN AS THE *"HITLESS WONDERS"* FOR THEIR INEPTITUDE AT THE PLATE.

THE SOX BATTED ONLY *.198* FOR THE SERIES, COMMITTED *FIFTEEN ERRORS*, AND STILL WON THE SERIES 4–2.

THE 1906 SERIES REMAINS PERHAPS THE *GREATEST UPSET* IN WORLD SERIES HISTORY.

BUT THE NEXT TWO YEARS WERE KINDER TO THE CUBS, AS THEY WON *BACK-TO-BACK WORLD SERIES*, BOTH AGAINST THE DETROIT TIGERS AND FIERY YOUNG SUPERSTAR TY COBB.

THE TIGERS' CHARLES "BOSS" SCHMIDT WOULD MAKE THE *FINAL OUT* OF BOTH SERIES.

Chicago Again World Champion

By defeating Detroit Yesterday, 2 to 0, the Chicago team

1908 BECAME A TALISMANIC NUMBER FOR CUBS FANS, SINCE IT STARTED A *108-YEAR DROUGHT* BETWEEN WORLD SERIES VICTORIES.

AFTER 1945, THE FUTILITY OF THEIR EFFORTS WAS TRADITIONALLY ASCRIBED TO THE CURSE OF *BILLY SIANIS*, OWNER OF THE LOCAL BILLY GOAT TAVERN. HE USED TO BRING HIS GOAT *MURPHY* TO GAMES, BUT WAS *KICKED OUT* OF GAME 4 OF THE 1945 SERIES.

AS REVENGE, SIANIS *CURSED* THE CUBS.

You are going to lose this World Series and you are never going to win another World Series STOP You are never going to win a World Series again because you insulted my goat STOP

BUT THE GOAT DOESN'T EXPLAIN HOW THE CUBS LOST *SEVEN* WORLD SERIES AFTER THEIR WIN IN 1908: 1910, 1918, 1929, 1932, 1935, 1938, AND 1945.

THE *1909 PIRATES* ARE ANOTHER TEAM THAT POPS UP IN "GREATEST OF ALL TIME" DISCUSSIONS. THEY RACKED UP 110 WINS IN THE BRAND-NEW FORBES FIELD, LED BY THE LEGENDARY *HONUS WAGNER*, AND CHARGED INTO THE WORLD SERIES AGAINST THE 98-WIN TIGERS, WHO WERE ITCHING TO MAKE UP FOR THEIR PREVIOUS SERIES LOSSES.

THE 1909 WORLD SERIES WAS THE ONLY TIME THAT THE *TWO GREATEST HITTERS OF THE DEAD BALL ERA* FACED EACH OTHER.

COBB WAS *TWENTY-TWO*, AND JUST COMING INTO HIS OWN. WAGNER WAS *THIRTY-FIVE*, AT THE END OF HIS PRIME.

PIRATES PLAYER-MANAGER *FRED CLARKE* WENT WITH A HUNCH AND STARTED ROOKIE PITCHER CHARLES BENJAMIN "BABE" ADAMS IN GAMES 1, 5, AND 7.

I'LL NEVER FORGET THE LOOK ON ADAMS'S FACE WHEN I TOLD HIM I WANTED HIM TO PITCH THE *OPENER.*

BUT ADAMS WON THAT OPENER, AND HIS OTHER TWO STARTS AS WELL. COBB WENT *1-FOR-11* AGAINST HIM OVER THOSE THREE STARTS, AND THE TIGERS WERE *DOOMED.*

COBB HIT *.231* FOR THE SERIES, WAGNER *.333*. THE OLD DOG STILL HAD A FEW TRICKS LEFT TO TEACH HIS SUCCESSOR.

WITH THAT LOSS, THE 1907-09 DETROIT TIGERS BECAME THE FIRST TEAM TO LOSE THE SERIES IN *THREE CONSECUTIVE YEARS*.

ALL THREE TIMES, THEY LOST THE FINAL GAME AT HOME.

TWO OF THOSE LOSSES CAME TO THE *PHILADELPHIA ATHLETICS*, THE FIRST TEAM TO WIN THREE SERIES (1910, 1911, AND 1913).

THE OTHER NOTEWORTHY OCCURRENCE OF 1909: THE CLEVELAND NAPS' NEAL BALL TURNED THE FIRST *UNASSISTED TRIPLE PLAY* IN MAJOR LEAGUE HISTORY.*

*WHEN A SINGLE FIELDER PUTS THREE BASERUNNERS OUT IN A SINGLE PLAY. THE *RAREST EVENT IN BASEBALL.*

Unbreakable Records: Dead Ball Era

The Dead Ball Era saw the establishment of four records widely considered unbreakable: Cy Young's *511 career wins*, Jack Chesbro's *41-win season*; Nap Lajoie's batting average of *.426* in 1901, and John Owen "Chief" Wilson's *36 triples* in 1912.

Cy Young pitched from 1890 to 1911, in an era when relief pitchers were extremely rare and a starter could take the mound for *fifty or more* games in a season. In today's game, pitchers rarely even make *thirty-five* starts, and relievers pile up wins and losses that in the Dead Ball Era went to starters. This makes Young's 511 wins one of baseball's *immortal numbers*. Three hundred wins is considered a guaranteed Hall of Fame career; only two men (Young and Walter Johnson) have 400; and when you get to 500, Young stands alone.

The same is likely true of Jack Chesbro's forty-one wins, a record achieved in 1904, when Chesbro also pitched *forty-eight complete games*. The record for wins since the mound was lowered in 1969 is twenty-seven.

Since the birth of the American League, the *single-season batting average record* is Nap Lajoie's .426 in 1901. Between 1901 and 1930, baseball saw thirteen .400 seasons. Since then, there's been one: Ted Williams' *.406 in 1941* (see page 77). Tony Gwynn Sr., at .394 in the strike-shortened season of 1994, and George Brett, at .390 in 1980, have gotten the closest. *No* currently active player places in the *top 100* of all-time season averages; Ichiro Suzuki's .372 in 2004 places the highest at #129. The game has changed. Scholars argue about why--bigger gloves? better athletes covering more ground? fewer bunts? better pitchers?--but the *results are clear*. The years 1970-2000 saw fewer .370+ seasons than 1901-30 saw .400+ seasons.

Pittsburgh Pirate outfielder Chief Wilson's thirty-six triples are an *underappreciated baseball milestone*. Only one other man has more than thirty (Baltimore's Henry Peter "Heinie" Reitz, in that batting-happy year of 1894). When you consider more recent history, Wilson's achievement is even more extraordinary. Only *six times* in the post-1961 expansion era has a player even reached *twenty triples*. For one thing, ballparks are different. Wilson hit in Pittsburgh's Forbes Field, which was *462* feet to center field. In today's parks, many of Wilson's triples would have been doubles (bouncing back off walls to outfielders) or home runs (over walls at a more reachable distance).

Honus Wagner

Honus Wagner was already a legendary player when he retired for the first time before the 1908 season. When Pirates owner Bernhard "Barney" Dreyfuss enticed him back to the diamond with a **$10,000 contract**, Wagner put together what some baseball statisticians consider **the greatest single season of all time**--not his greatest season; *the* greatest season. He led the league in batting, hits, total bases, doubles, triples, RBI, and stolen bases, while also playing a peerless shortstop.

He would record his **three thousandth hit** in 1914, becoming only the **second** member of that club (though Nap Lajoie would join him and Cap Anson a month later). Two years after that he became the oldest man to hit an inside-the-park home run. When Wagner retired in 1917 he was widely considered the **best ever to play the game**. (At the time, Babe Ruth was still a young pitcher.)

Apart from his on-the-field accomplishments, Wagner also made his mark in the **economics of baseball**. He was the first player to endorse the famous **Louisville Slugger** bat, and played a role in the growth of baseball's collector market when he made the American Tobacco Company (ATC) **stop producing cards with his image** because he did not want to be associated with smoking.

That card, the **T206**, became the most valuable baseball card on Earth by the 1930s. By 2007, a near-mint copy of the card sold for an incredible $2.8 million--quite a bit more than Wagner ever made playing the game.

Big Six

Christy Mathewson won 373 games during his seventeen-year career, putting him in the top five all time. Known for an *unhittable "fadeaway"* or screwball (which he might or might not have learned from the great Negro League pitcher *Rube Foster*), Mathewson more or less *single-handedly* won the 1905 World Series for the New York Giants, but didn't fare as well in the Giants' later Series appearances.

In the 1911 Series, he was half-responsible for one of the more ill-fitting nicknames ever bestowed on a player. The Philadelphia Athletics' Frank Baker, not known for his power, hit home runs in consecutive games off Rube Marquard and Mathewson, and was forever after known as *"Home Run Baker."*

Known as *"Big Six,"* Mathewson was a deeply religious man who *never pitched on Sundays*. Retiring as a player after 1916, he managed the Cincinnati Reds until his enlistment in the US Army during World War I. There, he helped train soldiers to defend against gas attacks. However, during the training, he was *accidentally gassed* himself. He died of tuberculosis in 1925, and was one of the *first five* players inducted into the Hall of Fame.

CHRISTY MATHE
NEW YORK, N.L., 190
CINCINNATI, N.L.
BORN FA TO VILLE, PA.,
GREATES ALL THE GR
THE CENTURY'S
P OUTS IN 190
FIRST OR THE CE
ME IN 3 SUCC VE ARS.
N 37 GAMES 1908
MATT WAS MASTER THEM

LESS WELL-KNOWN THAN THE EXPLOITS OF MAJOR LEAGUE TEAMS, BUT *JUST AS CRITICAL* TO BASEBALL'S FUTURE, WERE THE EXPLOITS OF THE GAME'S EARLY *AFRICAN AMERICAN STARS*.

A SUCCESSOR TO THE CUBAN GIANTS, THE *PHILADELPHIA CUBAN X-GIANTS*, WAS ONE OF THE EARLY GREAT TEAMS IN SO-CALLED *"BLACKBALL."* ONE OF BLACKBALL'S GREATEST PITCHERS WAS *RUBE FOSTER*.

THE *1885 CUBAN GIANTS* WERE THE FIRST *PROFESSIONAL AFRICAN AMERICAN TEAM*--"CUBAN" BEING AN EARLY MARKETING PLOY TO MAKE THE TEAM SOUND EXOTIC.

BORN ANDREW FOSTER, HE ACQUIRED THE NICKNAME "RUBE" AFTER *FACING AND BEATING RUBE WADDELL* IN AN EXHIBITION IN *1903*.

THE NEXT YEAR, ACCORDING TO ANECDOTAL HISTORIES, THE NEW YORK GIANTS' MANAGER *JOHN MCGRAW* GOT FOSTER TO TEACH YOUNG *CHRISTY MATHEWSON* THE *SCREWBALL*.

BY 1913, FOSTER WAS RUNNING THE *CHICAGO AMERICAN GIANTS*. HE CUT A DEAL WITH WHITE SOX OWNERSHIP TO MOVE INTO THE SOUTH SIDE PARK, WHICH THE SOX HAD JUST VACATED FOR THE NEW *COMISKEY PARK*.

NOW PRIMARILY AN OWNER, FOSTER SET ABOUT BUILDING BLACK BASEBALL INTO A *VIABLE AND ORGANIZED* BUSINESS.

FOSTER'S BUSINESS ACUMEN-- AND HIS ADVOCACY FOR *BLACK OWNERSHIP OF BLACK TEAMS*-- LAID THE FOUNDATION FOR WHAT WOULD BECOME THE *NEGRO NATIONAL LEAGUE* IN 1920.

(IF YOU'RE HEARING *ECHOES OF AL SPALDING'S STORY* HERE, YOU'RE CORRECT.)

AND WHO KNOWS, MAYBE HE REALLY DID TEACH CHRISTY MATHEWSON THE *FADEAWAY*.

The Old Arbitrator

WILLIAM J. KLEM
UMPIRE
- 1905 - 195
RATOR" UM
EDITED
INDIC
LS. P
A
S A
O

Known as the father of baseball umpires, Bill Klem was by all accounts a *pompous egomaniac* who thought that he never missed a call in his life. But he was also--by all accounts--an excellent umpire, and his credentials bear that out. He started umpiring professionally after meeting Silk O'Loughlin, and worked in the majors from 1905 to 1941, during which time Klem called balls and strikes in *eighteen* World Series. Among Klem's *innovations* were leaving his position behind the plate to get closer to a play in the field; standardizing arm signals; and straddling the foul lines to better see fair and foul balls. He was also probably the first umpire to stand off to the side of the catcher for a *better view* of the plate.

His *temper*, especially early in his career, led him to eject players and managers for minor dissent. One thing that ensured ejection was any player calling him *"Catfish,"* a nickname he hated.

Once players knew of his temper, of course, they did everything they could to get Klem *riled up*. Catcher Al López once pasted a newspaper clipping of Klem *blowing a call* to home plate and then covered it with dirt. Klem saw the clipping the first time he brushed the plate off--and immediately *ejected* López.

Over the years, Klem mellowed slightly. In his last seasons, he ejected fewer players and adopted the role of *mentor* to younger umpires. At the time of his retirement in 1941, he was widely credited with *professionalizing* the role of the umpire and making umps *respected* figures in the game.

THE INCREASING MONEY IN BASEBALL LED TO *BIGGER* INVESTMENTS IN *BETTER* BALLPARKS.

KNOWN AS *"JEWEL BOX"* PARKS, THESE WERE SMALL AND KEPT SPECTATORS CLOSE TO THE GAME.

FANS QUICKLY BECAME *SENTIMENTAL* ABOUT THESE PARKS, AND IN THE FUTURE WOULD FIGHT ANY EFFORT TO *DEMOLISH* THEM.

BUT OF ALL THE JEWEL BOX PARKS BUILT BY 1915, ONLY TWO SURVIVE: *WRIGLEY FIELD* AND *FENWAY PARK*.

BASEBALL OWNERS WERE ALSO STILL HARD AT WORK SPREADING THE *GOSPEL OF THE GAME*. THE GIANTS AND WHITE SOX WENT ON A *WORLD TOUR* IN 1913-14, PARTIALLY RETRACING THE STEPS OF SPALDING'S ORIGINAL TOUR OF *1888*.

BAD WEATHER PLAGUED THE TOUR, BUT THE TEAMS STILL MANAGED TO PLAY FORTY-SIX GAMES, INCLUDING THE *FIRST* MAJOR LEAGUE EXHIBITION IN JAPAN.

PLAYERS SAILED HOME FROM THE TOUR ON THE FAMOUS PASSENGER LINER *LUSITANIA*--WHICH, WHEN THE GERMANS *SANK* IT IN 1916, WOULD ACCELERATE AMERICA'S ENTRY INTO *WORLD WAR I*.

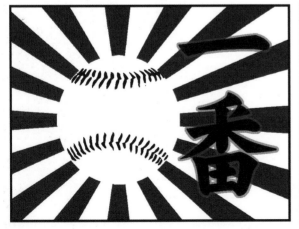

LOOK AT THAT *BEAUTY*. NOW WE GET TO HOBNOB WITH THE SWELLS.

MEANWHILE, BACK ON THE FIELD, A YOUNG *LEFT-HANDER* NAMED *GEORGE HERMAN "BABE" RUTH JR.* MADE HIS FIRST APPEARANCE WITH THE RED SOX, BEATING THE CLEVELAND NAPS.

THE SENATORS' *HUBERT "DUTCH" LEONARD* SET A RECORD FOR LOWEST EARNED RUN AVERAGE-- 0.96--THAT STILL STANDS TODAY.

FEW PEOPLE IN BOSTON NOTICED THIS ACCOMPLISHMENT, BECAUSE THE *BRAVES* WERE IN THE PROCESS OF PULLING OFF ONE OF BASEBALL'S *LEGENDARY* COMEBACKS.

AFTER THE ATHLETICS LOST THE WORLD SERIES TO THE BOSTON BRAVES, CONNIE MACK DECIDED TO *START FRESH.* HE PUT SOME OF HIS BEST PLAYERS ON WAIVERS, INCLUDING *EDDIE PLANK* AND *"CHIEF" BENDER.*

INFURIATED BECAUSE THE WAIVER SALE WOULD MEAN *PAY CUTS* THE NEXT YEAR, PLANK AND BENDER LOOKED FOR A WAY TO *OUTWIT* MACK.

THEY FOUND IT IN THE *FEDERAL LEAGUE.*

FOR SALE CHEAP!

Red Murray

A gifted outfielder for the New York Giants, known for his **cannon arm** and a penchant for spectacular catches, John Joseph "Red" Murray entered baseball lore on July 17, 1914, when he caught the last out of a twenty-one-inning game--and was immediately **struck by lightning.**

He **survived** to play until 1917 and then retired to run a tire store in his hometown of Elmira, New York.

Germany Schaefer

Known as the *"Clown Prince of Baseball"* (and probably the first to bear that title), William Herman "Germany" Schaefer was a mediocre player, but a big draw because of his on- and off-field antics. He once stole second base as part of a planned double steal and when the catcher didn't throw, on the next pitch Schaefer *ran back to first.* He then tried the double steal again and was pronounced safe at second again, becoming the *only man* ever to steal the same base *twice.* (Baseball outlawed this in 1920.)

Among Schaefer's other exploits: In 1906, he *announced* he was going to hit a home run, and did so *on the next pitch.* He then announced his own progress around the bases as if it were a horse race.

He was said to be the *inspiration* for the movie musical *Take Me Out to the Ball Game*, starring Gene Kelly and Frank Sinatra.

THE FEDERAL LEAGUE AND THE GREAT WAR

AS BASEBALL BECAME BIG BUSINESS, COMPETITION EMERGED IN THAT ASPECT. *MINOR LEAGUE* TEAMS PROLIFERATED, AS DID *AFRICAN AMERICAN* TEAMS. MAJOR LEAGUE OWNERS TRIED TO CONTROL MOST OF THESE TEAMS THROUGH BUSINESS ARRANGEMENTS.

IN 1913, A BASEBALL PROMOTER NAMED *JOHN POWERS* ANNOUNCED THE START OF THE *FEDERAL LEAGUE*, FEATURING TEAMS IN MIDWESTERN CITIES.

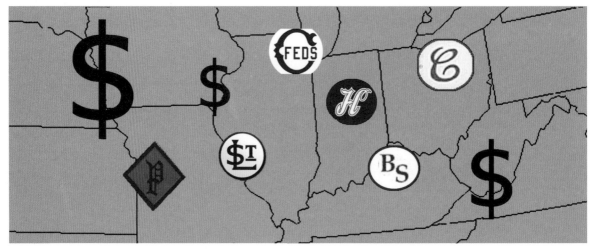

IN 1914, POWERS *TRIED AGAIN*, RECRUITING PLAYERS FROM THE AMERICAN AND NATIONAL LEAGUES BY PROMISING THEM *FREEDOM FROM THE RESERVE CLAUSE.*

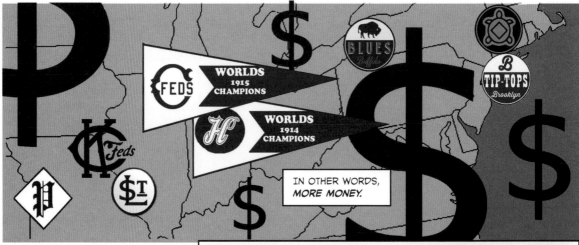

IN OTHER WORDS, *MORE MONEY.*

THE FEDERAL LEAGUE'S BIGGEST TARGET, WALTER JOHNSON, *RESISTED* THEIR EFFORTS AFTER THE SENATORS MADE HIM A LUCRATIVE COUNTEROFFER.

BUT THE FEDERALS LANDED A NUMBER OF OTHER BIG LEAGUE PLAYERS, INCLUDING THREE FINGER BROWN, CHIEF BENDER, *EDD ROUSH,* AND *EDDIE PLANK* (WHO WOULD WIN HIS THREE HUNDREDTH GAME WHILE PLAYING FOR THE ST. LOUIS TERRIERS).

BROWN AND OTHER FEDERAL RENEGADES EVEN TRIED TO MEET THE WHITE SOX AND GIANTS AS THEY RETURNED FROM A WORLD TOUR IN MARCH 1914.

RED SOX OWNER JAMES GAFFNEY--WHO WAS, SHALL WE SAY, CONNECTED--CALLED OUT **ARMED TAMMANY HALL THUGS** TO KEEP THEM AWAY.

AFTER THE 1915 SEASON, MAJOR LEAGUE OWNERS TOOK THE PRACTICAL ROUTE AND **BOUGHT OUT** HALF OF THE STRUGGLING FEDERAL LEAGUE TEAMS. TWO FEDERAL OWNERS BOUGHT MAJOR LEAGUE TEAMS, THE ST. LOUIS BROWNS AND THE CHICAGO CUBS

THE FINAL LEGACY OF THE FEDERAL LEAGUE WOULD BE A LONG-STANDING COURT CASE THAT CEMENTED BASEBALL'S EXEMPTION FROM THE **SHERMAN ANTI-TRUST ACT**.

FEDERAL JUDGE **KENESAW MOUNTAIN LANDIS** LET THE SUIT LANGUISH, HIS INACTION SLOWLY **STARVING** THE FEDERAL LEAGUE AND **ENSURING** THAT THE EXISTING MAJOR LEAGUES WOULD SURVIVE WITHOUT COMPROMISING THEIR BUSINESS PRACTICES--OR THE RESERVE CLAUSE.

YOU'LL BE HEARING A LOT MORE ABOUT **JUDGE LANDIS**.

Wrigley Field

A monument to *nostalgia* and *misery* due to the Cubs' century-long World Series drought, Wrigley Field was originally built as *Weeghman Field* for the Federal League's Chicago Whales. When the Federal League folded, the Cubs moved into the stadium. The park was known as Cubs Field until chewing-gum magnate *William Wrigley Jr.* named it after himself in 1926.

Among other things, Wrigley Field is known as the *last major league park to install lights* for night games, holding out until 1988. It's also renowned for its *ivy-covered* brick outfield walls, which were common when Weeghman Field was built, but are now seen only in the *"Friendly Confines"* (a nickname bestowed by famous Cubs second baseman Ernie Banks).

Another now-common practice originated with the field's namesake Charles Weeghman himself: he was the first to allow fans to *keep baseballs* hit into the stands. (Ironically, Wrigley Field was also where fans initiated the practice of *throwing back* home-run balls hit by other teams.)

1915 WAS A YEAR OF CONTINUITY IN MANY WAYS.

TYRUS RAYMOND "TY" COBB WON A *BATTING TITLE*... JUST LIKE IN 1914.

GROVER CLEVELAND ALEXANDER LED THE NL IN WINS AND STRIKEOUTS... JUST LIKE IN 1914.

WALTER JOHNSON LED THE AL IN *WINS*...JUST LIKE 1914.

THE RED SOX AND PHILLIES MET IN THE WORLD SERIES, THE SECOND YEAR IN A ROW THAT THOSE TWO CITIES WERE REPRESENTED.

AMERICAN CHAMPIONS LEAGUE 1915

✕RєδSoxx

MEANWHILE, THE ATHLETICS WENT FROM THE WORLD SERIES TO ONE OF THE WORST SEASONS IN BASEBALL HISTORY, GOING 43–109 TO FINISH 58½ *GAMES* OUT OF FIRST PLACE.

AND JUST AS THE BRAVES HAD BEATEN THE ATHLETICS IN 1914, THE RED SOX BEAT THE PHILLIES IN 1915.

ON MAY 6, 1915, BABE RUTH-- STILL A FULL-TIME PITCHER-- HIT HIS *FIRST CAREER HOME RUN*, OFF THE YANKEES' JACK WARHOP.

(YOU READ THAT RIGHT. BABE RUTH'S FIRST HOME RUN CAME *AGAINST* THE YANKEES.)

THE VERY NEXT DAY, A GERMAN U-BOAT TORPEDOED THE *LUSITANIA* OFF THE IRISH COAST, KILLING NEARLY *TWELVE HUNDRED* PEOPLE.

ALSO OF NOTE, IN 1915: THE DEATH OF *ALBERT SPALDING*. HAVING SPENT THE LATTER PART OF HIS LIFE DEVELOPING THE THEOSOPHICAL SOCIETY COMMUNITY KNOWN AS *LOMALAND* IN CALIFORNIA, SPALDING WAS NO LONGER INVOLVED WITH BASEBALL.

HE WOULD BE ELECTED TO THE BASEBALL HALL OF FAME IN *1939*, THE YEAR IT OPENED IN COOPERSTOWN-- THAT LOCATION, OF COURSE, LARGELY DUE TO HIS WORK ON BEHALF OF THE *DOUBLEDAY MYTH*.

Hail to the Chief

When **Nap Lajoie** left the Cleveland Naps after the 1914 season, the team's owner solicited ideas for a **new nickname.** After some debate, Indians was chosen (and unfortunately, the **racist caricature** Chief Wahoo was adopted as the logo). Common belief was that the choice was made in honor of **Louis Sockalexis**, probably the first Native American to play in the major leagues. A Penobscot from Indian Island, Maine, Sockalexis had a meteoric rise and fall with the Cleveland Spiders in 1897–99. He had **recently died** at the time of the renaming, and was apparently remembered with some fondness in Cleveland. (But the other story is that Cleveland chose "Indians" because they were inspired by the Boston Braves' **remarkable run** to the 1914 World Series.)

Following in Sockalexis's footsteps, a number of other **Native Americans** made their mark in the major leagues during the Dead Ball Era. Most of them, unfortunately, were nicknamed "Chief," and, like Sockalexis, faced **racism and patronizing treatment** from fans: Chief Bender, Chief Meyers, Chief Johnson, Chief Yellow Horse, Chief Youngblood...

Elon Chester "Chief" Hogsett, who played his final game in 1944, appears to be the **last Native American player** to have semiofficially borne this moniker. (Moses J. Yellow Horse, incidentally, grew up on an Oklahoma Pawnee reservation with future Dick Tracy cartoonist **Chester Gould**, who used Yellow Horse as the model for the character Yellow Pony.)

Other prominent Native American players have included Olympic legend **Jim Thorpe**, Rudy York, Jonny Leonard Roosevelt "Pepper" Martin, Allie Reynolds, and Cal McLish, who bore one of the great given names in the history of baseball: **Calvin Coolidge Julius Caesar Tuskahoma McLish.**

After World War II, Native American players became a rarity in the major leagues. **Chief Bender and Zack Wheat** are the only two Native Americans in the Baseball Hall of Fame.

The most prominent **current** Native American player is the Yankees' Jacoby Ellsbury, winner of two World Series with the Red Sox before he signed with the Yankees in 2014.

IF THE 1915 A'S WERE AWFUL, THE 1916 A'S WERE IN THE RUNNING FOR THE WORST MAJOR LEAGUE TEAM OF **ALL TIME**. THEY WENT 36-117, AND PLAYED IN SUCH MISERY THAT PLAYERS RETIRED MIDSEASON. EVEN THEIR **BATBOY** GREW SURLY AND HAD TO BE FIRED.

SINCE LOSING THE 1914 WORLD SERIES, THE A'S HAD A RECORD OF 89-226. IN TWO YEARS, THEY HAD WON ONE DECENT SEASON'S WORTH OF GAMES.

THE LONE BRIGHT SPOT WAS A *NO-HITTER* (SEE GLOSSARY) BY **LESLIE AMBROSE "BULLET JOE" BUSH** ON AUGUST 26--BUT BUSH ALSO LOST TWENTY-FOUR GAMES THAT YEAR.

CATCHER **WALTER HENRY "WALLY" SCHANG** ALSO BECAME THE FIRST MAN TO HIT HOME RUNS FROM **BOTH SIDES OF THE PLATE** IN ONE GAME.

BUT WHERE A MANAGER TODAY WOULD BE **FIRED** FOR TWO SEASONS LIKE THAT, CONNIE MACK WAS *UNTOUCHABLE.*

MACK EVEN GOT A **JOB OFFER** FROM THE BOSTON RED SOX, WHO HAD JUST WON THEIR SECOND STRAIGHT SERIES-- AND THIRD IN FIVE YEARS.

OH, AND WALTER JOHNSON LED THE LEAGUE IN **WINS AND STRIKEOUTS** FOR THE **THIRD** STRAIGHT YEAR.

The Big Train

Walter Johnson pitched twenty-one seasons for the *Washington Senators*, one of the more *hapless* franchises in baseball's early modern era. Despite his team's mediocrity, Johnson won *417* games, the second-highest total in major league history. Only *he and Cy Young* have more than 400 wins. Beginning his career in 1907, he finally won a World Series in 1924, the year after he became the first pitcher to record 3000 *strikeouts*. He would retire with 3508, a number unmatched until 1983--and no other pitcher would reach 3000 until the Cardinals' Bob Gibson did it in 1974. At the time of Johnson's retirement, in fact, only two other pitchers were *within 1000 strikeouts* of his total.

Well liked throughout the game, Johnson wasn't above going easy on some of his friends when the game wasn't on the line. He sometimes *let up* on the Tigers' Sam Crawford, a good friend, to pad Crawford's numbers--driving Crawford's teammate and rival Ty Cobb *crazy* in the process.

One of the first five players inducted into the Hall of Fame, Johnson managed the Senators and the Cleveland Indians before leaving baseball to involve himself in politics. He also took part in a *publicity stunt* in 1936, when the people of Fredericksburg, Virginia, decided to see if the legend of George Washington *throwing a silver piece* across the Rappahannock River was true. They asked Johnson to try it, and the Big Train came through. The distance of his throw? *Three hundred eighty-six feet.* Not bad for a forty-eight-year-old who was retired for almost a decade at the time.

BEFORE THE SINKING OF THE *LUSITANIA*, MOST AMERICANS HAD WANTED TO STAY OUT OF THE WAR IN EUROPE.

BUT *128 AMERICANS* WERE AMONG THE *LUSITANIA* DEAD, AND BRITAIN *STEPPED UP PRESSURE* ON THE UNITED STATES TO ENTER THE WAR OVER THE NEXT YEAR.

PRESIDENT WOODROW WILSON RESISTED, BUT THE TIDE WAS TURNING.

ON APRIL 6, 1917, WILSON GAVE THE BRITISH WHAT THEY WANTED. HE ASKED CONGRESS TO *DECLARE WAR* ON GERMANY.

FIVE DAYS LATER, BABE RUTH KICKED OFF THE BASEBALL SEASON WITH A 1-0 VICTORY OVER THE YANKEES.

RUTH LATER FIGURED IN ONE OF BASEBALL'S MOST *UNUSUAL* PITCHING FEATS. HE WALKED THE FIRST MAN HE FACED WHEN PITCHING AGAINST THE SENATORS ON JUNE 23, THEN GOT INTO AN ARGUMENT WITH UMPIRE CLARENCE BERNARD "BRICK" OWENS AND WAS *THROWN OUT* OF THE GAME.

ERNIE SHORE WAS BROUGHT IN TO RELIEVE RUTH. THE BASE RUNNER WAS CAUGHT STEALING, AND SHORE *RETIRED ALL TWENTY-SEVEN MEN* HE FACED FROM THAT POINT.

FOR MANY YEARS, SHORE'S ACCOMPLISHMENT WAS LISTED AS A *PERFECT GAME.* IT IS NOW CONSIDERED A *COMBINED NO-HITTER.*

BUT THE COMING WAR WAS ON EVERYONE'S MINDS.

ON JULY 15, *HANK GOWDY* OF THE BOSTON BRAVES BECAME THE FIRST MAJOR LEAGUER TO ENLIST. MANY OTHERS FOLLOWED, INCLUDING *FUTURE HALL OF FAMERS* EDDIE COLLINS SR., HARRY HEILMANN, AND GROVER CLEVELAND ALEXANDER.

ERNIE SHORE, WHO WE JUST MET, ALSO SIGNED UP EARLY IN 1918.

THE CHICAGO *WHITE SOX* BEAT THE NEW YORK GIANTS IN THE WORLD SERIES, JUST AS AMERICAN SOLDIERS WERE LEAVING FOR FRANCE. IT WOULD BE THE SOUTH SIDERS' *LAST* WORLD SERIES WIN UNTIL 2005.

Meanwhile in Cooperstown . . .

WE'LL CALL IT THE DOUBLEDAY MEMORIAL FUND.

The Mills Commission's 1907 pronouncement that baseball had *sprung fully formed* from the forehead of Abner Doubleday left prominent citizens of Cooperstown feeling like there ought to be some sort of *monument* to the great man. It took a while to get the movement going, but over the winter of 1917, five men--two of them former major leaguers Hardy Richardson and George Frederick "Deke" White--each *chipped in a quarter* and started the Doubleday Memorial Fund.

That summer they contacted sportswriter *Sam Crane*, who started banging the drum for their idea of a monument to Doubleday's moment of (mythical) inspiration. Soon, they had enough money to buy *Elihu Phinney's cow pasture*.

By 1919, the town had broken ground on what would become *Doubleday Field*, and the first game would be played there on September 6, 1920.

Doubleday Field now hosts the annual *Hall of Fame game*--but we're getting ahead of ourselves. We'll check back in the *1930s*, when the Hall of Fame really starts to take shape.

WITH THE WAR EFFORT ON, THE MINOR LEAGUES WERE *SHUT DOWN* AND THEIR PLAYERS EITHER *WENT TO WORK* IN WARTIME INDUSTRIES OR *SIGNED UP* TO FIGHT.

PLENTY OF MAJOR LEAGUERS WENT TOO. YOU'VE ALREADY MET SOME OF THEM.

THE UNITED STATES' ENTRY INTO WORLD WAR I CAUSED THE *SHORTENING* OF THE 1918 BASEBALL SEASON, WHICH ENDED ON SEPTEMBER 1.

WITH *BABE RUTH* PITCHING THEM TO VICTORIES IN GAMES 1 AND 4, THE RED SOX WON THEIR *FOURTH* WORLD SERIES SINCE 1912. (AND THEIR *LAST* UNTIL 2004.)

A NUMBER OF OTHER PLAYERS, INCLUDING *JOSEPH "SHOELESS JOE" JACKSON* (SEE PAGE 49), LEFT BASEBALL TO WORK IN WARTIME INDUSTRIES.

IN PARALLEL, THE *MASS MIGRATION* OF SOUTHERN BLACKS TO NORTHERN INDUSTRIAL CITIES ACCELERATED AS WARTIME INDUSTRY CREATED DEMAND FOR MORE WORKERS.

GAME 1 OF THIS SERIES WAS ALSO THE FIRST TIME *"THE STAR-SPANGLED BANNER"* WAS PLAYED AT A MAJOR LEAGUE GAME.

OTHER PROMINENT PLAYERS WHO ENLISTED INCLUDED *TY COBB, GEORGE SISLER, AND CHRISTY MATHEWSON.* ALL THREE HELPED TRAIN SOLDIERS TO PROTECT THEMSELVES AGAINST GAS ATTACKS.

THEY WOULD BE THE PRIMARY AUDIENCE FOR RUBE FOSTER'S ENVISIONED *NEGRO NATIONAL LEAGUE*--ONCE THE WAR WAS OVER.

OTHER PLAYERS WERE *WOUNDED IN ACTION*, INCLUDING GROVER CLEVELAND ALEXANDER, WHO NEVER RECOVERED FROM *MUSTARD GAS EXPOSURE* AND THE EFFECTS OF AN ARTILLERY BARRAGE. HE WOULD PITCH UNTIL 1930, BUT HIS BEST YEARS WERE BEHIND HIM.

ON THE HOME FRONT, INFLUENZA KILLED THOUSANDS OF AMERICANS, INCLUDING ONE OF BASEBALL'S MOST RESPECTED UMPIRES, *FRANCIS H."SILK" O'LOUGHLIN*.

STRIKE THREE!

HE WAS THE FIRST UMP TO *SHOUT OUT BALLS AND STRIKES* SO EVERYONE ON THE FIELD KNEW THE COUNT.

WITH THE WAR OVER, BASEBALL *REVVED BACK UP* ALONG WITH THE REST OF THE COUNTRY.

BABE RUTH SET A MAJOR LEAGUE RECORD FOR HOME RUNS, BELTING *TWENTY-NINE* AND BECOMING THE FIRST PLAYER TO HIT ONE IN *EVERY AMERICAN LEAGUE PARK* IN A SINGLE SEASON.

RUTH ALSO HIT HIS FIRST CAREER *GRAND SLAM* (HOME RUN WITH THE BASES LOADED). HE WOULD HIT FOUR DURING THE 1919 SEASON, SETTING A RECORD THAT STOOD UNTIL 1955.

ON AUGUST 24, WHILE PITCHING AGAINST PHILADELPHIA, INDIANS PITCHER RAY CALDWELL WAS *STRUCK BY LIGHTNING* WITH TWO OUTS IN THE NINTH.

HE RECOVERED TO GET THE FINAL OUT OF THE GAME...AND WOULD THROW A *NO-HITTER* TWO WEEKS LATER.

GIVE ME THE DANG BALL AND POINT ME TOWARD THE PLATE!

Yakyuu

The first **Japanese baseball teams** started to form in the 1870s, led by expatriate American teachers. The first matches between American and Japanese teams date to 1896.

In 1920, Japanese baseball took a big step forward with the the formation of **Nihon Undo Kyokai**, the Japanese Exercise Society. This was the country's first professional baseball club.

That same year, Herb Hunter led a team of mostly Pacific League players on a **tour of Japan**. He would return in 1922 and 1931--that last time with a team that included such greats as Mickey Cochrane, Lou Gehrig, and Lefty Grove.

On that 1922 tour, a Japanese team beat an American team for the first time, as the Mita Club took a 9-3 decision over Hunter's All Stars.

Teams of black players also toured Japan in the 1920s and '30s, and a black pitcher--**James Bonner**--played professionally in Japan **more than a decade before** Jackie Robinson took the field for the Dodgers.

THE BLACK SOX SCANDAL

THE CONSPIRACY STARTED EARLY IN 1919, BECAUSE A GROUP OF WHITE SOX PLAYERS WERE *RESENTFUL* OF OWNER *CHARLES COMISKEY*.

GAMBLER *JOSEPH J. "SPORT" SULLIVAN* WAS QUICK TO TAKE ADVANTAGE OF THIS RESENTMENT.

SAY, BOYS. YOU COULD MAKE A *LOT OF MONEY*, IF...

THE MAN BACKING SULLIVAN WAS ONE OF AMERICA'S MOST FEARED GANGSTERS: *ARNOLD ROTHSTEIN*.

EVEN *BEFORE* THE 1919 SERIES BEGAN, RUMORS FLEW ABOUT A FIX.

BOOKIES ACROSS THE COUNTRY NOTICED A *HUGE INFLUX* OF MONEY BEING PUT ON THE REDS.

BET THE REDS. YOU WANT REDS? I *GOT* 'EM.

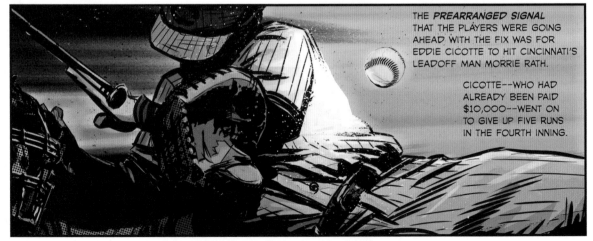

THE *PREARRANGED SIGNAL* THAT THE PLAYERS WERE GOING AHEAD WITH THE FIX WAS FOR EDDIE CICOTTE TO HIT CINCINNATI'S LEADOFF MAN MORRIE RATH.

CICOTTE--WHO HAD ALREADY BEEN PAID $10,000--WENT ON TO GIVE UP FIVE RUNS IN THE FOURTH INNING.

THE SCHEME *ALMOST* WENT OFF THE RAILS WHEN THE REST OF THE CONSPIRATORS *DIDN'T GET PAID*, ALLEGEDLY BECAUSE THE GAMBLERS HAD THEIR MONEY ALL TIED UP IN BETS ON *FUTURE* GAMES.

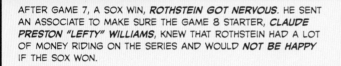

AFTER GAME 7, A SOX WIN, *ROTHSTEIN GOT NERVOUS*. HE SENT AN ASSOCIATE TO MAKE SURE THE GAME 8 STARTER, *CLAUDE PRESTON "LEFTY" WILLIAMS*, KNEW THAT ROTHSTEIN HAD A LOT OF MONEY RIDING ON THE SERIES AND WOULD *NOT BE HAPPY* IF THE SOX WON.

PAY WILLIAMS A VISIT. TELL HIM I'M *WORRIED* ABOUT HIS *WIFE.*

WILLIAMS WENT ON TO LOSE GAME 8 AND FINISH THE SERIES WITH AN 0-3 *RECORD* AND A 6.63 *ERA*--AFTER A REGULAR SEASON WHEN HE WENT 23-11 WITH A 2.64 ERA.

SUSPICION WAS IMMEDIATE THAT THE SOX HAD *THROWN THE SERIES*, JUST BECAUSE NOBODY COULD BELIEVE A TEAM *SO GOOD* COULD SUDDENLY PLAY *SO BAD.*

SOMETHING DOESN'T ADD UP HERE...

COLUMNIST HUGH FULLERTON STARTED DIGGING, AND PRETTY SOON THE *WHOLE CONSPIRACY* HAD COME TO LIGHT. THE NAME *"BLACK SOX,"* REFLECTING THE CORRUPTION OF THE WHITE SOX, SOON FOLLOWED.

The Commissioner

Shaken by the Black Sox scandal, baseball owners realized they needed to take drastic steps to *clean up the game*. Their solution was to hire the *first commissioner*-- Federal Judge Kenesaw Mountain Landis. They already knew him from his Federal League decision in 1915, and believed he was the man to *save baseball*.

Landis would only agree to take the job if he was granted the *sole power* to arbitrate decisions about baseball's rules. The owners agreed, and Landis immediately *banished eight White Sox players for life*. In 1922, Babe Ruth challenged his authority by barnstorming (see page 53) after Landis forbade it; the commissioner responded by *suspending* Ruth for six weeks.

KENESAW MOUNTAIN LANDIS
BASEBALL'S FIRST COMMISSIONER
ELECTED, 1920 — DIED IN OFFICE, 1944
HIS INTEGRITY AND LEADERSHIP
ESTABLISHED BASEBALL IN THE
RESPECT, ESTEEM AND AFFECTION
OF THE AMERICAN PEOPLE.

Throughout the 1920s and '30s, he ruled with an *iron fist*. Often considered unfair, Landis was also respected for restoring public faith in the *integrity* of baseball. He also oversaw the creation of the *farm system* as we know it today, knitting together hundreds of independent teams into a cohesive player-development system.

On the negative side of the ledger, Landis is generally believed to have *delayed* the breaking of baseball's *color line*. Accused by Dodger manager Leo Durocher of being complicit in *keeping baseball all-white* in 1942, he issued a statement denying it--but he also moved to stop Bill Veeck Jr. from buying the Phillies and stocking the team with Negro League stars. Whatever the truth of his intentions, baseball was not integrated until after Landis's death in 1944.

Say It Ain't So, Joe

Shoeless Joe Jackson was probably the **greatest hitter to never win a batting title.** From 1911 to 1913, his first three years in the majors, he finished second to Ty Cobb. Jackson's 1911 average of .408 is still a **rookie record**, but Cobb hit .420 that year. Jackson's lifetime average of .356 is third-best in baseball history, behind Cobb's .366 and Rogers Hornsby's .358. Cobb called Jackson "the **finest natural hitter** in the history of the game."

The **son of a sharecropper**, Jackson began working in textile mills when he was six years old and never attended school. His **illiteracy** was a source of embarrassment throughout his life. But his athletic talent led him from a mill team in 1900 to the Chicago White Sox eleven years later.

Despite **hitting .375** and playing **errorless ball** during the 1919 Series, Jackson received a **lifetime ban** along with the other players who admitted to their parts in the plot. He spent the next several years **playing incognito** with a series of semipro teams. Fans often recognized him and showered him with abuse. Eventually, he left the game and settled in South Carolina, where he ran a liquor store.

TOWARD THE END OF HIS LIFE, COBB RECALLED STOPPING BY THAT STORE IN THE 1940S.

JOE'S MARKET

DON'T YOU **KNOW** ME, JOE?

I KNOW YOU. BUT I WASN'T SURE YOU WANTED TO SPEAK TO **ME**. A LOT OF THEM DON'T.

Jackson died in 1951, **maintaining his innocence** to the end.

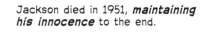

THE AFTERMATH OF THE BLACK SOX SCANDAL MARKED THE *END OF AN ERA.* BEFORE 1920, THE MOST SUCCESSFUL FRANCHISES IN BASEBALL HAD BEEN THE CUBS, WHITE SOX, AND RED SOX.

THEORIES ABOUND REGARD-ING THE END OF THE DEAD BALL ERA, BUT MOST PARTIES AGREE THAT ONE CONTRIBUTING FACTOR WAS THE *FATAL BEANING OF RAY CHAPMAN* ON AUGUST 16, 1920.

PITCHER CARL MAYS WAS A KNOWN *HEADHUNTER,** AND UNPOPULAR WITH FELLOW PLAYERS. WHEN CHAPMAN DIED EARLY THE NEXT MORNING, MAYS BECAME A PARIAH.

HE MAINTAINED TO THE END OF HIS LIFE THAT THE PITCH WAS A *STRIKE* AND THAT CHAPMAN WAS *LEANING OVER THE PLATE.*

THERE WERE *TWO IMME-DIATE CONSEQUENCES* OF CHAPMAN'S DEATH. FIRST, THE *SPITBALL* WAS OUTLAWED AFTER THE 1920 SEASON.*

NONE OF THOSE CLUBS WOULD WIN ANOTHER WORLD SERIES IN THE TWENTIETH CENTURY.

*A PITCHER KNOWN FOR THROWING AT BATTERS' HEADS.

*ALTHOUGH A CERTAIN NUMBER OF PITCHERS WERE GRANDFATHERED IN AND ALLOWED TO KEEP USING IT.

SECOND, BALLS WERE THEN *REPLACED* MUCH MORE FREQUENTLY. UNTIL 1920, BALLS WERE USED UNTIL THEY *FELL APART OR WERE LOST.* THIS MADE THEM PARTICULARLY *HARD* TO SEE LATE IN GAMES, WHEN THEY WERE DIRTY AND PITCHERS HAD LOADED THEM UP WITH *TOBACCO JUICE* FOR SEVERAL INNINGS.

GALVANIZED BY THE TRAGEDY, THE INDIANS WENT ON A *LATE-SEASON TEAR* AND WON THE WORLD SERIES THAT YEAR, BEATING THE DODGERS FIVE GAMES TO TWO IN ONE OF ONLY FOUR BEST-OF-NINE SERIES EVER PLAYED.

GAME 5 OF THAT SERIES ALSO SAW *SEVERAL FIRSTS*, ALL BY CLEVELAND PLAYERS. ELMER SMITH HIT THE FIRST WORLD SERIES GRAND SLAM, BILL WAMBSGANSS PULLED OFF THE ONLY UNASSISTED TRIPLE PLAY IN POSTSEASON HISTORY, AND JIM BAGBY SR. HIT THE FIRST SERIES HOME RUN BY A PITCHER.

THERE WAS ANOTHER FACTOR IN THE END OF THE DEAD BALL ERA. AFTER THE 1919 SEASON, THE RED SOX *SOLD BABE RUTH'S CONTRACT* TO THE YANKEES. HE WOULD ALMOST SINGLE-HANDEDLY DRAG BASEBALL THE REST OF THE WAY OUT OF THE DEAD BALL ERA AND ESTABLISH THE YANKEES AS THE *CENTER OF THE BASEBALL UNIVERSE.*

WORLD SERIES
19 20
CLEVELAND INDIANS

Dead or Alive?

In the early days of baseball, players often **made** their own balls, and teams chose balls that reflected their style of play. Good hitting clubs wanted a **livelier** ball; clubs reliant on pitching and fielding went with so-called **"dead" balls**. Design standards started to appear in the 1850s. In 1876, Spalding began manufacturing the **official ball** of the National League.

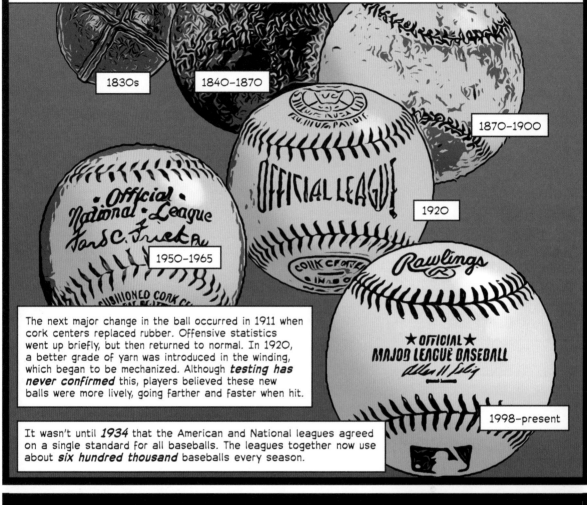

1830s

1840–1870

1870–1900

1920

1950–1965

The next major change in the ball occurred in 1911 when cork centers replaced rubber. Offensive statistics went up briefly, but then returned to normal. In 1920, a better grade of yarn was introduced in the winding, which began to be mechanized. Although **testing has never confirmed** this, players believed these new balls were more lively, going farther and faster when hit.

1998–present

It wasn't until **1934** that the American and National leagues agreed on a single standard for all baseballs. The leagues together now use about **six hundred thousand** baseballs every season.

No, Not Nanette

It is widely believed that Red Sox owner Harry Frazee sold Babe Ruth to the Yankees in order to finance the production of the musical **No, No, Nanette**. But that show didn't open until 1925. And in any case, there were plenty of other financial pressures on Frazee, who had big debts from his purchase of the Sox in 1916. (Ruth also wanted to **renegotiate** his contract.)

On the New York side, Yankees owner Jacob Ruppert Jr. was also facing financial pressures. A brewer by trade, he was expecting huge losses with the implementation of **Prohibition** on New Year's Day 1920. He also wanted to build the Yankees their own stadium. Calculating that **a star player** just might bring in enough spectators to offset those building costs, Ruppert took the plunge on Ruth...**and the rest, as they say, is history**.

Boston fans never trusted Frazee because he was a New Yorker, and their skepticism was probably justified. Over the next few years, Frazee made a number of **lopsided deals with the Yankees**, providing them with the core players of their pennant-winning 1921–23 teams, as the Red Sox began to fade. The Sox wouldn't have another winning season until 1935.

AS THE 1920 SEASON BEGAN, THE BIG NEWS AROUND BASEBALL WAS THE *DEBUT OF BABE RUTH WITH THE YANKEES.*

YANKEE MANAGER MILLER HUGGINS ALLOWED RUTH TO COMPLETE THE SWITCH HE'D BEGUN UNDER RED SOX MANAGER ED BARROW. RUTH WAS NOW A FULL-TIME SLUGGER, AND QUICKLY BECAME THE BEST THE GAME HAD EVER SEEN UP TO THAT POINT.

HE *OBLITERATED* HIS OWN HOME RUN RECORD, BELTING FIFTY-FOUR IN 1920-- MORE THAN MANY OTHER *MAJOR LEAGUE TEAMS'* COMBINED TOTALS.

THE YANKEES BECAME THE FIRST TEAM TO DRAW A *MILLION FANS* THAT YEAR, AS NEW YORKERS *SWARMED* TO THE POLO GROUNDS TO SEE THE PHENOMENON THAT WAS "THE BABE."

RUTH'S EXPLOITS GAVE BASEBALL FANS *SOMETHING TO BELIEVE IN*, AS THE BLACK SOX SCANDAL LED TO CRIMINAL CHARGES AGAINST EIGHT PLAYERS--INCLUDING SHOELESS JOE JACKSON.

SAY IT AIN'T SO, JOE.*

*THIS ACTUALLY *NEVER HAPPENED*; (*EVERYTHING* IN BASEBALL GETS MYTHOLOGIZED.)

RUTH WOULD HIT *FIFTY-NINE* HOME RUNS IN 1921, AND AFTER A HICCUP IN 1922--DURING WHICH HE WAS SUSPENDED FOR SIX WEEKS FOR OFF-SEASON *BARNSTORMING*-- HE WOULD RETURN TO FORM, HITTING .393 WITH FORTY-ONE HOME RUNS IN 1923...

*THIS WAS THE PRACTICE OF *TOURING* IN THE OFF-SEASON TO PLAY EXHIBITION GAMES FOR *EXTRA MONEY*, BACK IN THE DAYS *BEFORE* MILLION-DOLLAR CONTRACTS.

...IN THE BRAND-NEW *YANKEE STADIUM.*

THE YANKEES CHRISTENED THEIR NEW STADIUM WITH THEIR *FIRST SERIES WIN* IN 1923.

RUTH'S POWER AND PERSONA WERE REVOLUTIONIZING THE GAME. OTHER PLAYERS WHO HAD COME UP DURING THE DEAD BALL ERA STRUGGLED TO ADJUST.

OTHER CHANGES BREWED ACROSS THE BASEBALL LANDSCAPE. RUBE FOSTER, BUILDING ON HIS SUCCESS IN CHICAGO, FOUNDED THE *NEGRO NATIONAL LEAGUE* IN 1920. THE *FOUNDING TEAMS* WERE THE CHICAGO AMERICAN GIANTS, CHICAGO GIANTS, CUBAN STARS, DAYTON MARCOS, DETROIT STARS, INDIANAPOLIS ABCS, KANSAS CITY MONARCHS, AND ST. LOUIS GIANTS.

OVER THE NEXT THREE YEARS, OTHER BLACK LEAGUES--THE EASTERN COLORED LEAGUE AND THE SOUTHERN NEGRO LEAGUE--FORMED RIVALRIES WITH THE NEGRO NATIONAL LEAGUE. THIS COMPETITION CULMINATED IN THE FIRST *COLORED WORLD SERIES* IN 1924.

THE KANSAS CITY MONARCHS BEAT HILLDALE OF PENNSYLVANIA FIVE GAMES TO FOUR.

CUT OFF FROM THE MAJOR LEAGUES, THE FIRST GENERATION OF *GREAT AFRICAN AMERICAN PLAYERS* CAME OF AGE IN THE 1920S IN THESE LEAGUES. AMONG THE FUTURE HALL OF FAMERS:

JAMES THOMAS "COOL PAPA" BELL WHOSE SPEED SPAWNED A THOUSAND TALES.

OSCAR CHARLESTON, A CAREER .354 HITTER WHO WOULD LATER BE PLAYER-MANAGER WITH THE LEGENDARY PITTS-BURGH CRAWFORDS TEAMS OF THE 1930S. MAJOR LEAGUE PLAYERS OFTEN SAID CHARLESTON WAS *AMONG THE BEST PLAYERS--WHITE OR BLACK--THEY EVER SAW.*

JOHN HENRY "POP" LLOYD, THE *GREATEST SHORTSTOP* IN THE HISTORY OF THE NEGRO LEAGUES. LLOYD WAS OFTEN COMPARED TO HONUS WAGNER, AND BABE RUTH SAID LLOYD WAS THE *BEST PLAYER* HE HAD EVER SEEN.

WILLIAM JULIUS "JUDY" JOHNSON, THE CEREBRAL THIRD BASEMAN WHO ANCHORED THE KANSAS CITY MONARCHS AND HOMESTEAD GRAYS.

BASEBALL IS LIKE EVERYTHING ELSE. YOU GOT TO *STUDY EVERY ANGLE* TO WIN.

THE NEGRO LEAGUE PLAYERS ALSO PLAYED *UNOFFICIAL* GAMES WITH WHITE TEAMS DURING *SPRING TRAINING* AND IN THE *OFF-SEASON.*

BABE RUTH, IN PARTICULAR, WHO HAD HIS *PICK* OF BARNSTORMING DATES, ALWAYS *MADE A POINT* OF SCHEDULING GAMES AGAINST ALL-BLACK TEAMS.

NEARLY *ASPHYXIATED* BY A GAS LEAK IN 1925, RUBE FOSTER SUFFERED BRAIN DAMAGE AND HIS INCREASING *PARANOIA AND ERRATIC BEHAVIOR* RESULTED IN HIM BEING INSTITU-TIONALIZED. HE DIED IN 1930, AND THE NEGRO NATIONAL LEAGUE *DISINTEGRATED* THE NEXT YEAR.

MAJOR LEAGUERS MIGHT NOT HAVE WANTED THE BIG LEAGUES INTEGRATED, BUT THEY *KNEW AND RESPECTED* THE ABILITIES OF NEGRO LEAGUE PLAYERS.

HE WAS ELECTED TO THE HALL OF FAME IN 1981.

RADIO AND THE ROARING TWENTIES

AS THE YANKEES GEARED UP FOR THEIR DECADES-LONG RUN AT THE TOP OF THE GAME, A FEW *OTHER TEAMS* MANAGED TO MAKE THEIR MARKS AS WELL.

IN 1924, WALTER JOHNSON FINALLY WON A WORLD SERIES (NEITHER HE NOR THE SENATORS WOULD EVER WIN ANOTHER).

JOHNSON WOULD WIN HIS *FOUR HUNDREDTH* GAME TWO YEARS LATER, REACHING A PLATEAU OCCUPIED ONLY BY HIMSELF AND CY YOUNG.

THAT WOULD LEAVE TY COBB AS THE ONLY ONE OF THE *FIRST FIVE** TO NEVER WIN A WORLD SERIES.

THE WASHINGTON SENATORS ARE *WORLD SERIES CHAMPIONS* FOR THE FIRST...

*SEE PAGE 72.

IN 1926, THE ST. LOUIS CARDINALS TOOK HOME THEIR FIRST SERIES TROPHY.

FOR THE YANKEES, BABE RUTH RECORDED THE *FIRST THREE-HOME-RUN GAME* IN WORLD SERIES HISTORY.

HE ALSO MADE THE *FINAL OUT* OF THE SERIES WHILE ATTEMPTING TO STEAL SECOND BASE.

HORNSBY

RUTH

IT WOULD BE *FORTY-THREE YEARS* BEFORE ANOTHER FIRST-TIME TEAM WON A SERIES--THE *"MIRACLE" METS* IN 1969. (SEE PAGE 126.)

ANOTHER OF BASEBALL'S GREAT FEATS BEGAN UNNOTICED ON JUNE 2, 1925, WHEN YANKEE FIRST BASEMAN *WALLY PIPP* SUFFERED A RECURRENCE OF THE HEADACHES THAT HAD PLAGUED HIM SINCE CHILDHOOD.

WALLY, TAKE THE DAY OFF. WE'LL TRY THE KID AT FIRST AND GET YOU BACK IN THERE TOMORROW.

THE KID--LOU GEHRIG--WOULD END UP PLAYING 2,130 STRAIGHT GAMES. (SEE PAGE 75.)

PIPP WOULD BE TRADED TO CINCINNATI IN THE OFF-SEASON.

MEANWHILE, JUDGE LANDIS--WHO HAD ALREADY CRACKED DOWN ON BARNSTORMING AND GAMBLING--SET HIS SIGHTS ON THE MINOR LEAGUES.

LANDIS *PROHIBITED* MINOR LEAGUE TEAMS FROM STOCKPILING PLAYERS WHO OTHERWISE WOULD HAVE A SHOT AT OTHER MAJOR LEAGUE TEAMS.

BY BRINGING *TRANSPARENCY* TO THE MINORS, LANDIS ALSO HELPED TO CREATE A NATIONAL BASEBALL CULTURE. FANS OF MINOR LEAGUE TEAMS COULD TRACK THEIR FAVORITE PLAYERS AS THEY MADE THE JUMP TO *"THE SHOW."*

BOY, THAT KID SURE CAN HIT.

Old Pete

One of the true greats of the transition era between the Dead Ball Era and the new age of the slugger, Grover Cleveland Alexander--known as "Old Pete" for reasons that remain obscure--won the same number of games as Christy Mathewson, putting him in a tie for *third winningest pitcher* of all time. Alexander led the National League in wins and strikeouts from 1914 to 1917, then spent most of 1918 in France during World War I. There he suffered wounds that left him *epileptic* for the rest of his life--a problem made worse by his heavy drinking. During the 1926 World Series with the Cardinals, he won Games 2 and 6 and got the final outs of Game 7, despite a *brutal hangover* from the previous night's celebrations.

GROVER CLEVELAND ALEXANDER

GREAT NATIONAL LEAGUE PITC
FOR TWO DECADES WIT
CUBS AND CARDIN
IN 1911. WON 1926
FOR CARDIN
LAZZERI W
FINAL CRISIS

ALEXANDER WASN'T DRUNK OUT THERE ON THE MOUND THE WAY PEOPLE THOUGHT. HE WAS AN EPILEPTIC. OLD PETE WOULD FALL DOWN WITH A SEIZURE BETWEEN INNINGS, THEN GO BACK OUT AND PITCH ANOTHER SHUTOUT.

Roger Hornsby

Ty Cobb

I'D RATHER HAVE HIM PITCH A CRUCIAL GAME FOR ME DRUNK THAN ANYONE ELSE SOBER. HE WAS THAT GOOD.

After leaving the big leagues, Alexander later turned up as part of the legendary *House of David* barnstorming squad (see page 67).

WIDELY CONSIDERED THE GREATEST BASEBALL TEAM EVER ASSEMBLED, THE 1927 YANKEES BOASTED SIX FUTURE HALL OF FAMERS. THEIR BATTING ORDER BECAME KNOWN AS *MURDERERS' ROW.**

THEY ALSO FEATURED A PLAYER WITH ONE OF BASEBALL'S ALL-TIME NOTABLE NAMES: *URBAN SHOCKER*

*ALTHOUGH THE TERM HAD PREVIOUSLY BEEN APPLIED TO OTHER DANGEROUS LINEUPS, THE YANKEES HAVE OWNED IT EVER SINCE.

THE YANKEES WON 110 GAMES THAT YEAR AND OUTSCORED THEIR OPPONENTS BY NEARLY *FOUR HUNDRED RUNS*. THE SENATORS' JOE JUDGE SPOKE FOR MANY OF THEIR OPPONENTS.

THOSE GUYS DON'T JUST BEAT YOU. THEY BREAK YOUR HEART.

A YANKEE FINISHED FIRST IN *EVERY OFFENSIVE CATEGORY* EXCEPT BATTING AVERAGE AND STOLEN BASES (WHERE GEHRIG AND BOB MEUSEL FINISHED SECOND, RESPECTIVELY).

THEIR PITCHERS WERE ALSO GOOD, BUT WITH THAT LINEUP, THEY DIDN'T HAVE TO BE, AS YANKEE STARTER WAITE HOYT UNDERSTOOD.

THE SECRET OF SUCCESS AS A PITCHER LIES IN GETTING A JOB WITH THE YANKEES.

BABE RUTH HIT SIXTY HOME RUNS, MORE THAN EVERY OTHER *TEAM* IN THE MAJORS.

SIXTY! COUNT 'EM, SIXTY! LET'S SEE SOME SONOFAB*TCH MATCH THAT!

IN THE WORLD SERIES, THE YANKEES DEMOLISHED A GOOD PIRATES TEAM THAT FEATURED FUTURE HALL OF FAMERS *PIE TRAYNOR* AND BROTHERS *PAUL "BIG POISON"* AND *LLOYD "LITTLE POISON" WANER.*

THE 1927 SERIES IS THE ONLY ONE EVER TO END WITH A RUNNER SCORING ON A *WILD PITCH.*

Ink-Stained Wretches

Other writers' work on baseball has become justly famous, from Henry Chadwick through Grantland Rice to John Updike and Roger Angell, but nobody ever did it better than columnist *Ring Lardner*. His stories collected in *You Know Me Al* are still some of the best and funniest baseball writing ever done. (The book even attracted the admiration of Virginia Woolf.)

Woolf recognized––as had other observers on this side of the Atlantic––that baseball was one of the threads knitting together the American *sense of self*. That was true in 1925, and it's still true today.

IN OUR SUN-DOWN PERAMBULATIONS OF LATE, THROUGH THE OUTER PARTS OF BROOKLYN, WE HAVE OBSERVED SEVERAL PARTIES OF YOUNGSTERS PLAYING "BASE", A CERTAIN GAME OF 'BALL'...LET US GO FORTH AWHILE, AND GET BETTER AIR IN OUR LUNGS. LET US LEAVE OUR CLOSE ROOMS...THE GAME OF BALL IS *GLORIOUS.*

HE WRITES THE *BEST PROSE* THAT HAS COME OUR WAY...OFTEN IN A LANGUAGE WHICH IS *NOT* ENGLISH.

MR. LARDNER'S INTEREST IN GAMES HAS SOLVED ONE OF THE MOST DIFFICULT PROBLEMS OF THE AMERICAN WRITER; IT HAS GIVEN HIM A CLUE, A CENTRE, A MEETING PLACE FOR THE DIVERSE ACTIVITIES OF PEOPLE WHOM A VAST CONTINENT ISOLATES, WHOM NO TRADITION CONTROLS.

IN MAY OF 1929, THE YANKEES BECAME THE FIRST TEAM TO PUT NUMBERS ON THEIR UNIFORMS.*

THIS PRACTICE WOULD LATER BE A HUGE LEAP FORWARD FOR MERCHANDISING, BUT AT THE TIME IT WAS A WAY FOR FANS IN THE *CHEAP SEATS* TO RECOGNIZE THEIR FAVORITE PLAYERS.

BY THE EARLY 1930S, EVERY TEAM WOULD EMPLOY NUMBERS, AND MANY BEGAN ADDING PLAYERS' NAMES SOON AFTER.

*THEY HAVE SINCE RETIRED TWENTY-TWO OF THEM, INCLUDING THE NUMBER 8 *TWICE.*

AT THE END OF OCTOBER 1929 CAME THE STOCK MARKET CRASH KNOWN AS *BLACK MONDAY.* WITHIN A FEW MONTHS, THE BOTTOM HAD DROPPED OUT OF THE AMERICAN ECONOMY.

THE *GREAT DEPRESSION* BROUGHT DIFFICULT TIMES. BUT EVEN PEOPLE WHO COULDN'T AFFORD A TICKET COULD SOMETIMES CATCH A GAME...

...THANKS TO THE RELATIVELY RECENT INVENTION OF *RADIO.*

BY 1928, 30 PERCENT OF AMERICAN HOUSEHOLDS HAD RADIOS.

THAT NUMBER WOULD CLIMB TO *80 PERCENT* BY 1938.

THE FIRST STATION TO BROADCAST A MAJOR LEAGUE GAME WAS *KDKA PITTSBURGH.**

AND IT'S A BASE HIT TO CENTER!

CRACK!

*ALTHOUGH *WWJ IN DETROIT* DISPUTES THIS CLAIM.

MOST STATIONS DIDN'T SEND CREWS TO AWAY GAMES. INSTEAD THEY RELIED ON *TELEGRAPH FEEDS* TO RE-CREATE THE GAME IN-STUDIO.

AND IT'S A BASE HIT TO CENTER!

CRACK!

The Georgia Peach

WHAT A HELL OF A LEAGUE THIS IS. I HIT .387, .408, AND .395 THE LAST THREE YEARS AND I AIN'T WON *NOTHIN'* YET!

Admired for his immense talent and demonic energy—and *reviled* for his violent tendencies and jealous rivalries—Detroit Tigers outfielder Ty Cobb set approximately **ninety major league records** over the course of his twenty-five-year career. His career batting average of .366 is one of baseball's immortal records, and several of his lesser-known marks are even less likely to be broken. He stole home **fifty-four times** over his career, and once stole second, third, and home on **three consecutive pitches**. He is also the only man ever to lead the major leagues in home runs without hitting a ball out of the park, recording nine inside-the-park round-trippers in 1909. He hit .300 or better for twenty-three straight seasons, and won **twelve out of thirteen** American League batting titles in the years 1907–1919. (In three of those years, Shoeless Joe Jackson—whom Cobb admired—finished second.)

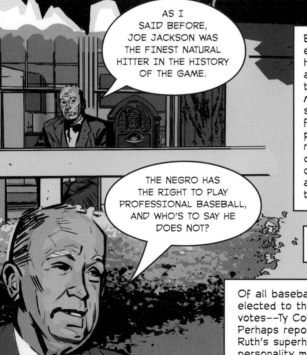

AS I SAID BEFORE, JOE JACKSON WAS THE FINEST NATURAL HITTER IN THE HISTORY OF THE GAME.

THE NEGRO HAS THE RIGHT TO PLAY PROFESSIONAL BASEBALL, AND WHO'S TO SAY HE DOES NOT?

But Cobb's personality overshadowed his excellence, particularly at the time of his death when reporter Al Stump published a **wildly sensationalized** biography of Cobb that cemented his reputation as a **violent racist** hated by his fellow ballplayers. That story took hold, despite Stump's obvious fabrications. Cobb's **great-grandfather** preached against slavery; his **grandfather** refused to fight in the Confederate Army during the Civil War, and his father was credited with breaking up a lynch mob. He also made a point of saying he supported the integration of the major leagues.

In 1952, Cobb said **Willie Mays** was the only player he would pay money to see.

Of all baseball's greats—he was among the First Five elected to the Hall of Fame, with 98 percent of the votes—Ty Cobb has gotten the rawest deal from history. Perhaps reporters needed an **antihero** to balance Babe Ruth's superhuman persona, or perhaps Cobb's prickly personality made it easy to believe terrible things about him. Whatever the case, Stump himself later recanted much of what he had written.

AS THE COUNTRY SANK INTO THE DEPTHS OF THE DEPRESSION, THE ONCE-WOEFUL PHILADELPHIA ATHLETICS HEADED IN THE OPPOSITE DIRECTION.

AFTER THEIR COMICALLY BAD SEASONS IN THE LATE 1910S, THE ATHLETICS SLOWLY PUT THEMSELVES BACK TOGETHER AND FINISHED SECOND TO THE MIGHTY YANKEES IN 1927 AND 1928.

THEN THEY LEAPED AHEAD OF THE BRONX BOMBERS TO WIN THREE STRAIGHT PENNANTS FROM 1929 TO 1931, WITH BACK-TO-BACK WORLD SERIES IN '29 AND '30...

...ALL, INCREDIBLY, UNDER THE *SAME MANAGER* WHO HAD SEEN THEM THROUGH THEIR FIRST RUN OF SUCCESS TWO DECADES BEFORE: CONNIE MACK.

MACK BUILT THE TEAM AROUND THE HALL-OF-FAME-BOUND QUARTET OF AL SIMMONS, MICKEY COCHRANE, JIMMIE FOXX, AND LEFTY GROVE.

FOXX, KNOWN AS *"DOUBLE X"* AND "THE BEAST," STRUCK PARTICULAR FEAR INTO OPPOSING PITCHERS, FINISHING HIS CAREER WITH 534 HOME RUNS* AND NEARLY WINNING BACK-TO-BACK *TRIPLE CROWNS*** IN 1932 AND 1933.

HE ALSO HIT 60 HOME RUNS IN 1932, WHICH WOULD HAVE TIED BABE RUTH'S RECORD, BUT TWO OF THEM WERE *ERASED* BY RAINED-OUT GAMES. (IF FIVE INNINGS OF A GAME AREN'T COMPLETED, NONE OF THE STATISTICS FROM THAT GAME COUNT.)

HE HAS MUSCLES IN HIS HAIR.

FOXX

LEFTY

*SECOND TO BABE RUTH, UNTIL WILLIE MAYS PASSED HIM IN 1966.

**WHEN A HITTER LEADS THE LEAGUE IN BATTING AVERAGE, HOME RUNS, AND RUNS BATTED IN.

THE A'S WERE EVERY BIT THE EQUAL OF THE LEGENDARY YANKEES OF THE SAME ERA. BUT WHEN IT CAME TO *REPUTATION*, THE YANKEES HAD THE DECISIVE ADVANTAGE OF PLAYING IN NEW YORK.

BY 1934, WITH REVENUES FALLING IN THE MIDST OF THE DEPRESSION, MACK HAD *SOLD OFF* ALL THE A'S BEST PLAYERS AND THE TEAM ENTERED ANOTHER LONG DECLINE.

BUT BASEBALL WAS NOW A FULLY ENTRENCHED BIG BUSINESS. STAR PLAYERS, THEN AS NOW, WERE *IMMUNE* TO ECONOMIC PRESSURES FELT BY THEIR FANS. IN 1932, BABE RUTH WAS ASKED WHAT HE THOUGHT ABOUT HIS SALARY OF $80,000 *EXCEEDING* THE $75,000 EARNED BY PRESIDENT HERBERT HOOVER.*

WHAT THE HELL DOES HOOVER HAVE TO DO WITH IT? ANYWAY, I HAD A *BETTER YEAR* THAN HE DID.

*WHO LOVED BASEBALL AND WAS THE SUBJECT OF THE FIRST PRINT APPEARANCE OF THE PHRASE *"AS AMERICAN AS BASEBALL OR APPLE PIE,"* IN MARCH OF 1928.

John McGraw

Fearless and pugnacious as both a player and manager, John McGraw acquired the nickname "Little Napoleon" even before the end of his playing days. His steely determination was forged early in life, as he ran away from an abusive home at the age of twelve and made his way through a succession of minor league teams before signing on with the Baltimore Orioles (later to become the New York Yankees) in 1891. As a shortstop, McGraw became known for both his glove and for his willingness to bend the rules. Becoming a player-manager with the New York Giants by 1902, McGraw went on to win 2,763 games over the course of thirty-four seasons, a total exceeded only by his rival Connie Mack—who was also McGraw's greatest admirer among his managing peers.

Hated by some of his players for his strictness (McGraw forbade them to smile in the dugout), he also earned their respect for his courage.

He was also known as a smart and fair appraiser of talent. He considered fellow shortstop Honus Wagner to be by far the greatest player in the history of the game.

VIRGINIA WOOLF'S OBSERVATION ABOUT SPORTS AND AMERICAN CULTURE (SEE PAGE 59) WAS NOWHERE MORE TRUE THAN IN THE NEGRO LEAGUES, WHERE GAMES AND TEAMS BECAME *IMPORTANT TOUCHSTONES* OF LOCAL AFRICAN AMERICAN COMMUNITIES.

THAT WAS PARTICULARLY APPARENT IN *PITTSBURGH.*

IN THE 1930S, BASEBALL'S BEST RIVALRY WASN'T RED SOX VS. YANKEES OR GIANTS VS. CARDINALS.

IT WAS *GRAYS VS. CRAWFORDS.*

THESE TWO PITTSBURGH-BASED NEGRO LEAGUE TEAMS SHARED AN INTENSE RIVALRY BETWEEN 1931 AND 1938, FEATURING A *WHO'S WHO* OF THAT GENERATION'S GREATEST AFRICAN AMERICAN PLAYERS.

AFTER GAMES, PLAYERS WERE PART OF THE THRIVING INTEGRATED SOCIAL SCENE AT GUS GREENLEE'S *CRAWFORD GRILL*, A GATHERING SPOT FOR PITTSBURGH'S SOCIAL ELITE ON ANY GIVEN NIGHT, YOU MIGHT FIND...

...*JOSH GIBSON* KNOWN AS THE *"BLACK BABE RUTH"* FOR HIS POWER AND CHARISMA--THOUGH SEVERAL OBSERVERS SUGGESTED THAT PERHAPS RUTH SHOULD HAVE BEEN KNOWN AS THE *"WHITE JOSH GIBSON."*

BUCK LEONARD, KNOWN AS THE LOU GEHRIG TO GIBSON'S "BLACK BABE RUTH." A PERENNIAL NEGRO LEAGUE ALL-STAR, LEONARD *TURNED DOWN* A MAJOR LEAGUE OFFER IN 1952 BECAUSE HE FELT HE WAS TOO OLD TO PLAY WELL.

LEON DAY, A PREMIER PITCHER FOR THE BROOKLYN AND NEWARK EAGLES. AFTER SERVING IN WORLD WAR II, HE WOULD PLAY AN UNEXPECTED ROLE IN *THE FIRST EUROPEAN BASEBALL CHAMPIONSHIP, THE ETO WORLD SERIES. (SEE PAGE 84.)*

TURKEY STEARNES, A WIDE-RANGING OUTFIELDER AND LIFETIME .344 HITTER. IN MANY OFF-SEASONS, HE WORKED IN AN AUTO PLANT OWNED BY WILLIAM BRIGGS, WHO ALSO OWNED THE DETROIT TIGERS-- A TEAM STEARNES WAS *BARRED* FROM JOINING.

BRILLIANT ON THE FIELD AND ENDLESSLY QUOTABLE OFF IT, SATCHEL PAIGE PROBABLY PITCHED FOR MORE TEAMS IN *MORE PLACES* THAN ANY OTHER BALLPLAYER IN HISTORY.

JOE DIMAGGIO CALLED PAIGE THE BEST PITCHER HE EVER FACED. THE EVER-QUOTABLE DIZZY DEAN (MORE ABOUT HIM ON PAGE 67), WHO BARNSTORMED WITH PAIGE DURING THE 1930S, SAID...

IF SATCH AND I WERE PITCHING ON THE SAME TEAM, WE'D HAVE THE PENNANT CINCHED BY JULY 4 AND GO FISHING UNTIL WORLD SERIES TIME.

Cumberland Posey and Gus Greenlee

Cumberland Posey was born to a prominent African American family in Homestead, Pennsylvania, outside Pittsburgh. His father was a riverboat engineer who later owned the Diamond Coke and Coal Company. A superb basketball player in the era before the integration of the *National Basketball Association*, he was also good enough at *baseball* to sign with the Homestead Grays in 1911.

CUMBERLAND WILLIS POSEY, JR.
'CUM"
PRE-N[...] LEAGUES, 1911-1919
HOME[...]AD GRAYS, 1920-1946
SUCCESSFUL ENTR[...] PERENNIAL POWERHOUSE HOMESTEAD
GRAYS, WINNING [...] EGRO NATIONAL LEAGUE PENNANTS,
1937-1945, AND T[...] ORLD SERIES TITLES. BEGAN AS SEMI-
PROFESSIONAL O[...] BECAME BUSINESS MANAGER, THEN
MANAGER, AND [...] M 1920 TO 1946. GRAYS REIGNED AS
MOST FORMIDAB[...] M OF 1920s, WINNING MORE THAN 80
PERCENT OF GA[...] ESSIVE TALENT SCOUT, SIGNED TOP
STARS, DRAWIN[...] HOME GAMES AT FORBES FIELD IN
PITTSBURGH AND[...] WAS[...]

Ten years later, Posey owned the team, and later he became a forceful executive in the Negro National League of the 1930s. He died in 1946 and is the only man elected to the Hall of Fame in *both* baseball and basketball.*

Gus Greenlee came north from North Carolina to Pittsburgh as part of the *great migration* of African Americans during the 1910s and 1920s. Settling in Pittsburgh, he worked in steel mills and ran a numbers racket. His gambling enterprise made him *rich and influential*, and he bought the Pittsburgh Crawfords in 1930. Then, incensed that his players couldn't use the dressing rooms at Forbes Field, Greenlee built his own stadium, *Greenlee Field*. Controlling his own revenues, he stocked the Crawfords with great players and also rented out the stadium to football's *Pittsburgh Steelers* as a practice facility. After the 1938 season, Greenlee sold the Crawfords and tore down the stadium. He died in 1952.

*One other Basketball Hall of Famer occupies a strange place in baseball history. *Bill Sharman*, a Celtics stalwart during the 1950s, was also a long-time Brooklyn Dodgers farmhand, called up to the big leagues during the 1951 pennant race. He never appeared in a game, but was *ejected* while sitting on the bench on September 27 of that year...becoming in all likelihood the only player ever *ejected* from a major league game while never *appearing* in one.

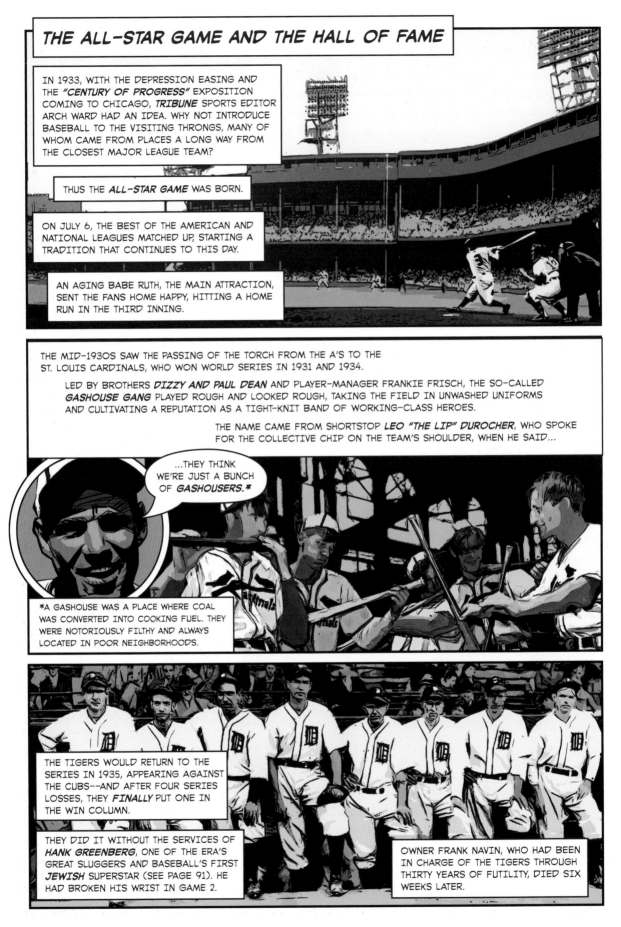

THE ALL-STAR GAME AND THE HALL OF FAME

IN 1933, WITH THE DEPRESSION EASING AND THE *"CENTURY OF PROGRESS"* EXPOSITION COMING TO CHICAGO, *TRIBUNE* SPORTS EDITOR ARCH WARD HAD AN IDEA. WHY NOT INTRODUCE BASEBALL TO THE VISITING THRONGS, MANY OF WHOM CAME FROM PLACES A LONG WAY FROM THE CLOSEST MAJOR LEAGUE TEAM?

THUS THE *ALL-STAR GAME* WAS BORN.

ON JULY 6, THE BEST OF THE AMERICAN AND NATIONAL LEAGUES MATCHED UP, STARTING A TRADITION THAT CONTINUES TO THIS DAY.

AN AGING BABE RUTH, THE MAIN ATTRACTION, SENT THE FANS HOME HAPPY, HITTING A HOME RUN IN THE THIRD INNING.

THE MID-1930S SAW THE PASSING OF THE TORCH FROM THE A'S TO THE ST. LOUIS CARDINALS, WHO WON WORLD SERIES IN 1931 AND 1934.

LED BY BROTHERS *DIZZY AND PAUL DEAN* AND PLAYER-MANAGER FRANKIE FRISCH, THE SO-CALLED *GASHOUSE GANG* PLAYED ROUGH AND LOOKED ROUGH, TAKING THE FIELD IN UNWASHED UNIFORMS AND CULTIVATING A REPUTATION AS A TIGHT-KNIT BAND OF WORKING-CLASS HEROES.

THE NAME CAME FROM SHORTSTOP *LEO "THE LIP" DUROCHER*, WHO SPOKE FOR THE COLLECTIVE CHIP ON THE TEAM'S SHOULDER, WHEN HE SAID...

...THEY THINK WE'RE JUST A BUNCH OF *GASHOUSERS.**

*A GASHOUSE WAS A PLACE WHERE COAL WAS CONVERTED INTO COOKING FUEL. THEY WERE NOTORIOUSLY FILTHY AND ALWAYS LOCATED IN POOR NEIGHBORHOODS.

THE TIGERS WOULD RETURN TO THE SERIES IN 1935, APPEARING AGAINST THE CUBS--AND AFTER FOUR SERIES LOSSES, THEY *FINALLY* PUT ONE IN THE WIN COLUMN.

THEY DID IT WITHOUT THE SERVICES OF *HANK GREENBERG*, ONE OF THE ERA'S GREAT SLUGGERS AND BASEBALL'S FIRST *JEWISH* SUPERSTAR (SEE PAGE 91). HE HAD BROKEN HIS WRIST IN GAME 2.

OWNER FRANK NAVIN, WHO HAD BEEN IN CHARGE OF THE TIGERS THROUGH THIRTY YEARS OF FUTILITY, DIED SIX WEEKS LATER.

Dizzy Dean

TEACH, *YOU* LEARN 'EM ENGLISH, AND *I'LL* LEARN 'EM BASEBALL.

A meteor streaking across the sky of 1930s baseball, Jay Hanna "Dizzy" Dean put together four dominant seasons from 1934 to 1937, including a *thirty-win season* for the Gashouse Gang in 1934. A *broken toe* made him change his pitching motion, which ruined his arm by 1938, though he scuffled through another decade before retiring. He then became an announcer, enlivening the airwaves from 1941 to 1968. Fans loved his *cheerful mangling* of the English language. When an English teacher wrote him a critical letter, Dean issued a famous riposte over the air.

Dean was inducted into the Hall of Fame in 1953.

The House of David

In the same year as the first World Series, a religious colony known as the *Israelite House of David* was founded in Benton Harbor, Michigan. Its members were forbidden to *shave or cut their hair*, among other prohibitions. The colony quickly grew to include its own zoo, cannery, and an amusement park on the shores of Lake Michigan. In 1913, its founders hit upon another way to spread the word: a barnstorming baseball team.

As the team's fame grew, its owners brought in *big-name talent:* Grover Cleveland Alexander, Three Finger Brown, Chief Bender, and Satchel Paige were among the stars who donned the House of David uniform over the years. (Not all of them grew beards; the team provided *false whiskers* for those who wished to remain clean-shaven.)

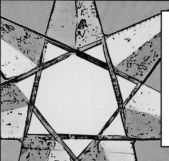

Babe Didrikson Zaharias, probably the most famous female athlete of the prewar era, played for the team in the 1930s.

AS BASEBALL MATURED IN THE UNITED STATES, IT ALSO BEGAN TO TAKE HOLD AROUND THE WORLD--MOST NOTABLY IN *JAPAN.**

THE FIRST JAPANESE BASEBALL TEAMS STARTED TO FORM IN THE 1870S, LED BY EXPATRIATE AMERICAN TEACHERS. THE FIRST MATCHES BETWEEN AMERICAN AND JAPANESE TEAMS DATE TO 1896.

THE GAME WAS KNOWN AS *YAKYUU*, OR "FIELD BALL," ALTHOUGH THE VERBAL APPROXIMATION *BESUBORU* WAS ALSO USED.

*ALSO LATIN AMERICA-- SEE PAGES 112–113.

IN 1920, JAPANESE BASEBALL TOOK A BIG STEP FORWARD WITH THE FORMATION OF *NIHON UNDO KYOKAI*, THE COUNTRY'S FIRST PROFESSIONAL BASEBALL CLUB.

THAT SAME YEAR, HERB HUNTER LED A TEAM ON A TOUR OF JAPAN. HUNTER WOULD RETURN IN 1922 AND 1931--THAT LAST TIME WITH A TEAM THAT INCLUDED SUCH GREATS AS MICKEY COCHRANE, LOU GEHRIG, AND LEFTY GROVE.

TEAMS OF BLACK PLAYERS ALSO TOURED JAPAN IN THE 1920S AND '30S, AND A BLACK PITCHER--*JAMES BONNER*-- PLAYED BRIEFLY IN JAPAN MORE THAN A DECADE BEFORE JACKIE ROBINSON TOOK THE FIELD FOR THE DODGERS.

THE LOS ANGELES NIPPONS, COMPOSED OF *JAPANESE AMERICAN PLAYERS*, ALSO TOURED THE ISLANDS IN 1931.

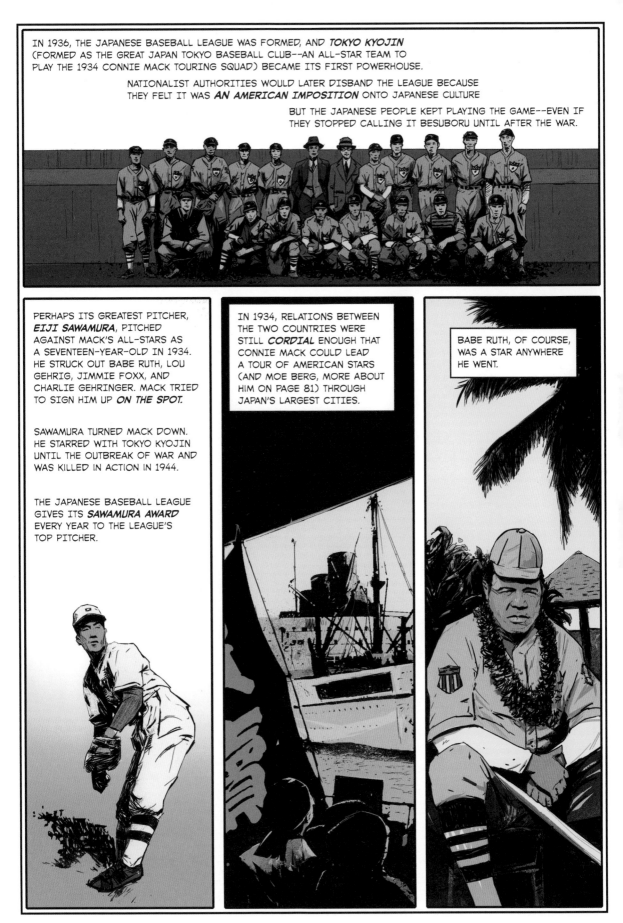

IN 1936, THE JAPANESE BASEBALL LEAGUE WAS FORMED, AND *TOKYO KYOJIN* (FORMED AS THE GREAT JAPAN TOKYO BASEBALL CLUB--AN ALL-STAR TEAM TO PLAY THE 1934 CONNIE MACK TOURING SQUAD) BECAME ITS FIRST POWERHOUSE.

NATIONALIST AUTHORITIES WOULD LATER DISBAND THE LEAGUE BECAUSE THEY FELT IT WAS *AN AMERICAN IMPOSITION* ONTO JAPANESE CULTURE

BUT THE JAPANESE PEOPLE KEPT PLAYING THE GAME--EVEN IF THEY STOPPED CALLING IT BESUBORU UNTIL AFTER THE WAR.

PERHAPS ITS GREATEST PITCHER, *EIJI SAWAMURA*, PITCHED AGAINST MACK'S ALL-STARS AS A SEVENTEEN-YEAR-OLD IN 1934. HE STRUCK OUT BABE RUTH, LOU GEHRIG, JIMMIE FOXX, AND CHARLIE GEHRINGER. MACK TRIED TO SIGN HIM UP *ON THE SPOT.*

SAWAMURA TURNED MACK DOWN. HE STARRED WITH TOKYO KYOJIN UNTIL THE OUTBREAK OF WAR AND WAS KILLED IN ACTION IN 1944.

THE JAPANESE BASEBALL LEAGUE GIVES ITS *SAWAMURA AWARD* EVERY YEAR TO THE LEAGUE'S TOP PITCHER.

IN 1934, RELATIONS BETWEEN THE TWO COUNTRIES WERE STILL *CORDIAL* ENOUGH THAT CONNIE MACK COULD LEAD A TOUR OF AMERICAN STARS (AND MOE BERG, MORE ABOUT HIM ON PAGE 81) THROUGH JAPAN'S LARGEST CITIES.

BABE RUTH, OF COURSE, WAS A STAR ANYWHERE HE WENT.

The Sultan of Swat

It is probably *impossible* to overstate the influence George Herman Ruth Jr. had on the development of baseball in the critical years of the 1920s. A sport crippled by the fallout from the Black Sox scandal was *rejuvenated* by the exploits of the Babe, who transformed how the game was played and appreciated.

THE HOME RUN BECAME GLORIFIED WITH BABE RUTH. STARTING WITH HIM, BATTERS HAVE BEEN THINKING IN TERMS OF *HOW FAR* THEY COULD HIT THE BALL, NOT *HOW OFTEN.*

A larger-than-life figure in every way, with *legendary appetites* for food, liquor, women, and baseball, Ruth became a cultural hero at exactly the moment the first Yankee dynasty was embodying the brashness and energy of the *Roaring Twenties.* The Babe roared louder than anyone else.

His statistics are incredible on their own, but his legend is better served by the stories, none of which has endured like the *Called Shot.*

In the 1932 World Series, angered at abuse from the Cubs bench, Ruth appeared to *point out to center field* first with his bat and then with his hand. He hit the next pitch about as far as anyone has ever hit a pitch in Wrigley Field. It would be his last World Series home run, and the *capstone* on the *Babe Ruth legend.*

Did he really call the shot? Opinions differ. The Cubs say *no*. People at the game, including future Supreme Court Justice John Paul Stevens, say yes. Either way, the story entered the popular imagination and has never left.

Sensing an opportunity, the Curtiss Candy Company, at the time located across the street from Wrigley Field, put up a rooftop billboard advertising its *Baby Ruth* bar (which was actually named after President Grover Cleveland's daughter). The billboard, a sore spot with some Cubs fans as their World Series drought continued, was torn down in the 1970s.

After Ruth's retirement in 1935, he tried for the rest of his life to get a job managing a big league club. No one would hire him because no baseball executive trusted him to rein himself in enough to handle other players. This concern was probably well-founded, as Ruth's behavior was *notoriously* intemperate.

COBB CANNOT BE FULLY APPRECIATED UNLESS YOU ARE A STUDENT OF BASEBALL. RUTH APPEALS TO *EVERYBODY.*

During World War II, Ruth worked tirelessly making appearances to rally support for the troops, even as he continued to hope for a chance to manage a team. By 1946, *cancer* began to sap him of his physique and energy. He made a final appearance at Yankee Stadium with the rest of the 1923 team before dying in 1948.

COOPERSTOWN HOTELIER STEPHEN CARLTON CLARK MADE THE FIRST *OFFICIAL* PLANS TO BUILD A HALL OF FAME IN THE EARLY 1930S.

HE HOPED TO REJUVENATE COOPERSTOWN'S TOURIST TRADE, DEVASTATED BY THE DEPRESSION AND PROHIBITION.

IN 1936, HE AND HIS GROUP HONORED THE *FIRST FIVE...*

THE HALL ALSO VOTED IN NEW MEMBERS FOR 1937--39, AS THE BUILDING WAS UNDER CONSTRUCTION AND PREPARATIONS WERE MADE FOR ITS OFFICIAL OPENING.

NATIONAL BASEBALL MUSEUM

THE *GRAND OPENING* AND FIRST INDUCTION CEREMONY TOOK PLACE ON JUNE 12, 1939, WITH MOST OF THE SURVIVING INDUCTEES IN ATTENDANCE.

IT'S A PLEASURE FOR ME TO COME UP HERE AND BE PICKED IN THE HALL OF FAME.

Rogers Hornsby

Rogers Hornsby carved out a spot on baseball's Mount Rushmore with his 1924 season, during which he hit *.424*, and through his unparalleled achievement of 1922––when he hit .401 *and* launched forty home runs. No other player has ever matched that particular feat. Nicknamed "Rajah" or *"The Rajah,"* to reflect his regal game (and *his royal self-regard*), Hornsby put together one of the great five-year stretches in the history of the game from 1921 to 1925, *averaging* .402 over that period. The next closest period of sustained hitting brilliance is Ty Cobb's 1909–13 seasons, during which Cobb managed a measly .396. Hornsby's overall career batting average of .358 is second only to Cobb's.

Hornsby was never personally popular because he knew how good he was and didn't bother to be *modest* about it. But his immense talent gained him the respect of fellow players, and even umpires.

SON, IF YOU PITCH A STRIKE, MR. HORNSBY WILL LET YOU KNOW.

HERE YOU SEE RAJAH AND MR. CUB IN THE LATE 1950S.

He also *mentored* a number of young hitters in the 1940s and '50s, and even compared notes with sluggers at the top of their games.

Never a fan of the modern game (see page 116 for his comments on Roger Maris breaking Babe Ruth's home-run mark), Hornsby died in 1963 with his hitting records and his acerbic personality intact.

THE ESTABLISHMENT OF THE HALL OF FAME GAVE BASEBALL A SENSE OF *HISTORY,* AND IN AMERICAN CULTURE MORE BROADLY, THE GAME GAINED A DEEPER HOLD THAN IT EVER HAD. ONE BIG REASON: *BROADCAST MEDIA.*

THE 1939 YANKEES WERE--ALONG WITH THE '27 EDITION AND THE 1909 PIRATES--ONE OF THE GREATEST TEAMS EVER TO TAKE THE FIELD.

WITHOUT THE STAR POWER OF THE 1927 TEAM, THIS YEAR'S YANKEES FEATURED *OVERALL EXCELLENCE AT EVERY POSITION.*

THE *BRONX BOMBERS** ROLLED TO 106 WINS AND THEIR FOURTH STRAIGHT WORLD SERIES TRIUMPH, THIS TIME OVER THE CINCINNATI REDS. (WHO WOULD RETURN TO THE SERIES AND WIN IT IN 1940.)

IN 1938, THE LAST HOLDOUTS COLLAPSED AND EVERY MAJOR LEAGUE TEAM HAD A RADIO BROADCASTING DEAL. NATIONAL NETWORKS ADDED BASEBALL TO THEIR WEEKLY SCHEDULES.

BASEBALL WAS NOW AVAILABLE TO PEOPLE WHO COULD NOT ATTEND GAMES.

*THIS NICKNAME WAS COINED IN 1936 BY NEW YORK WORLD-TELEGRAM WRITER DANIEL M. DANIELS, WHO WAS PUNNING ON "THE BROWN BOMBER," HEAVYWEIGHT CHAMP JOE LOUIS'S NICKNAME.

AS BARNSTORMING DECLINED, *RADIO* TOOK OVER THE FUNCTION OF CREATING BASEBALL FANS IN PLACES *FAR AWAY* FROM THE NEAREST TEAM.

ANOTHER LANDMARK IN BASEBALL'S MEDIA HISTORY OCCURRED ON AUGUST 26, 1939, AS THE REDS AND DODGERS PLAYED THE FIRST TELEVISED MAJOR LEAGUE GAME.

BASEBALL BEGAN TO BE A PART OF THE BROADCAST *ENTERTAINMENT INDUSTRY*--WHICH, BECAUSE IT WAS CENTERED IN NEW YORK, TENDED TO FAVOR THE YANKEES, WHO ALSO HAPPENED TO BE IN THE MIDDLE OF AN *UNPRECEDENTED* PERIOD OF DOMINANCE.

A WEEK LATER, HITLER INVADED POLAND AND EUROPE WAS PLUNGED INTO *WORLD WAR II.*

AS A RESULT, WHETHER YOU LOVED THEM OR HATED THEM, THE YANKEES BECAME *AMERICA'S TEAM.*

GERMAN ARMY ATTACKS
CITIES BOMBED, PORT B[...]
DANZIG IS ACCEPTED

The Luckiest Man On The Face Of The Earth

LADIES AND GENTLEMEN, THIS IS THE FIRST TIME LOU GEHRIG'S NAME WILL NOT APPEAR ON THE YANKEES LINEUP IN *2,130 CONSECUTIVE GAMES.*

Known as the *"Iron Horse,"* Lou Gehrig batted *cleanup* behind Babe Ruth for ten years, from 1925 to 1934. A fearsome player in his own right, Gehrig *outhit Ruth* and drove in more runs over those ten seasons, while Ruth basked in the spotlight of his home-run power and his outsized persona. A New York native, Gehrig signed with the Yankees out of Columbia University in 1923 and never played for another team.

He began noticing his physical deterioration in 1938, and by the following year took himself out of the Yankees' lineup, ending a consecutive-games streak that *dated back to 1925.* During that time he played through head injuries and broken bones, but amyotrophic lateral sclerosis––now commonly known as *Lou Gehrig's disease*––finally wore him down.

His was the first *number retired* in the history of baseball, at Lou Gehrig Appreciation Day on July 4, 1939. There he delivered one of the most famous speeches in the history of American sport–– and reconciled with Babe Ruth.

TODAY I CONSIDER MYSELF THE LUCKIEST MAN ON THE FACE OF THE EARTH...

He died two years later.

IN RETROSPECT, THE 1941 SEASON SEEMS LIKE A *NATURAL BREAK POINT* IN THE HISTORY OF BASEBALL. TWO RECORDS WERE SET THAT SEEM UNBREAKABLE: .406 AND 56. LOU GEHRIG DIED OF THE DISEASE THAT WOULD COME TO BEAR HIS NAME. THE BROOKLYN DODGERS BECAME THE FIRST TEAM TO WEAR *BATTING HELMETS*, AND THE LAST ALL–NEW YORK WORLD SERIES UNTIL 1999 WAS PLAYED BETWEEN THOSE DODGERS AND THE MIGHTY YANKEES, WHO WON IN FIVE GAMES. (THERE'S ALSO A BEGINNING THERE, SINCE IN BASEBALL NOTHING EVER REALLY ENDS WITHOUT SOMETHING ELSE BEGINNING; THAT SERIES KICKED OFF A RUN OF DODGERS' *NEAR-GREATNESS* THAT SAW THEM LOSE FIVE SERIES IN TWELVE YEARS...*ALL TO THE YANKEES*.)

406

E TO REGISTRAN TO APPEAR FOR PHYSICAL EXAM

uly 4, 1941
(Date)

J. Yarn
(examining physician)

ALSO, IN JUNE OF THAT YEAR, PHILLIES RIGHT-HANDER *HUGH MULCAHY* BECAME THE FIRST BIG-LEAGUER *DRAFTED* BECAUSE OF WORLD WAR II.

Failure to do so is an act punishable

Not A Record, But You'll Never See It Again: .406

When Ted Williams took the field on the last day of the 1941 season, his batting average stood at .3995--in other words, technically .400. But Williams refused to sit out and protect his average, and during that season-ending double-header the Splendid Splinter went 6 for 8 to finish at .406. This was the first .400 season since Bill Terry's in 1930.

The feat has not been accomplished since.

I HOPE SOMEBODY HITS .400 SOON. THEN PEOPLE CAN START PESTERING THAT GUY WITH QUESTIONS ABOUT THE LAST GUY TO HIT .400.

Top Ten Averages Since 1941

Tony Gwynn Sr., San Diego (1994) .394, George Brett, Kansas City (1980) .390, Ted Williams, Boston (1957) .388, Rod Carew, Minnesota (1977) .388, Larry Walker, Colorado (1999) .379, Stan Musial, St. Louis (1948) .376, Tony Gwynn Sr., San Diego (1997) .372, Nomar Garciaparra, Boston (2000) .372, Todd Helton, Colorado (2000) .372, Ichiro Suzuki, Seattle (2004) .372

Unbreakable Records: 56

Other than Cy Young's 511 wins, no baseball record is considered more secure than Joe DiMaggio's *56-game hitting streak* from May to July of 1941. The *Yankee Clipper*, so named for his grace on the field, was no stranger to hitting streaks; he'd hit in 61 straight games in the minor leagues in 1933. But at that time, the longest streak in major league history was Wee Willie Keeler's *44 games* in 1897. The longest one since DiMaggio? Pete Rose's *44 games* in 1978 (a *symmetry* compounded by the fact that 1897 and 1978 are numeric anagrams).

A fifty-six-game hitting streak is, in all likelihood, the *most improbable feat* in the history of organized sports.

The incredible nature of the streak was enough to propel DiMaggio to a *Most Valuable Player* (MVP) win over Ted Williams, despite Williams hitting .406 that year. (The fact that Williams was *notoriously prickly* with reporters probably made a difference too.)

And the notoriety of the streak--plus DiMaggio's overall excellence--couldn't have hurt his prospects with Marilyn Monroe, either.

DIMAGGIO'S MARRIAGE TO MARILYN MONROE DIDN'T LAST, BUT HIS STREAK PROBABLY WILL.

BASEBALL IN WARTIME

THEN, TWO MONTHS AFTER THE END OF THE 1941 SEASON... *PEARL HARBOR.*

THE NEXT DAY, PRESIDENT FRANKLIN DELANO ROOSEVELT DELIVERED HIS FAMOUS SPEECH DECLARING DECEMBER 7, 1941...

...A DATE WHICH WILL *LIVE IN INFAMY...*

FDR ASKED CONGRESS FOR A DECLARATION OF WAR.

LEISURE ACTIVITIES AND TRAVEL WERE SHARPLY CURTAILED DURING THE WAR, BUT FDR DEEMED BASEBALL *ESSENTIAL TO HOME-FRONT MORALE.*

SO WHILE HUNDREDS OF BALLPLAYERS JOINED THE *MILLIONS OF AMERICANS* SERVING IN EUROPE AND IN THE PACIFIC...

...THE GAME WENT ON AT HOME.

THE *FAT GUYS* VERSUS THE *TALL GUYS* AT THE OFFICE PICNIC.

IN TRUTH, THE GAME SUFFERED, BOTH FROM THE *MANPOWER SHORTAGE* AND FROM OTHER CHANGES ENFORCED BY LIFE DURING WARTIME.

ONE POSITIVE CHANGE WAS THE INTRODUCTION OF NIGHT GAMES. IN 1935, THE CINCINNATI REDS HAD BEEN THE FIRST MAJOR LEAGUE TEAM TO PLAY AN OFFICIAL NIGHT GAME. BY 1941, HALF OF MAJOR LEAGUE BALLPARKS HAD LIGHTS, BUT NIGHT GAMES WERE STILL RARE.

DURING THE WAR, THESE GAMES BECAME MUCH MORE COMMON SO THAT PEOPLE WORKING THE DAY SHIFT COULD STILL CATCH A BALL GAME. BASEBALL WAS A NEEDED DISTRACTION AND MORALE BOOSTER.

Under The Lights

Along with barnstorming clubs, teams in the minor leagues and Negro Leagues *pioneered night baseball* around 1930. Enthusiastic early adopters included the Kansas City Monarchs and the House of David, whose owners figured out that by playing at night they could fit in more games on a tour--sometimes playing each other--and thereby *increase gate receipts.* The initial lighting setups were a far cry from today's floodlit stadiums. The lights were portable, powered by generators, and provided *barely enough* illumination to make the games playable.

Major league owners *disdained* night baseball until the minors had proved it worthwhile. By 1948, every big-league ballpark (except Wrigley Field) had lights. It wasn't until *1988* that the *"Friendly Confines"* hosted its first night game.

IN ADDITION TO MANPOWER SHORTAGES, MATERIAL SHORTAGES ALSO MEANT NO SPRING TRAINING AND CURTAILED TRAVEL.

CORK FILLED

RUBBER FILLED

RUBBER SHORTAGES ALSO LED TO REDESIGNED BASEBALLS THAT FORCIBLY BROUGHT THE DEAD BALL ERA BACK TO LIFE FOR THE FIRST PART OF THE WAR.

THE INTRODUCTION OF SYNTHETIC RUBBER IN 1944 RETURNED THINGS TO NORMAL.

AT HOME AND ABROAD, CIVILIANS AND SOLDIERS IN BOTH THE UNITED STATES AND JAPAN KEPT ON PLAYING BASEBALL.

EVEN INTERNED JAPANESE AMERICANS COULD TAKE THEIR MINDS OFF THE INJUSTICE OF THEIR PLIGHT WHILE THEY WERE ON THE FIELD.

Moe Berg

When Jimmy Doolittle and his bomber squadron pulled off an *air raid on Tokyo* in 1943, the mission's success was a big shot in the arm for American morale.

Part of the reason for that success was film footage of Tokyo shot during a 1934 barnstorming tour by one *Morris J. Berg*, a catcher for the Boston Red Sox--of whom it was said he could *speak a dozen languages* but couldn't *hit* in any of them. Berg turned the footage over to the government after the tour, hoping it might be of strategic use.

(Or, if you are of a *conspiratorial* bent: the government sent him to shoot that footage, because who in his right mind would put Moe Berg on a touring baseball all-star team?)

During the war, Berg joined the OSS (later to become the CIA) and conducted a number of intelligence operations. The most important of those occurred in 1943, when Berg was sent to attend a speech given by physicist Werner Heisenberg (you have perhaps heard of his uncertainty principle). Armed with a gun and a suicide pill, Berg was supposed to shoot Heisenberg if he thought the lecture's contents suggested the Nazis were close to completing an atomic bomb. After some internal debate--Berg scribbled a joke about the uncertainty principle in the lecture program's margin--he let Heisenberg live. The Nazis never got their bomb.

After leaving intelligence work behind in the 1950s, Berg never held another job. He died in 1972, and his last words were apparently a question about how the Mets had done that day.

THE CARDINALS WERE THE BEST OF THE WARTIME CLUBS. THEY WENT TO THREE STRAIGHT WORLD SERIES FROM 1942 TO 1944.

LED BY THE YOUNG *STAN MUSIAL*, THE CARDINALS SANDWICHED TWO WINS AROUND A YANKEE SERIES TRIUMPH IN '43.

THE LAST OF THESE WINS, IN 1944, WAS PART OF THE ONLY *ALL-ST. LOUIS SERIES* EVER PLAYED. THE BROWNS LOST AND NEVER WON ANOTHER PENNANT BEFORE MOVING TO BALTIMORE IN 1953.

WARTIME CIRCUMSTANCES CREATED NEW POSSIBILITIES IN BASEBALL JUST AS IN OTHER PARTS OF AMERICAN CULTURE. IN 1943, CUBS OWNER PHILIP K. WRIGLEY STARTED THE *ALL-AMERICAN GIRLS PROFESSIONAL BASEBALL LEAGUE* (AAGPBL).

A TRANSPARENT *PUBLICITY STUNT*, THE NEW LEAGUE ALSO REFLECTED THE *SLOW EMERGENCE OF WOMEN* INTO AREAS OF AMERICAN LIFE PREVIOUSLY CLOSED OFF TO THEM.

AFTER ALL, IF WOMEN COULD BUILD *BOMBERS*, WHY COULDN'T THEY *PLAY BASEBALL?*

BASED IN SMALL MIDWESTERN CITIES, THE AAGPBL CONTINUED INTO THE 1950S. MANY OF THE LEAGUE'S SKEPTICS CAME AWAY *IMPRESSED* BY THE QUALITY OF THE PLAYERS.

SHORTSTOP DOTTIE SCHROEDER WAS THE ONLY PLAYER TO PARTICIPATE IN ALL TWELVE OF ITS FULL SEASONS.

I'D PAY $50,000 FOR HER IF SHE WAS A BOY.*

*THAT NEVER HAPPENED, BUT AT LEAST THREE WOMEN ARE KNOWN TO HAVE PLAYED FOR NEGRO LEAGUE TEAMS. SEE PAGE 105.

WARTIME INDUSTRIES ALSO PUT UNPRECEDENTED AMOUNTS OF MONEY IN THE POCKETS OF **BLACK FAMILIES**, AND AS A RESULT THEY FLOCKED TO BALL GAMES--BOTH NEGRO LEAGUE AND MAJOR LEAGUE. THIS DID NOT ESCAPE THE ATTENTION OF BASEBALL EXECUTIVES.

(INCLUDING THE DODGERS' BRANCH RICKEY AND WOULD-BE OWNER BILL VEECK--MORE ABOUT HIM ON PAGE 93.)

Monarchs vs. Eagles

EBBETS FIELD

VEECK TRIED TO BUY THE MORIBUND PHILLIES IN 1942 AND STOCK THE TEAM WITH **NEGRO LEAGUE PLAYERS**, BUT COMMISSIONER LANDIS AND NATIONAL LEAGUE PRESIDENT FORD FRICK **STONEWALLED HIM** UNTIL SOMEONE ELSE BOUGHT THE A'S.

HE WANTS TO DO WHAT!? GET BILL COX ON THE PHONE.

(OR SO VEECK CLAIMED. SEE PAGE 48.)

RICKEY HAD A DIFFERENT PLAN.

MONARCHS

HE KNEW IT WOULD TAKE A CERTAIN KIND OF PERSON TO WITHSTAND THE PRESSURES OF **INTEGRATING THE MAJOR LEAGUES.**

SO HE STARTED LOOKING FOR THAT PERSON. BY 1945, HE'D CONSIDERED A NUMBER OF PLAYERS, BUT THE ONE HE SETTLED ON WAS A SHORTSTOP FOR THE KANSAS CITY MONARCHS...

...BY THE NAME OF **JACK ROOSEVELT ROBINSON.**

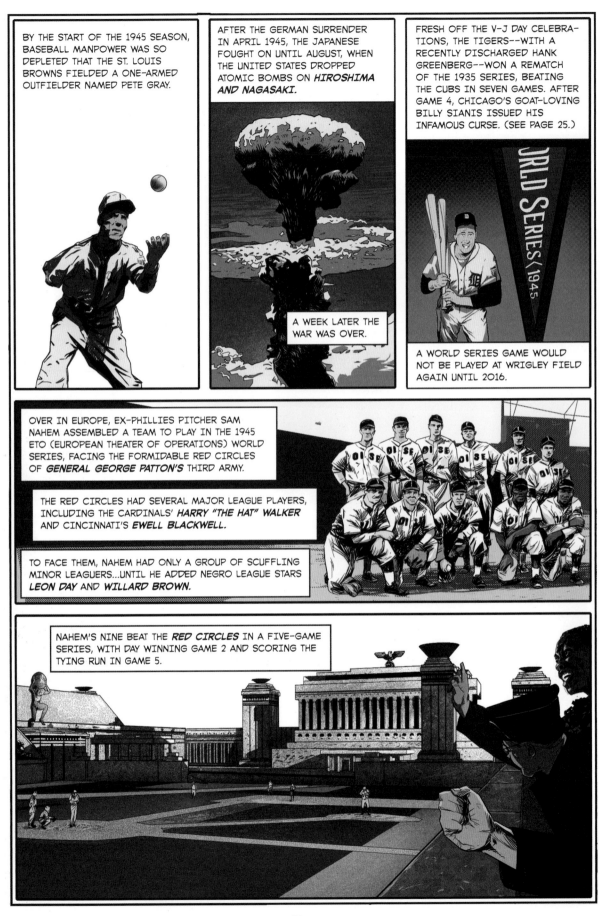

BY THE START OF THE 1945 SEASON, BASEBALL MANPOWER WAS SO DEPLETED THAT THE ST. LOUIS BROWNS FIELDED A ONE-ARMED OUTFIELDER NAMED PETE GRAY.

AFTER THE GERMAN SURRENDER IN APRIL 1945, THE JAPANESE FOUGHT ON UNTIL AUGUST, WHEN THE UNITED STATES DROPPED ATOMIC BOMBS ON *HIROSHIMA AND NAGASAKI.*

A WEEK LATER THE WAR WAS OVER.

FRESH OFF THE V-J DAY CELEBRATIONS, THE TIGERS--WITH A RECENTLY DISCHARGED HANK GREENBERG--WON A REMATCH OF THE 1935 SERIES, BEATING THE CUBS IN SEVEN GAMES. AFTER GAME 4, CHICAGO'S GOAT-LOVING BILLY SIANIS ISSUED HIS INFAMOUS CURSE. (SEE PAGE 25.)

WORLD SERIES 1945

A WORLD SERIES GAME WOULD NOT BE PLAYED AT WRIGLEY FIELD AGAIN UNTIL 2016.

OVER IN EUROPE, EX-PHILLIES PITCHER SAM NAHEM ASSEMBLED A TEAM TO PLAY IN THE 1945 ETO (EUROPEAN THEATER OF OPERATIONS) WORLD SERIES, FACING THE FORMIDABLE RED CIRCLES OF *GENERAL GEORGE PATTON'S* THIRD ARMY.

THE RED CIRCLES HAD SEVERAL MAJOR LEAGUE PLAYERS, INCLUDING THE CARDINALS' *HARRY "THE HAT" WALKER* AND CINCINNATI'S *EWELL BLACKWELL.*

TO FACE THEM, NAHEM HAD ONLY A GROUP OF SCUFFLING MINOR LEAGUERS...UNTIL HE ADDED NEGRO LEAGUE STARS *LEON DAY* AND *WILLARD BROWN.*

NAHEM'S NINE BEAT THE *RED CIRCLES* IN A FIVE-GAME SERIES, WITH DAY WINNING GAME 2 AND SCORING THE TYING RUN IN GAME 5.

84

TWO WEEKS AFTER THE 1945 SEASON ENDED, THE BROOKLYN DODGERS ANNOUNCED THE SIGNING OF JACKIE ROBINSON TO A MINOR LEAGUE CONTRACT WITH THE MONTREAL ROYALS.

AN *INTEGRATED TEAM* HAD REPRESENTED THE ARMED FORCES IN EUROPE, AND NOW BRANCH RICKEY FORCED MAJOR LEAGUE BASEBALL'S HAND.

ALL IN ALL, HUNDREDS OF PROFESSIONAL AND SEMIPRO PLAYERS SERVED IN WORLD WAR II.

THESE ARE THE MOST FAMOUS FACES OF BASEBALL'S WAR...AND THE FACES OF THE MEN WHO SURVIVED.

UNLIKE BERRA, GREENBERG, WILLIAMS, AND BASEBALL'S OTHER STARS WHO MADE IT HOME, A NUMBER OF BIG LEAGUERS AND NEGRO LEAGUERS MADE THE *ULTIMATE SACRIFICE.*

HERE RESTS IN HONORED GLORY
A COMRADE IN ARMS
KNOWN BUT TO GOD

DOZENS OF *JAPANESE BASEBALL LEAGUE* PLAYERS DIED IN THE WAR AS WELL, INCLUDING SEVERAL OF THE LEAGUE'S TOP STARS.

195

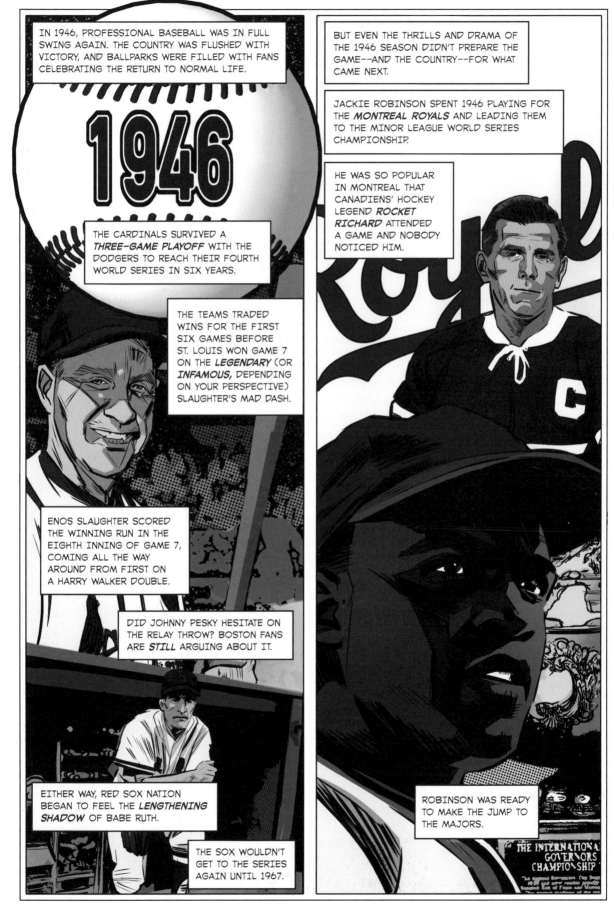

IN 1946, PROFESSIONAL BASEBALL WAS IN FULL SWING AGAIN. THE COUNTRY WAS FLUSHED WITH VICTORY, AND BALLPARKS WERE FILLED WITH FANS CELEBRATING THE RETURN TO NORMAL LIFE.

1946

THE CARDINALS SURVIVED A *THREE-GAME PLAYOFF* WITH THE DODGERS TO REACH THEIR FOURTH WORLD SERIES IN SIX YEARS.

THE TEAMS TRADED WINS FOR THE FIRST SIX GAMES BEFORE ST. LOUIS WON GAME 7 ON THE *LEGENDARY* (OR *INFAMOUS,* DEPENDING ON YOUR PERSPECTIVE) SLAUGHTER'S MAD DASH.

ENOS SLAUGHTER SCORED THE WINNING RUN IN THE EIGHTH INNING OF GAME 7, COMING ALL THE WAY AROUND FROM FIRST ON A HARRY WALKER DOUBLE.

DID JOHNNY PESKY HESITATE ON THE RELAY THROW? BOSTON FANS ARE *STILL* ARGUING ABOUT IT.

EITHER WAY, RED SOX NATION BEGAN TO FEEL THE *LENGTHENING SHADOW* OF BABE RUTH.

THE SOX WOULDN'T GET TO THE SERIES AGAIN UNTIL 1967.

BUT EVEN THE THRILLS AND DRAMA OF THE 1946 SEASON DIDN'T PREPARE THE GAME--AND THE COUNTRY--FOR WHAT CAME NEXT.

JACKIE ROBINSON SPENT 1946 PLAYING FOR THE *MONTREAL ROYALS* AND LEADING THEM TO THE MINOR LEAGUE WORLD SERIES CHAMPIONSHIP.

HE WAS SO POPULAR IN MONTREAL THAT CANADIENS' HOCKEY LEGEND *ROCKET RICHARD* ATTENDED A GAME AND NOBODY NOTICED HIM.

ROBINSON WAS READY TO MAKE THE JUMP TO THE MAJORS.

THE INTERNATIONAL GOVERNORS CHAMPIONSHIP

Teddy Ballgame

Ted Williams was said to have eyes so sharp he could count the stitches on a baseball as it came toward the plate. A student of the game, Williams sought out great hitters of previous generations while he was in the minor leagues. Among others, he consulted with .400 hitters Hugh Duffy, Rogers Hornsby, Bill Terry, and Ty Cobb--and had the confidence to argue with Cobb. The advice stood "Teddy Ballgame" in good stead, as he racked up his immortal .406 in 1941, only his third major league season.

Williams won the Triple Crown the next year, then spent three years as a fighter pilot during World War II. He also flew combat missions during the Korean War--often as wingman to future astronaut and U.S. Senator John Glenn. Ultimately, he lost almost five years of his baseball career to military service.

Returning to the Red Sox in 1946, he led the team to the World Series and was named American League MVP. He won another Triple Crown in 1947 (only he and Rogers Hornsby have achieved the feat twice).

Perhaps the best pure hitter in the game since its first generation of immortals, Williams would surely have eclipsed six hundred home runs and two thousand RBIs had military service not taken so many of his prime years. In his last at-bat in 1960, Williams hit a home run and then refused to come out for a curtain call, inspiring writer John Updike's famous quip: "Gods do not answer letters."

I HOPE SOMEDAY SATCHEL PAIGE AND JOSH GIBSON WILL BE VOTED INTO THE HALL OF FAME AS SYMBOLS OF THE GREAT NEGRO PLAYERS WHO ARE NOT HERE ONLY BECAUSE THEY WEREN'T GIVEN THE CHANCE.

After his retirement, he briefly managed the Washington Senators before leaving out of frustration that the players couldn't match his single-minded pursuit of excellence. In the 1960s, he advocated for the admission of former Negro League stars to the Hall of Fame. His call doubtless spurred the Hall to begin including Negro Leaguers sooner than it otherwise would have.

HERE'S TO YOU, MR. ROBINSON

WHEN JACKIE ROBINSON TROTTED OUT ONTO THE FIELD WITH THE BROOKLYN DODGERS ON APRIL 15, 1947, BASEBALL'S *UNOFFICIAL COLOR LINE* WAS BROKEN ONCE AND FOR ALL.

ROBINSON WASN'T THE BEST NEGRO LEAGUE PLAYER--OR EVEN THE BEST-KNOWN. HE WASN'T EVEN BRANCH RICKEY'S FIRST CHOICE. BUT RICKEY COULD SEE HE HAD *COURAGE.*

HE HAD DEMONSTRATED IT IN THE ARMY, WHEN HE WAS *COURT-MARTIALED* FOR REFUSING TO MOVE TO THE BACK OF A BUS WHILE TRAINING AS A TANK OFFICER IN 1944.

THAT INCIDENT DERAILED HIS MILITARY CAREER, BUT IT ALSO TOLD RICKEY THAT ROBINSON HAD THE COURAGE TO SURVIVE WHAT BASEBALL'S *ENTRENCHED RACISM* WOULD THROW AT HIM.

RICKEY TOLD ROBINSON AS MUCH IN A MEETING, THE YEAR BEFORE HE SIGNED ROBINSON TO PLAY FOR THE MONTREAL ROYALS.

YOU MEAN YOU WANT A BLACK MAN WHO *WON'T FIGHT BACK?*

I NEED A MAN WITH THE GUTS NOT TO FIGHT BACK.

ROBINSON KNEW THE FIRST AFRICAN AMERICAN IN THE MAJOR LEAGUES WOULD CARRY A UNIQUE BURDEN.

AND HE DECIDED TO ACCEPT IT.

DURING SPRING TRAINING, SEVERAL DODGER PLAYERS CIRCULATED A PETITION *AGAINST* ROBINSON MAKING THE TEAM. FURIOUS, DODGER MANAGER LEO DUROCHER TOOK A STAND.

I DON'T CARE IF THE GUY IS YELLOW OR BLACK, OR IF HE HAS *STRIPES* LIKE A F*CKIN' ZEBRA! *I'M* THE MANAGER OF THIS TEAM, AND I SAY HE *PLAYS!*

DIXIE WALKER, WHO STARTED THE PETITION, WAS TRADED AFTER THAT SEASON.

OTHER DODGERS RALLIED AROUND ROBINSON, NOTABLY *EDDIE STANKY* AND TEAM CAPTAIN *PEE WEE REESE.*

WHY DON'T YOU GUYS GO TO WORK ON SOMEBODY WHO CAN FIGHT BACK? THERE ISN'T ONE OF YOU HAS THE GUTS OF A *LOUSE!*

STANKY CALLED OUT THE *ENTIRE PHILLIES TEAM* DURING A GAME EARLY IN THE SEASON, AFTER PHILLIES MANAGER BEN CHAPMAN LED A BARRAGE OF RACIST ABUSE FROM THEIR DUGOUT.

REESE FAMOUSLY CROSSED THE INFIELD TO DRAPE AN ARM OVER ROBINSON'S SHOULDER DURING A GAME IN CINCINNATI IN 1947.*

*OR BOSTON IN 1948. ACCOUNTS DIFFER.

ALL THE SAME, ROBINSON WENT THROUGH AN ORDEAL *UNLIKE* ANY ATHLETE BEFORE OR SINCE.

PITCHERS ROUTINELY *THREW AT* HIM, OPPOSING TEAMS AND FANS *ABUSED* HIM, BASE RUNNERS *SPIKED* HIM AS THEY SLID INTO SECOND BASE.

IN CINCINNATI, HE RECEIVED THE FIRST OF WHAT WOULD BE MANY *DEATH THREATS.*

HE TOOK IT ALL, AND HE *PERSEVERED.*

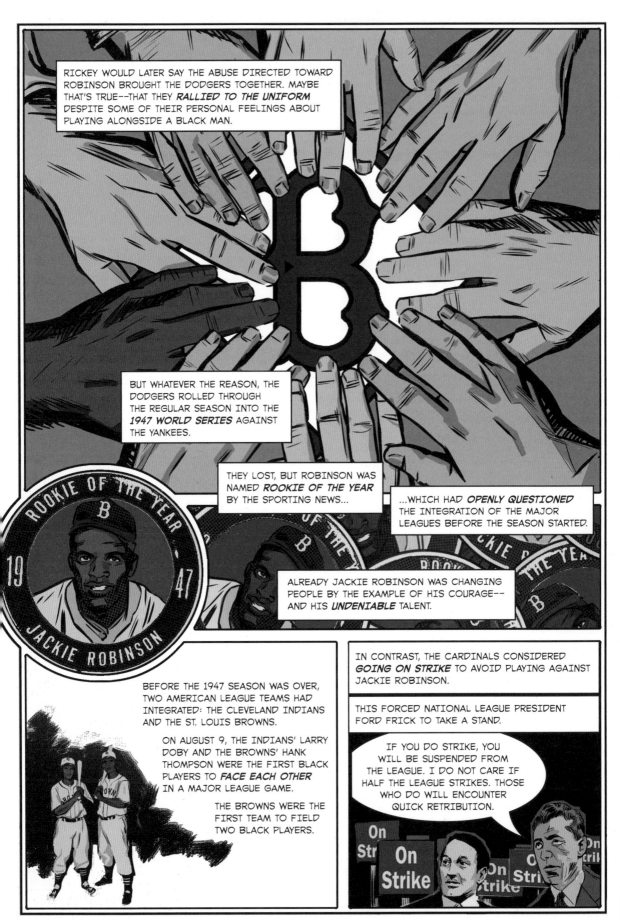

RICKEY WOULD LATER SAY THE ABUSE DIRECTED TOWARD ROBINSON BROUGHT THE DODGERS TOGETHER. MAYBE THAT'S TRUE--THAT THEY *RALLIED TO THE UNIFORM* DESPITE SOME OF THEIR PERSONAL FEELINGS ABOUT PLAYING ALONGSIDE A BLACK MAN.

BUT WHATEVER THE REASON, THE DODGERS ROLLED THROUGH THE REGULAR SEASON INTO THE *1947 WORLD SERIES* AGAINST THE YANKEES.

THEY LOST, BUT ROBINSON WAS NAMED *ROOKIE OF THE YEAR* BY THE SPORTING NEWS...

...WHICH HAD *OPENLY QUESTIONED* THE INTEGRATION OF THE MAJOR LEAGUES BEFORE THE SEASON STARTED.

ROOKIE OF THE YEAR
19 47
JACKIE ROBINSON

ALREADY JACKIE ROBINSON WAS CHANGING PEOPLE BY THE EXAMPLE OF HIS COURAGE-- AND HIS *UNDENIABLE* TALENT.

BEFORE THE 1947 SEASON WAS OVER, TWO AMERICAN LEAGUE TEAMS HAD INTEGRATED: THE CLEVELAND INDIANS AND THE ST. LOUIS BROWNS.

ON AUGUST 9, THE INDIANS' LARRY DOBY AND THE BROWNS' HANK THOMPSON WERE THE FIRST BLACK PLAYERS TO *FACE EACH OTHER* IN A MAJOR LEAGUE GAME.

THE BROWNS WERE THE FIRST TEAM TO FIELD TWO BLACK PLAYERS.

IN CONTRAST, THE CARDINALS CONSIDERED *GOING ON STRIKE* TO AVOID PLAYING AGAINST JACKIE ROBINSON.

THIS FORCED NATIONAL LEAGUE PRESIDENT FORD FRICK TO TAKE A STAND.

IF YOU DO STRIKE, YOU WILL BE SUSPENDED FROM THE LEAGUE. I DO NOT CARE IF HALF THE LEAGUE STRIKES. THOSE WHO DO WILL ENCOUNTER QUICK RETRIBUTION.

On Strike

On Strike

On Strike

On Strike

HENRY BENJAMIN GREENBERG

The first *Jewish star* in American sports, Hank Greenberg blazed a trail to the major leagues from his Bronx childhood, breaking in with the Detroit Tigers in 1933 and immediately establishing himself as one of the game's *elite sluggers,* along with Ruth, Gehrig, and Foxx. The next year he led his team to its first World Series since 1909, although he caused controversy by *refusing to play* on Rosh Hashanah or Yom Kippur.

Eventually he compromised, playing on Rosh Hashanah. After a Tigers win, the *Detroit Free Press* celebrated, with "Happy New Year" printed in *Hebrew* on its front page.

Falling to the Gashouse Gang Cardinals in 1934, the Tigers returned to the Series in 1935 against the Cubs, riding Greenberg's *MVP season* to the franchise's first World Series win.

Greenberg was always conscious of his status as a Jewish icon, and he took justifiable pride in proving that Jews could be powerful and athletic, contrary to the *stereotypes* of the day. He tore big-league pitching apart in the late 1930s before the threat of war with Japan led him to register for the draft after the 1940 season.

As war loomed, no one tried harder than Hank Greenberg to do his part. Classified 4-F because of flat feet, he appealed to the draft board and was enlisted. Then, after he was released in 1941 because of his age, he went back and *reenlisted,* serving until early 1945. All told, he lost more playing time than any other major league player.

He finished his career with the Pittsburgh Pirates, and was one of the white players *Jackie Robinson* remembered having encouraged him during his rookie season. Greenberg, having played through *anti-Semitic abuse,* understood what Robinson was going through.

After retiring, Greenberg joined the Cleveland Indians as general manager. He led efforts to bring in more African Americans, and as a result the Indians were the first American League team to field a black player: Larry Doby. Greenberg's *biggest mistake* as an executive was *declining* to sign three players Doby recommended from his Negro League days. Their names? *Ernie Banks, Willie Mays, and Hank Aaron.* All three are in the Hall of Fame.

THE STORY OF THE 1948 SEASON WAS THAT OF THE CLEVELAND INDIANS, *PERENNIAL ALSO-RANS* SINCE THEIR REMARKABLE WORLD SERIES WIN IN 1920.

THE TEAM'S MOST FAMOUS PLAYER WAS PITCHER *BOB FELLER*, WHO IN 1946 HAD BROKEN WALTER JOHNSON'S SEASON STRIKEOUT RECORD.

FELLER WAS ALSO KNOWN FOR HIS OPINION THAT FEW IF ANY BLACK PLAYERS HAD WHAT IT TOOK TO MAKE IT IN THE MAJORS.*

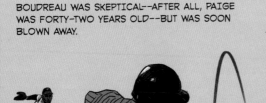

*HE WOULD LATER CHANGE HIS TUNE, AND GET SOME DESERVED CREDIT FOR EXPOSING NEGRO LEAGUE STARS TO WIDER AUDIENCES DURING BARNSTORMING TOURS IN THE 1940S.

IN JULY, WITH THE TEAM IN A TIGHT PENNANT RACE WITH THE RED SOX AND YANKEES, INDIANS PLAYER-MANAGER LOU BOUDREAU GOT A CALL FROM OWNER BILL VEECK, ASKING HIM TO COME IN AND WORK OUT A "NEW" PITCHER.

BOUDREAU SHOWED UP AND DISCOVERED THE PITCHER IN QUESTION WAS *SATCHEL PAIGE*.

BOUDREAU WAS SKEPTICAL--AFTER ALL, PAIGE WAS FORTY-TWO YEARS OLD--BUT WAS SOON BLOWN AWAY.

THE WAY VEECK TOLD THE STORY LATER, BOUDREAU MADE SOLID CONTACT WITH ONLY ONE OF PAIGE'S PITCHES.

VEECK KNEW A *GATE ATTRACTION* WHEN HE SAW ONE, AND BOUDREAU KNEW *GOOD PITCHING*.

DON'T LET HIM GET AWAY. WE CAN USE HIM.

PAIGE BECAME AN INCREDIBLE ATTRACTION. HIS STARTS SET *ATTENDANCE RECORDS* BOTH AT HOME AND ON THE ROAD.

HE ALSO WON GAMES, GOING 6-1 TO HELP THE INDIANS TAKE THE PENNANT.

THE INDIANS' IMPROBABLE RUN CONCLUDED WITH A WORLD SERIES WIN OVER THE BOSTON BRAVES.

AN IMAGE OF PITCHER STEVE GROMEK CELEBRATING WITH LARRY DOBY BECAME ICONIC BECAUSE, AS DOBY WOULD LATER SAY, IT WAS JUST *TWO TEAMMATES* "HAPPY THAT THEY WON A BALL GAME."

AN INTEGRATED TEAM HAD WON THE WORLD SERIES.

PAIGE PITCHED ONLY TWO-THIRDS OF AN INNING IN THAT SERIES. FOR THE REST OF HIS LIFE, HE WOULD BE ANGRY OVER THE SLIGHT.

Veeck As In Wreck

Baseball has seen its share of characters, but no owner has ever been quite as flamboyantly chaotic as *William Veeck*. His first contribution to the game was the idea to *plant ivy* on the outfield walls at Wrigley Field. During World War II, he lost a leg to a recoiling artillery piece. When he got an artificial leg, he carved a hole in it to use as an *ashtray.*

IF JACKIE ROBINSON WAS THE IDEAL MAN TO BREAK THE COLOR LINE, BROOKLYN WAS THE IDEAL PLACE. I WASN'T SURE ABOUT CLEVELAND.

Veeck had wanted to be a team owner for years, and he also wanted to integrate the majors. He got the chance to do both when he bought the Cleveland Indians in 1946 and signed Larry Doby the next year. It was a *risky move,* and Veeck knew it.

Veeck sold the Indians to finance a *divorce settlement* in 1949 and bought the St. Louis Browns in 1951, then sold that club two years later. He also owned the Chicago White Sox *twice.*

Master Melvin

The first two members of basesball's 500 home-run club--Mel Ott and Babe Ruth.

ELVIN T. (MEL

192

Without question, 1947 was the Year of Jackie Robinson, but it also saw the retirement of one of baseball's quietest greats: *Melvin Thomas Ott.* Signed as a sixteen-year-old out of Gretna, Louisiana, Ott never played in the minor leagues. By his eighteenth birthday, he was the Giants' everyday center fielder. *Overshadowed* in the media because of the flashier players on the Yankees and Dodgers, Mel Ott was a Giants legend well before he became only the *second* player in major league history with five hundred home runs on August 1, 1945. The source of his power was a mystery, as he stood only 5'9" and weighed only 170 pounds, but he always pointed to a difference in his swing--Ott was one of the first players to incorporate a *step* into their swing.

LED IN MOST RUNS SCO
IN, TOTA
B ES O
BA ING
MES AND IN TH

Cynics attributed his home-run totals to the short right-field fence at the Polo Grounds, but Ott always had a ready answer: if it was that *easy,* why didn't *other* hitters do it?

He would remain the *only* National League player with five hundred home runs until *Willie Mays* passed him in 1966.

Satchel Paige

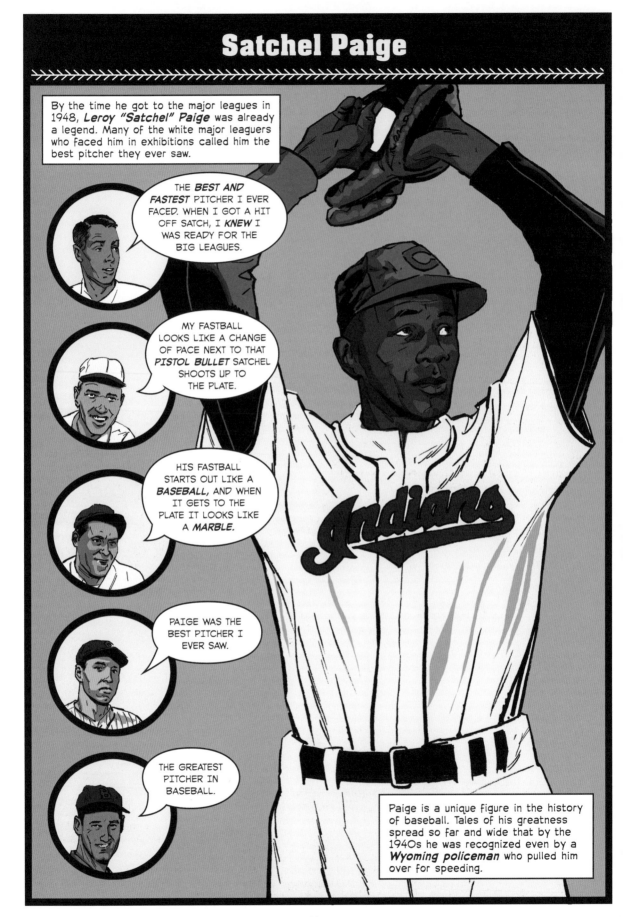

By the time he got to the major leagues in 1948, *Leroy "Satchel" Paige* was already a legend. Many of the white major leaguers who faced him in exhibitions called him the best pitcher they ever saw.

THE *BEST AND FASTEST* PITCHER I EVER FACED. WHEN I GOT A HIT OFF SATCH, I *KNEW* I WAS READY FOR THE BIG LEAGUES.

MY FASTBALL LOOKS LIKE A CHANGE OF PACE NEXT TO THAT *PISTOL BULLET* SATCHEL SHOOTS UP TO THE PLATE.

HIS FASTBALL STARTS OUT LIKE A *BASEBALL,* AND WHEN IT GETS TO THE PLATE IT LOOKS LIKE A *MARBLE.*

PAIGE WAS THE BEST PITCHER I EVER SAW.

THE GREATEST PITCHER IN BASEBALL.

Paige is a unique figure in the history of baseball. Tales of his greatness spread so far and wide that by the 1940s he was recognized even by a *Wyoming policeman* who pulled him over for speeding.

PAIGE LEFT THE INDIANS AFTER THE 1949 SEASON, BUT WAS BACK IN THE BIG LEAGUES AS A FEARED RELIEF PITCHER IN 1951--AT *FORTY-FIVE YEARS OLD.*

IF THE YANKEES DON'T GET AHEAD IN THE FIRST SIX INNINGS, THE BROWNS BRING IN THAT *DAMNED OLD MAN*, AND WE'RE SUNK.

AND OFF THE FIELD, HE BECAME ONE OF THE GAME'S MOST BELOVED PERSONALITIES.

AIN'T NO MAN CAN AVOID BEING BORN *AVERAGE*, BUT THERE AIN'T NO MAN GOT TO BE *COMMON.*

AGE IS A CASE OF MIND OVER MATTER. IF YOU DON'T *MIND*, IT DON'T *MATTER.*

JUST TAKE THE BALL AND THROW IT WHERE YOU WANT TO. HOME PLATE DON'T MOVE.

ALTHOUGH PAIGE UNDERSTOOD BRANCH RICKEY'S REASONING, HE ALWAYS FELT IT SHOULD HAVE BEEN *HIM* TO INTEGRATE THE BIG LEAGUES INSTEAD OF JACKIE ROBINSON.

SIGNING JACKIE LIKE THEY DID STILL *HURT ME* DEEP DOWN. *I'D* BEEN THE ONE WHO STARTED ALL THAT BIG TALK ABOUT LETTING US IN THE BIG TIME.

I'D BEEN THE ONE WHO'D OPENED UP MAJOR LEAGUE PARKS TO COLORED TEAMS. *I'D* BEEN THE ONE WHO THE WHITE BOYS WANTED TO GO BARNSTORMING AGAINST.

PAIGE WROTE ABOUT THIS WHILE ON THE ROAD IN THE 1940S AND '50S, NEVER GOING ANYWHERE WITHOUT A TYPEWRITER.

SIGNING JACKIE LIKE THEY DID STILL HURT ME DEEP DOWN. I'D BEEN THE ONE WHO STARTED ALL THAT BIG TALK ABOUT LETTING US IN THE BIG TIME. I'D BEEN THE ONE WHO'D OPENED UP MAJOR LEAGUE PARKS TO COLORED TEAMS. I'D BEEN THE ONE WHO THE WHITE BOYS WANTED TO GO BARNSTORMING AGAINST.

AFTER 1948, THE BASEBALL WORLD CENTERED ITSELF IN NEW YORK AGAIN, AND WOULD *STAY* THERE FOR TWENTY YEARS. THE NUMBERS ARE FRANKLY *MIND-BOGGLING:*

BETWEEN 1947 AND 1956, *SEVEN OUT OF TEN* WORLD SERIES WERE CONTESTED BETWEEN NEW YORK TEAMS. THE YANKEES WON FIVE STRAIGHT BETWEEN 1949 AND 1953 (THREE OF THEM OVER THE DODGERS).

BETWEEN 1949 AND 1964, *FIFTEEN OUT OF SIXTEEN* WORLD SERIES FEATURED AT LEAST ONE NEW YORK TEAM.

THE YANKEES APPEARED IN *FOURTEEN* SERIES DURING THAT SPAN, AND WON NINE.

IT WAS A *GOLDEN AGE* FOR NEW YORK BASEBALL, AND BECAUSE OF NEW YORK'S SIZE AND MEDIA CLOUT, IT BECAME THE GOLDEN AGE OF ALL OF BASEBALL IN THE POPULAR MEMORY.

LET'S TAKE A LOOK AT 1951, WHEN THIS GOLDEN AGE WAS JUST GETTING INTO FULL SWING...

A YOUNG *MICKEY MANTLE* WAS JUST BREAKING INTO A YANKEE TEAM ALREADY LOADED WITH STARS LIKE YOGI BERRA, PHIL RIZZUTO, AND JOE DIMAGGIO.

THE DODGERS' IMMORTAL DOUBLE-PLAY COMBINATION OF *ROBINSON AND REESE* WAS JOINED BY FEARLESS CATCHER ROY CAMPANELLA AND POWER-HITTING CENTER FIELDER DUKE SNIDER.

IN UPPER MANHATTAN, SEASONED GIANTS VETS EDDIE STANKY AND SAL "THE BARBER" MAGLIE WERE MENTORING *WILLIE MAYS AND MONTE IRVIN* AT THE BEGINNINGS OF THEIR HALL OF FAME CAREERS.

The Tall Tactician

Cornelius McGillicuddy became known as *Connie Mack* even before he made his playing debut with the Washington Nationals (not the current version) in 1886. A *clever* but *modestly talented* catcher, he became the first manager of the Philadelphia Athletics in 1901 and did not let go of the job until after the 1950 season.

Over that fifty-year period, Mack both won (3,731) and lost (3,948) more games than any other manger in history. He won *five World Series titles*, and his teams finished *last* seventeen times-- another record.

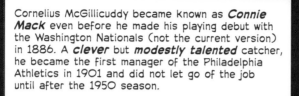

CONNIE MACK

SHIBE HAS A *WHITE ELEPHANT* ON HIS HANDS.

Early in his career, Mack had a *fierce rivalry* with Giants manager John McGraw, who in 1902 already thought A's owner Ben Shibe had kept Mack on too long.

Mack immediately made a white elephant the *team logo*, and even gave McGraw a stuffed elephant before the first game of the 1905 World Series. He also made no secret of his admiration for McGraw's skills in the dugout.

THERE IS ONLY ONE MANAGER, AND THAT'S JOHN MCGRAW.

HERE'S MACK WITH HIS GREATEST HOME-RUN HITTER, JIMMIE FOXX.

Of course, that was easy for Mack to say, since he won nearly *one thousand* more games than McGraw did. (McGraw would probably have shot back that Mack also had *two thousand more losses* than he did.)

AND OF COURSE THERE WERE GREAT PLAYERS *OUTSIDE* THE FIVE BOROUGHS, TOO.

FOR A SPAN OF SEVEN YEARS—FROM 1946 TO 1952—NONE WAS BETTER THAN PITTSBURGH'S *RALPH KINER.*

KINER LED THE MAJORS IN HOME RUNS FOR ALL SEVEN OF THOSE YEARS (WITH THREE TIES). EVEN BABE RUTH HAD ONLY MANAGED SIX STRAIGHT.

THANKS TO PIRATES PART-OWNER *BING CROSBY*, KINER ALSO GOT A LITTLE TASTE OF THE CELEBRITY SCENE.

BEFORE HIS CAREER WAS CUT SHORT BY BACK PROBLEMS AND A FEUD WITH BRANCH RICKEY, RALPH KINER WAS AS *FEARED* A POWER HITTER AS THERE WAS IN THE GAME.

HE WOULD LATER BECOME A BROADCASTER FOR THE EXPANSION NEW YORK METS, WHOSE GAMES HE BROADCAST FOR *FIFTY-THREE YEARS.*

IN OTHER CASES, THE INTERSECTION OF BASEBALL AND CELEBRITY HAD MORE TRAGIC RESULTS.

IN 1949, A CUBS FAN BY THE NAME OF *RUTH ANN STEINHAGEN* GOT OBSESSED WITH EX-CUB *EDDIE WAITKUS* AND LURED HIM TO HER HOTEL ROOM USING THE NAME OF A HIGH SCHOOL FRIEND OF HIS.

WAITKUS WENT TO THE HOTEL ROOM AND STEINHAGEN *SHOT* HIM.

IN ADDITION TO INSPIRING BERNARD MALAMUD, STEINHAGEN ALSO ENTERED THE LEXICON OF BASEBALL SLANG. *"BASEBALL ANNIE"* HAS BEEN A COMMON TERM FOR A GROUPIE EVER SINCE. (SEE SUSAN SARANDON'S CHARACTER IN *BULL DURHAM* FOR THE MOST FAMOUS EXAMPLE.)

WAITKUS'S STORY ALSO ENTERED LITERARY (AND LATER FILM) HISTORY THANKS TO HIS TEAMMATES' NICKNAME FOR HIM...

THE NATURAL.

HUH.

PULITZER PRIZE winner and two-time winner of the NATIONAL BOOK AWARD

Bernard Malamud The Natural

Introduction by KEVIN BAKER

Girl Fan Wounds Philly Ball Player Seriously

Eddie Waitkus Shot In Chest With Rifle In Chicago Hotel

BETWEEN 1941 AND 1956, THE *YANKEES* AND *DODGERS* PLAYED SEVEN WORLD SERIES AGAINST EACH OTHER.

THE YANKEES WON SIX OF THE SEVEN.

THIS WAS ONE REASON WHY THE DODGERS WERE ALSO KNOWN AS THE *BUMS.*

THE YANKEES WERE THE TEAM OF BROADWAY (EVEN THOUGH THEY PLAYED IN THE BRONX), WHILE THE DODGERS WERE THE HEART AND SOUL OF WORKING-CLASS BROOKLYN.

LIKE THE DODGERS, THE GIANTS WERE OVERSHADOWED BY THE YANKEES--DESPITE THE ARRIVAL OF THEIR ELECTRIC ROOKIE CENTER FIELDER *WILLIE MAYS IN 1951.*

NEW YORK'S MARKET--AND SOME OF BASEBALL'S OTHER TWO-TEAM MARKETS--WERE STARTING TO SEEM A LITTLE *CROWDED.*

IN PARALLEL, MORE AND MORE PEOPLE WERE MOVING OUT OF THE CROWDED OLD EAST COAST CITIES. *TEXAS, FLORIDA,* AND *CALIFORNIA* BOOMED. PEOPLE IN THOSE STATES WERE HUNGRY FOR BASEBALL, WHICH THEY COULD ONLY HEAR ON THE RADIO.

WHETHER OR NOT THIS WAS A GOLDEN AGE ON THE FIELD, IT CERTAINLY WAS ON THE *AIRWAVES.* THE GREATEST GENERATION OF BASEBALL ANNOUNCERS WAS WORKING, AND THEIR *TRADEMARK PHRASES* WERE ENTERING THE AMERICAN LEXICON.

HOW ABOUT THAT!?

IT'S TIME FOR *DODGER BASEBALL!*

THAT BALL IS GOING...-GOING...IT IS GONE!

HE STOOD THERE LIKE THE HOUSE BY THE SIDE OF THE ROAD, AND WATCHED IT GO BY.

THE INTEGRATION OF THE BIG LEAGUES IRONICALLY LED TO *FEWER* AFRICAN AMERICANS PLAYING BASEBALL. MANY MAJOR LEAGUE CLUBS TENDED TO FEEL THAT THEY HAD DONE ENOUGH IF THEY HAD ONE OR TWO BLACK PLAYERS--AND VERY FEW OF THEM HAD ANY INTEREST IN HIRING THE BLACK *COACHES AND SCOUTS* WHO HAD MADE THE NEGRO LEAGUES GREAT.

THE NEGRO LEAGUES THEMSELVES WERE IN DIRE TROUBLE. BY THE EARLY 1950S, ONLY *A FEW TEAMS* SURVIVED.

MAJOR LEAGUE TEAMS HAD RAIDED THEIR BEST PLAYERS--NEARLY ALWAYS WITHOUT *COMPENSATING* THE TEAMS--AND THE ONCE-THRIVING LEAGUE WAS A SHELL OF ITS FORMER SELF.

The Old Perfessor: Casey Stengel

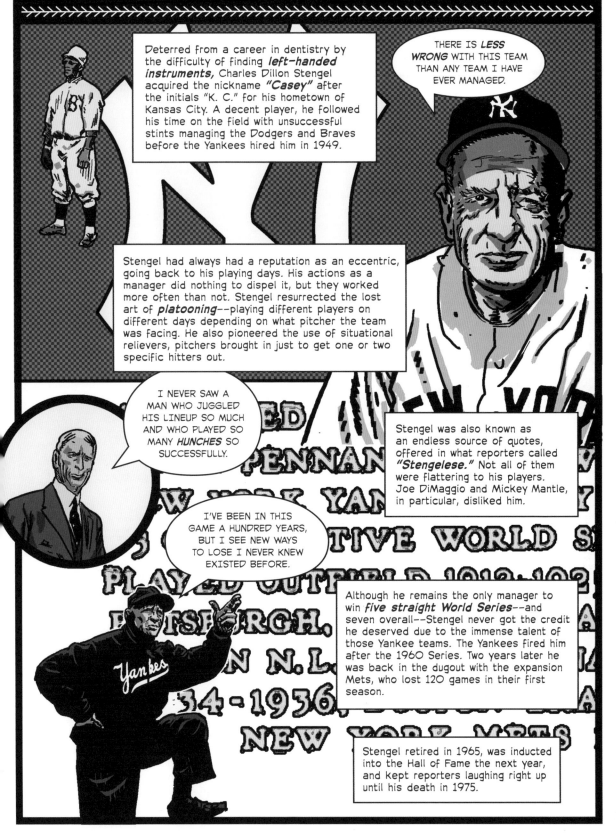

Deterred from a career in dentistry by the difficulty of finding *left-handed instruments,* Charles Dillon Stengel acquired the nickname *"Casey"* after the initials "K. C." for his hometown of Kansas City. A decent player, he followed his time on the field with unsuccessful stints managing the Dodgers and Braves before the Yankees hired him in 1949.

THERE IS *LESS WRONG* WITH THIS TEAM THAN ANY TEAM I HAVE EVER MANAGED.

Stengel had always had a reputation as an eccentric, going back to his playing days. His actions as a manager did nothing to dispel it, but they worked more often than not. Stengel resurrected the lost art of *platooning*--playing different players on different days depending on what pitcher the team was facing. He also pioneered the use of situational relievers, pitchers brought in just to get one or two specific hitters out.

I NEVER SAW A MAN WHO JUGGLED HIS LINEUP SO MUCH AND WHO PLAYED SO MANY *HUNCHES* SO SUCCESSFULLY.

Stengel was also known as an endless source of quotes, offered in what reporters called *"Stengelese."* Not all of them were flattering to his players. Joe DiMaggio and Mickey Mantle, in particular, disliked him.

I'VE BEEN IN THIS GAME A HUNDRED YEARS, BUT I SEE NEW WAYS TO LOSE I NEVER KNEW EXISTED BEFORE.

Although he remains the only manager to win *five straight World Series*--and seven overall--Stengel never got the credit he deserved due to the immense talent of those Yankee teams. The Yankees fired him after the 1960 Series. Two years later he was back in the dugout with the expansion Mets, who lost 120 games in their first season.

Stengel retired in 1965, was inducted into the Hall of Fame the next year, and kept reporters laughing right up until his death in 1975.

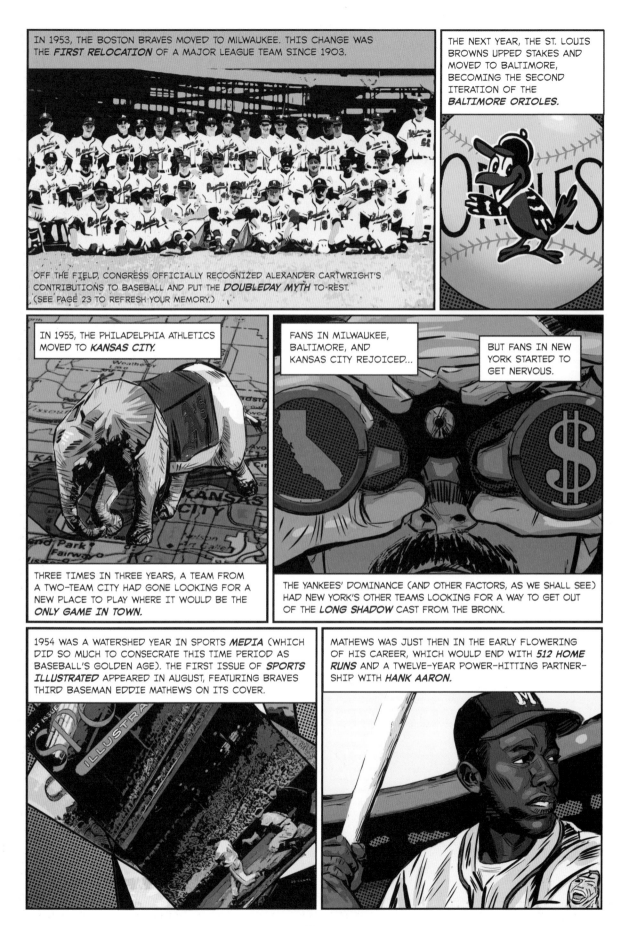

IN 1953, THE BOSTON BRAVES MOVED TO MILWAUKEE. THIS CHANGE WAS THE *FIRST RELOCATION* OF A MAJOR LEAGUE TEAM SINCE 1903.

OFF THE FIELD, CONGRESS OFFICIALLY RECOGNIZED ALEXANDER CARTWRIGHT'S CONTRIBUTIONS TO BASEBALL AND PUT THE *DOUBLEDAY MYTH* TO REST. (SEE PAGE 23 TO REFRESH YOUR MEMORY.)

THE NEXT YEAR, THE ST. LOUIS BROWNS UPPED STAKES AND MOVED TO BALTIMORE, BECOMING THE SECOND ITERATION OF THE *BALTIMORE ORIOLES.*

IN 1955, THE PHILADELPHIA ATHLETICS MOVED TO *KANSAS CITY.*

THREE TIMES IN THREE YEARS, A TEAM FROM A TWO-TEAM CITY HAD GONE LOOKING FOR A NEW PLACE TO PLAY WHERE IT WOULD BE THE *ONLY GAME IN TOWN.*

FANS IN MILWAUKEE, BALTIMORE, AND KANSAS CITY REJOICED...

BUT FANS IN NEW YORK STARTED TO GET NERVOUS.

THE YANKEES' DOMINANCE (AND OTHER FACTORS, AS WE SHALL SEE) HAD NEW YORK'S OTHER TEAMS LOOKING FOR A WAY TO GET OUT OF THE *LONG SHADOW* CAST FROM THE BRONX.

1954 WAS A WATERSHED YEAR IN SPORTS *MEDIA* (WHICH DID SO MUCH TO CONSECRATE THIS TIME PERIOD AS BASEBALL'S GOLDEN AGE). THE FIRST ISSUE OF *SPORTS ILLUSTRATED* APPEARED IN AUGUST, FEATURING BRAVES THIRD BASEMAN EDDIE MATHEWS ON ITS COVER.

MATHEWS WAS JUST THEN IN THE EARLY FLOWERING OF HIS CAREER, WHICH WOULD END WITH *512 HOME RUNS* AND A TWELVE-YEAR POWER-HITTING PARTNERSHIP WITH *HANK AARON.*

Moon Shots

Telling stories about how far a home run traveled is baseball's version of the fishermen's tales of the ones that got away. The tradition has existed since Babe Ruth was clouting balls where they had never before been clouted, but it kicked into another gear on April 17, 1953, when **Mickey Mantle** hit a ball that skimmed off a billboard in Griffiths Stadium and disappeared into the row houses beyond the stadium's bleachers. (Or so the story went.) Yankees PR man **Red Patterson** claimed he was going to get a tape measure--he didn't--and measure the distance after finding a local boy who had found the ball. His conclusion, based on pacing off the distance? Mantle had hit the ball **565 feet.** *Tape measure home run* entered the lexicon the next day when Patterson got word to the beat writers following the team.

This story stood more or less unchallenged for fifty years, until a reporter tracked down the kid who had found the ball. As it turns out, the original story was *malarkey*, but Mantle still hit the ball more than 500 feet. Few players in the history of the game have had that kind of power.

LED BY A DOMINANT QUARTET OF STARTING PITCHERS, AND THE BATS OF *LARRY DOBY* AND *AL ROSEN,* THE 1954 CLEVELAND INDIANS PUT TOGETHER ONE OF THE GREATEST REGULAR SEASONS IN BASEBALL HISTORY.

THEY RACKED UP *111 WINS* AND TOOK THE AMERICAN LEAGUE PENNANT BY EIGHT GAMES OVER THE YANKEES.

THEN THEY WERE *SWEPT* IN THE WORLD SERIES BY THE GIANTS IN ONE OF THE FALL CLASSIC'S GREAT *UPSETS.*

IN GAME 1, WILLIE MAYS MADE WHAT WOULD FOREVER AFTER BE KNOWN AS *"THE CATCH,"* RUNNING DOWN A 460-FOOT LINE DRIVE OFF THE BAT OF VIC WERTZ.

MAYS WAS BACK FROM TWO YEARS IN THE ARMY, AND COMING OFF AN MVP SEASON.

IT WOULD BE LEO DUROCHER'S ONLY WORLD SERIES WIN AS A MANAGER.

THE GIANTS HADN'T WON THE SERIES SINCE 1933, AND WOULDN'T WIN AGAIN UNTIL 2010.

THE INDIANS WOULDN'T MAKE IT BACK TO THE SERIES UNTIL 1995. THEY *STILL* HAVEN'T WON ANOTHER ONE.

IN THE OFFSEASON, THE PITTSBURGH PIRATES PLUCKED A LITTLE-KNOWN OUTFIELDER BY THE NAME OF ROBERTO CLEMENTE FROM THE YANKEES' LIST OF UNPROTECTED MINOR LEAGUE PLAYERS.

THE YEAR 1954 ALSO SAW THE FINAL GAME PLAYED IN THE TWELVE-YEAR HISTORY OF THE ALL-AMERICAN GIRLS PROFESSIONAL BASEBALL LEAGUE. THE *KALAMAZOO LASSIES* TOOK HOME THEIR ONLY TITLE OVER THE FORT WAYNE DAISIES.

A-A
GPBL

NO PROFESSIONAL LEAGUE FOR WOMEN WOULD EXIST AGAIN UNTIL THE *NATIONAL PRO FASTPITCH* SOFTBALL LEAGUE WAS ESTABLISHED IN 2004.

BUT A FEW WOMEN DID PLAY WITH NEGRO LEAGUE TEAMS IN THEIR FINAL YEARS. *TONI STONE, CONNIE MORGAN, AND MAMIE "PEANUT" JOHNSON* ALL APPEARED FOR THE INDIANAPOLIS CLOWNS IN THE MID-1950S.

WILLIE, MICKEY, AND THE DUKE

IF NEW YORK WAS THE CENTER OF THE BASEBALL UNIVERSE IN THE 1950S, THE CENTER OF NEW YORK BASEBALL WAS IN *CENTER FIELD.*

THE YANKEES, GIANTS, AND DODGERS ALL FEATURED IMMORTALS AT THE POSITION: *WILLIE, MICKEY, AND THE DUKE.*

MANTLE AND MAYS WERE FOREVER LINKED BY TWO THINGS.

ONE: IT WAS MAYS WHO HIT THE FLY BALL THAT MANTLE *WRECKED HIS KNEE* TRYING TO CATCH DURING THE 1951 SERIES.

JOE DIMAGGIO--IN HIS LAST YEAR--CALLED OFF THE ROOKIE AT THE *LAST SECOND,* AND MANTLE *CAUGHT HIS SPIKES* IN AN UNCOVERED DRAIN AS HE TRIED TO STOP.

HE WOULD NEVER PLAY WITHOUT PAIN AGAIN.

TWO: THROUGHOUT THE 1950S, AND EVER SINCE, THE QUESTION OF WHICH WAS A GREATER PLAYER HAS RAGED AMONG FANS.

MICKEY!

WILLIE!

DUKE.

SNIDER, FIVE YEARS OLDER THAN MANTLE AND MAYS, ALWAYS TENDED TO COME IN THIRD IN THOSE CONVERSATIONS--*UNLESS* YOU WERE FROM BROOKLYN.

MANTLE, LIKE SO MANY OF BASEBALL'S IMMORTALS, HAD A DARK SIDE, TOO. THE COUNTRY BOY ACQUIRED A TASTE FOR CITY PLEASURES, AND IN *WHITEY FORD* AND *BILLY MARTIN* HE FOUND TWO ENTHUSIASTIC DRINKING BUDDIES.

IF I HADN'T MET *THOSE TWO GUYS* AT THE START OF MY CAREER, I WOULD HAVE LASTED ANOTHER FIVE YEARS.

YANKEE MANAGEMENT TOLERATED IT BECAUSE MICKEY MANTLE WAS THE *BIGGEST STAR* IN THE GAME...

...EVEN WHEN HE WAS *HUNGOVER*, WHICH WAS OFTEN.

MOST OF THE PLAYERS' EXPLOITS WERE KEPT OUT OF THE PAPERS...UNTIL THE SO-CALLED *"COPA INCIDENT"* OF 1957, IN WHICH SEVERAL YANKEES--INCLUDING MANTLE--WERE INVOLVED IN A FIGHT DURING A *BIRTHDAY PARTY* FOR MARTIN. THE STORY GOT OUT DESPITE THE PLAYERS' CLAIM THAT NOTHING HAD HAPPENED.

YANKS COPA BRAWL

NOBODY DID NOTHIN' TO NOBODY.

NOW THAT BASEBALL PLAYERS WERE *HOBNOBBING WITH CELEBRITIES,* THEIR OWN CELEBRITY LED THE PRESS TO DIG INTO THEIR FEET OF CLAY.

MAJOR LEAGUE PLAYERS ALSO BEGAN TO ORGANIZE IN THE MID-1950S, WITH INDIANS PITCHER *BOB FELLER* CHOSEN AS THE FIRST *PLAYER REPRESENTATIVE* IN 1956.

THE PLAYERS BEGAN TO REALIZE THEIR POWER. *MILLIONS OF FANS* CAME TO THE PARKS AND LISTENED TO THE RADIO FOR THEM...AND NOW THESE PLAYERS STARTED TO *LEVERAGE* THAT POWER.

THE FIRST *COLLECTIVE BARGAINING AGREEMENT* WAS STILL A DECADE AWAY, BUT THE OLD WAR BETWEEN CAPITAL AND LABOR LOOMED OVER THE NATIONAL PASTIME.

I Didn't Really Say Everything I Said

Famously jocular off the field, *Lawrence Peter "Yogi" Berra* was a hard-nosed competitor when he strapped on his catcher's gear. He was on more World Series-winning teams than any other player in baseball history, with ten--and another three as a coach.

> *NINETY PERCENT* OF BASEBALL IS MENTAL. THE *OTHER HALF* IS PHYSICAL.

Berra was the *greatest catcher* in the history of the game, a power hitter with a strong and accurate arm who was also known for his handling of pitchers. He was particularly known for his clutch hitting and his superb bat control. Five times in his career, he tallied *more home runs than strikeouts* in a season.

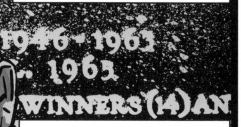

After his playing days, Berra coached and managed for a variety of teams while dispensing the *"Yogi-isms"* that so endeared him to reporters and the public. The most famous was uttered in July 1973 when the Mets were far behind the Cubs in the National League East.

> IT AIN'T OVER 'TIL IT'S OVER.

COACHES

ROY McMILLAN

JOE PIGNATANO

RUBE WALKER

EDDIE YOST

YOGI BERRA
NEW YORK METS

MANAGER

The Mets then pulled off an inspiring comeback to reach the World Series. They *lost*, but this particular Yogi-ism has become an American folk saying.

THE GIANTS HAD GOTTEN THEIR TASTE OF WORLD SERIES GLORY IN 1954, AND IN '55 IT WAS THE *DODGERS' TURN*. JACKIE ROBINSON (AND DUKE SNIDER) AT LAST BEAT THE YANKEES, AFTER SIX TRIES. THE BUMS WERE THE CHAMPS.

ROY CAMPANELLA'S HALL OF FAME CAREER WOULD BE CUT SHORT AFTER THE 1957 SEASON BY A *CAR ACCIDENT* THAT LEFT HIM *PARALYZED,* BUT IN 1955 HE WAS THE BEST CATCHER IN THE GAME...EVEN WITH YOGI BERRA IN THE OTHER DUGOUT.

IN 1957, THE NEW MILWAUKEE BRAVES ANNOUNCED THEMSELVES AS A POWERHOUSE, TAKING HOME THE FRANCHISE'S FIRST SERIES WIN SINCE *1914.*

IT WAS ALSO THE FIRST TIME IN TEN YEARS THAT A NEW YORK TEAM *HADN'T* WON.

THE BRAVES, LIKE MANY OTHER NATIONAL LEAGUE TEAMS, WERE LED BY A DYNAMIC YOUNG PLAYER SIGNED FROM THE NEGRO LEAGUES: IN THIS CASE *HENRY "HANK" AARON.*

EIGHT OF THE TEN NATIONAL LEAGUE MVP AWARDS IN THE 1950S WENT TO FORMER NEGRO LEAGUE PLAYERS.

IN THE MORE *CONSERVATIVE* (AND YANKEE-DOMINATED) AMERICAN LEAGUE, IT WAS A DIFFERENT STORY.

BUT THE CONVERSATION ABOUT WHETHER BLACK PLAYERS COULD CUT IT IN THE BIG LEAGUES WAS OVER.

THE BRAVES WERE ALSO LED BY THE AGELESS WONDER, *WARREN SPAHN.*

IN 1957, SPAHN WAS THIRTY-SIX YEARS OLD, WITH TWELVE YEARS OF MAJOR LEAGUE BALL ALREADY BEHIND HIM.*

HE HAD BEEN THE BRAVES' ACE FOR MOST OF THAT TIME.

*HE WAS A COMBAT ENGINEER IN WORLD WAR II DURING THE 1943-45 SEASONS.

HIS CAREER WAS *ALMOST* TORPEDOED BEFORE IT BEGAN, WHEN HE REFUSED CASEY STENGEL'S ORDER TO *THROW AT* PEE WEE REESE.

I SAID *"NO GUTS"* TO A KID WHO WENT ON TO BECOME A WAR HERO AND ONE OF THE GREATEST LEFT-HANDED PITCHERS YOU EVER SAW. YOU CAN'T SAY I DON'T *MISS* 'EM WHEN I *MISS* 'EM.

SPAHN WOULD LATER PLAY FOR STENGEL AGAIN, WHEN BOTH WERE WITH THE METS IN 1965.

I'M PROBABLY THE ONLY GUY WHO WORKED FOR STENGEL *BEFORE AND AFTER* HE WAS A GENIUS.

SPAHN WON MORE GAMES THAN *ANY LEFTY* IN THE HISTORY OF BASEBALL: 363. THAT'S ALSO BY FAR THE HIGHEST TOTAL OF ANY PITCHER WHO PITCHED HIS FULL CAREER *AFTER* THE DEAD BALL ERA WAS OVER.

HE ALSO GOT BETTER AS HE GOT OLDER, THROWING HIS *FIRST NO-HITTER* AT THE AGE OF *THIRTY-NINE*...AND HIS SECOND THE NEXT YEAR, JUST AFTER HE TURNED FORTY.

AS MORE BLACK PLAYERS MADE THEIR MARK IN THE MAJOR LEAGUES, THE DOORS ALSO OPENED WIDER FOR PLAYERS OF *LATIN* DESCENT.

BUT ALL OF THEM STOOD ON THE SHOULDERS OF *PIONEERS* LIKE MARTÍN DIHIGO, ADOLFO LUQUE, AND MIGUEL ANGEL GONZÁLEZ.

THE CLEVELAND INDIANS WERE ONCE AGAIN PIONEERS, SIGNING THE *FIRST BLACK LATIN* PLAYER IN 1949: *MINNIE MIÑOSO.*

MIÑOSO OPENED DOORS FOR AN *INFLUX* OF LATINOS WHO FOLLOWED IN THE 1950S.

THE *CUBAN EMBARGO*, ENFORCED AFTER *FIDEL CASTRO* CAME TO POWER IN 1953, ENDED ACCESS TO THAT COUNTRY'S ESTABLISHED LEAGUE AND PLAYER POOL.

THE EMBARGO ALSO HAD THE UNINTENDED CONSE-QUENCE OF FORCING MAJOR LEAGUE TEAMS TO FIND SOMEWHERE ELSE TO PLAY *WINTER BALL.*

BIENVE
SANTO
CONCEJC

THAT IN TURN LED TO HEAVIER SCOUTING OF *PUERTO RICO*, THE *DOMINICAN REPUBLIC,* AND LATER *VENEZUELA*—ALL OF WHICH WOULD PROVE TO BE RICH IN BASEBALL TALENT.

BY 1959, *EVERY* MAJOR LEAGUE TEAM HAD AT LEAST ONE BLACK PLAYER.

BY THIS TIME, MOST TEAMS ALSO HAD AT LEAST ONE LATIN PLAYER—AND WITH *EXPANSION* COMING IN 1961, THESE PLAYERS' NUMBERS WOULD INCREASE DRAMATICALLY.

THE BOSTON RED SOX WERE LAST, ADDING *PUMPSIE GREEN* TO THEIR ROSTER ON JULY 21 OF THAT YEAR. HE JOINED THE BASEBALL'S *FIRST MEXICAN STAR*, BOBBY AVILA, THEN IN HIS LAST BIG-LEAGUE YEAR AFTER A STRONG CAREER WITH—YOU GUESSED IT—THE CLEVELAND INDIANS.

Una Historia Del Beisbol

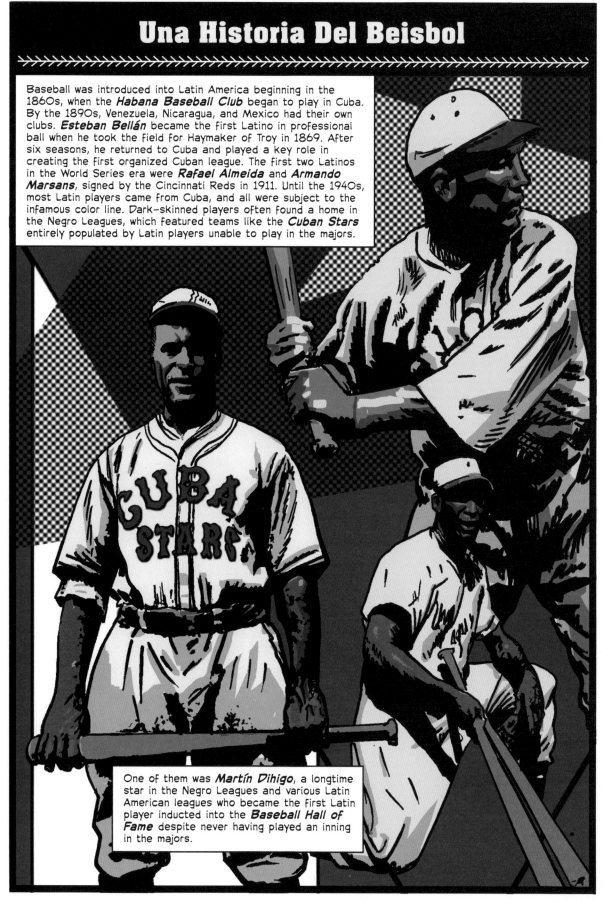

Baseball was introduced into Latin America beginning in the 1860s, when the **Habana Baseball Club** began to play in Cuba. By the 1890s, Venezuela, Nicaragua, and Mexico had their own clubs. **Esteban Bellán** became the first Latino in professional ball when he took the field for Haymaker of Troy in 1869. After six seasons, he returned to Cuba and played a key role in creating the first organized Cuban league. The first two Latinos in the World Series era were **Rafael Almeida** and **Armando Marsans**, signed by the Cincinnati Reds in 1911. Until the 1940s, most Latin players came from Cuba, and all were subject to the infamous color line. Dark-skinned players often found a home in the Negro Leagues, which featured teams like the **Cuban Stars** entirely populated by Latin players unable to play in the majors.

One of them was **Martín Dihigo**, a longtime star in the Negro Leagues and various Latin American leagues who became the first Latin player inducted into the **Baseball Hall of Fame** despite never having played an inning in the majors.

THEN, AFTER THE 1957 SEASON, BOTH THE DODGERS AND THE GIANTS LEFT NEW YORK, BREAKING THE HEARTS OF MILLIONS OF FANS.

DODGERS OWNER O'MALLEY WANTED TO BUILD A NEW STADIUM, AND COULDN'T--SO HE UPPED STAKES AND HEADED WEST.

THE POPULATION OF LOS ANGELES HAD JUMPED FROM 100,000 IN 1900 TO 2 MILLION IN 1950. IT WAS A MARKET NO ONE COULD IGNORE, AND ONE HUNGRY FOR BASEBALL.

KNOWING A WEST COAST RIVALRY WOULD BE GOOD FOR BOTH TEAMS, O'MALLEY CONVINCED GIANTS OWNER HORACE STONEHAM TO HEAD WEST AS WELL.

DODGER
L.A. NE
Move Ends

IT'S OFFICIA
GO TO SAN

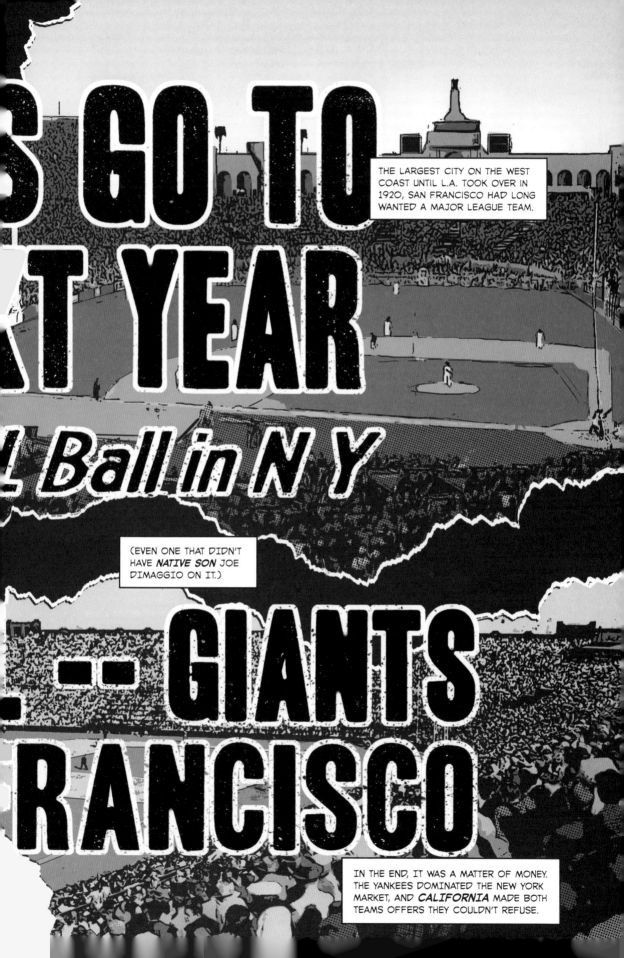

GO TO
...T YEAR

...l Ball in N Y

THE LARGEST CITY ON THE WEST COAST UNTIL L.A. TOOK OVER IN 1920, SAN FRANCISCO HAD LONG WANTED A MAJOR LEAGUE TEAM.

(EVEN ONE THAT DIDN'T HAVE *NATIVE SON* JOE DIMAGGIO ON IT.)

...- GIANTS
...RANCISCO

IN THE END, IT WAS A MATTER OF MONEY. THE YANKEES DOMINATED THE NEW YORK MARKET, AND *CALIFORNIA* MADE BOTH TEAMS OFFERS THEY COULDN'T REFUSE.

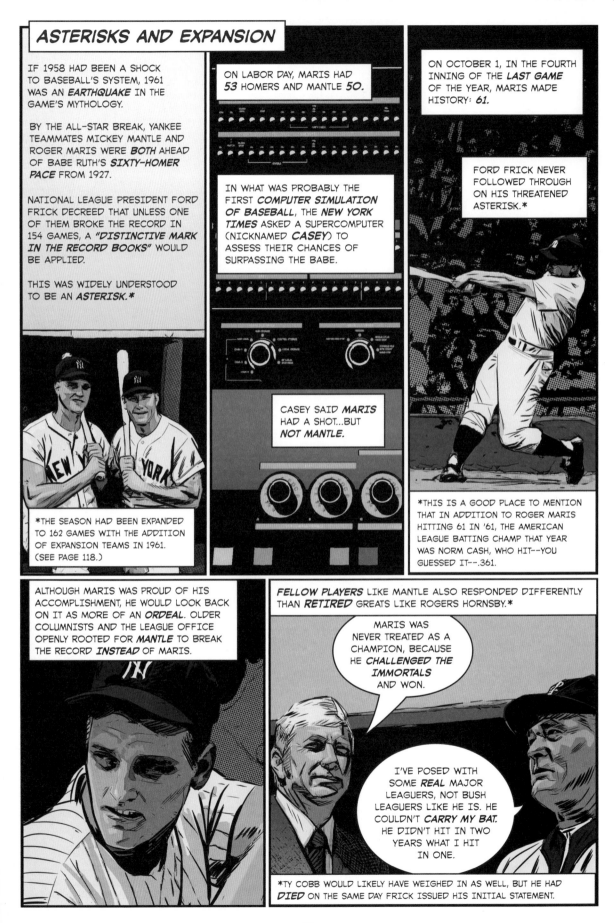

ASTERISKS AND EXPANSION

IF 1958 HAD BEEN A SHOCK TO BASEBALL'S SYSTEM, 1961 WAS AN *EARTHQUAKE* IN THE GAME'S MYTHOLOGY.

BY THE ALL-STAR BREAK, YANKEE TEAMMATES MICKEY MANTLE AND ROGER MARIS WERE *BOTH* AHEAD OF BABE RUTH'S *SIXTY-HOMER PACE* FROM 1927.

NATIONAL LEAGUE PRESIDENT FORD FRICK DECREED THAT UNLESS ONE OF THEM BROKE THE RECORD IN 154 GAMES, A *"DISTINCTIVE MARK IN THE RECORD BOOKS"* WOULD BE APPLIED.

THIS WAS WIDELY UNDERSTOOD TO BE AN *ASTERISK.**

*THE SEASON HAD BEEN EXPANDED TO 162 GAMES WITH THE ADDITION OF EXPANSION TEAMS IN 1961. (SEE PAGE 118.)

ON LABOR DAY, MARIS HAD *53* HOMERS AND MANTLE *50.*

IN WHAT WAS PROBABLY THE FIRST *COMPUTER SIMULATION OF BASEBALL*, THE *NEW YORK TIMES* ASKED A SUPERCOMPUTER (NICKNAMED *CASEY*) TO ASSESS THEIR CHANCES OF SURPASSING THE BABE.

CASEY SAID *MARIS* HAD A SHOT...BUT *NOT MANTLE.*

ON OCTOBER 1, IN THE FOURTH INNING OF THE *LAST GAME* OF THE YEAR, MARIS MADE HISTORY: *61.*

FORD FRICK NEVER FOLLOWED THROUGH ON HIS THREATENED ASTERISK.*

*THIS IS A GOOD PLACE TO MENTION THAT IN ADDITION TO ROGER MARIS HITTING 61 IN '61, THE AMERICAN LEAGUE BATTING CHAMP THAT YEAR WAS NORM CASH, WHO HIT--YOU GUESSED IT--.361.

ALTHOUGH MARIS WAS PROUD OF HIS ACCOMPLISHMENT, HE WOULD LOOK BACK ON IT AS MORE OF AN *ORDEAL.* OLDER COLUMNISTS AND THE LEAGUE OFFICE OPENLY ROOTED FOR *MANTLE* TO BREAK THE RECORD *INSTEAD* OF MARIS.

FELLOW PLAYERS LIKE MANTLE ALSO RESPONDED DIFFERENTLY THAN *RETIRED* GREATS LIKE ROGERS HORNSBY.*

MARIS WAS NEVER TREATED AS A CHAMPION, BECAUSE HE *CHALLENGED THE IMMORTALS* AND WON.

I'VE POSED WITH SOME *REAL* MAJOR LEAGUERS, NOT BUSH LEAGUERS LIKE HE IS. HE COULDN'T *CARRY MY BAT.* HE DIDN'T HIT IN TWO YEARS WHAT I HIT IN ONE.

*TY COBB WOULD LIKELY HAVE WEIGHED IN AS WELL, BUT HE HAD *DIED* ON THE SAME DAY FRICK ISSUED HIS INITIAL STATEMENT.

Arguments over how to handle records from different periods date back at least to the 1920s, when the end of the Dead Ball Era transformed the way the game was played. Once it was a big deal to hit *ten home runs;* after Babe Ruth, it took *fifty* to really get the public's attention. The same is true of batting averages. Is *Hugh Duffy's .440* really better than *Ted Williams's .406*, since Williams faced much better pitching? On the pitching front, was it harder for *Warren Spahn* to win 363 games in the mid-twentieth century than it was for *Pud Galvin* to win 364 in the late nineteenth? Probably. But how can that difference be codified?

There's no way to know. (Although *sabermetricians* are trying. See page 143.)

More recently, this argument flared up around the inflated power numbers of the *steroid era,* during which Maris's home run record was broken several times. See page 154.

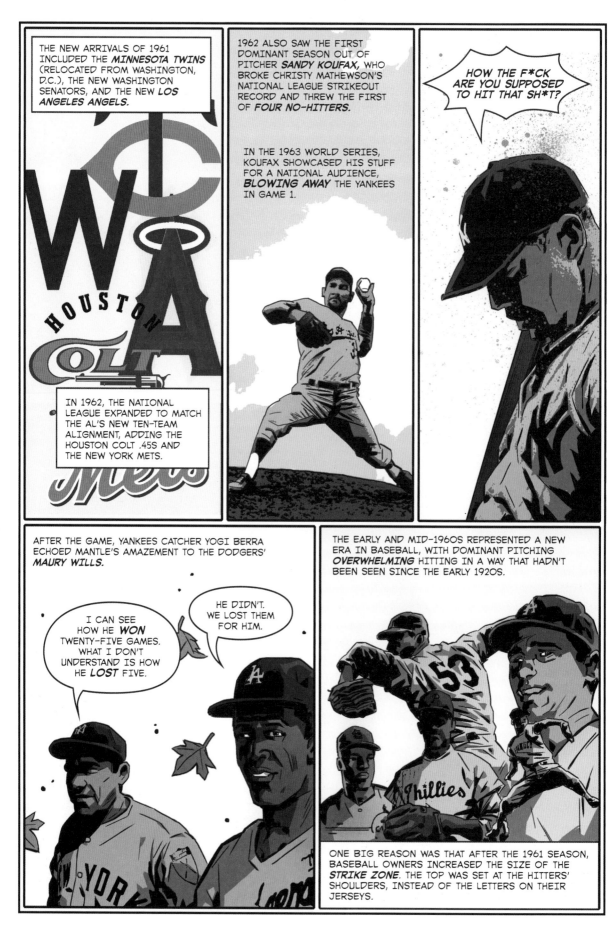

THE NEW ARRIVALS OF 1961 INCLUDED THE **MINNESOTA TWINS** (RELOCATED FROM WASHINGTON, D.C.), THE NEW WASHINGTON SENATORS, AND THE NEW **LOS ANGELES ANGELS**.

IN 1962, THE NATIONAL LEAGUE EXPANDED TO MATCH THE AL'S NEW TEN-TEAM ALIGNMENT, ADDING THE HOUSTON COLT .45S AND THE NEW YORK METS.

1962 ALSO SAW THE FIRST DOMINANT SEASON OUT OF PITCHER **SANDY KOUFAX,** WHO BROKE CHRISTY MATHEWSON'S NATIONAL LEAGUE STRIKEOUT RECORD AND THREW THE FIRST OF **FOUR NO-HITTERS.**

IN THE 1963 WORLD SERIES, KOUFAX SHOWCASED HIS STUFF FOR A NATIONAL AUDIENCE, **BLOWING AWAY** THE YANKEES IN GAME 1.

HOW THE F*CK ARE YOU SUPPOSED TO HIT THAT SH*T?

AFTER THE GAME, YANKEES CATCHER YOGI BERRA ECHOED MANTLE'S AMAZEMENT TO THE DODGERS' **MAURY WILLS.**

I CAN SEE HOW HE **WON** TWENTY-FIVE GAMES. WHAT I DON'T UNDERSTAND IS HOW HE **LOST** FIVE.

HE DIDN'T. WE LOST THEM FOR HIM.

THE EARLY AND MID-1960S REPRESENTED A NEW ERA IN BASEBALL, WITH DOMINANT PITCHING **OVERWHELMING** HITTING IN A WAY THAT HADN'T BEEN SEEN SINCE THE EARLY 1920S.

ONE BIG REASON WAS THAT AFTER THE 1961 SEASON, BASEBALL OWNERS INCREASED THE SIZE OF THE **STRIKE ZONE.** THE TOP WAS SET AT THE HITTERS' SHOULDERS, INSTEAD OF THE LETTERS ON THEIR JERSEYS.

SANDY KOUFAX INJURED HIS ARM IN 1964 AND WAS OUT OF THE GAME TWO YEARS LATER, BUT NOT BEFORE STRIKING OUT A RECORD *382* BATTERS IN 1965.

DON DRYSDALE WON THREE WORLD SERIES WITH THE DODGERS, TEAMING WITH KOUFAX TO GIVE THE TEAM BASEBALL'S BEST PITCHING DUO.

DRYSDALE WOULD ALSO STEP IN WHEN KOUFAX DECLINED TO PITCH IN GAME 1 OF THE 1965 SERIES BECAUSE IT FELL ON *YOM KIPPUR.*

SEVEN RUNS IN THE FIRST THREE INNINGS.

HE GAVE UP.

BOB GIBSON WAS A DOMINANT FORCE IN THREE WORLD SERIES, AND THE FIRST PITCHER SINCE WALTER JOHNSON TO REACH *THREE THOUSAND STRIKEOUTS.*

JIM BUNNING THREW TWO NO-HITTERS AND RETIRED WITH THE *SECOND-HIGHEST* CAREER STRIKEOUT TOTAL IN THE HISTORY OF BASEBALL (UNTIL GIBSON PASSED HIM).

JUAN MARICHAL IS THE ONLY PITCHER OTHER THAN KOUFAX WITH *THREE 25-WIN SEASONS* IN THE LIVE BALL ERA.

AT THE END OF 1963, *STAN MUSIAL* AND *EARLY WYNN* RETIRED. THEY WERE THE LAST REMAINING PLAYERS WHO HAD STARTED THEIR CAREERS *BEFORE* WORLD WAR II.

WYNN WON HIS THREE HUNDREDTH GAME IN HIS *LAST CAREER START*.

MUSIAL WAS A .331 LIFETIME HITTER AND THE NATIONAL LEAGUE'S *ALL-TIME LEADER IN HITS* WITH 3,630.

HIS LAST MAJOR LEAGUE HIT WAS A GROUND BALL PAST YOUNG SECOND-BASEMAN *PETE ROSE*--WHO WOULD LATER SURPASS BOTH MUSIAL AND TY COBB'S HIT TOTALS.

IN BASEBALL, EVERY *ENDING* IS ALSO A BEGINNING.

WITH YOUNG SPEEDSTER *LOU BROCK* REPLACING MUSIAL AND BOB GIBSON DOMINATING THE AGING YANKEES, THE CARDINALS WON THE 1964 WORLD SERIES.

THE YANKEES HAD APPEARED IN *FOURTEEN OUT OF SIXTEEN* SERIES BETWEEN 1949 AND 1964.

THEY WOULDN'T MAKE IT *BACK* TO THE FALL CLASSIC UNTIL 1976.

THE CARDINALS--AND DODGERS AND GIANTS-- WERE PLAYING A *NEW* KIND OF BASEBALL.

THE INCREASING PRESENCE OF *BLACK PLAYERS* IN THE NATIONAL LEAGUE BROUGHT SOME OF THE *STYLE* OF THE NEGRO LEAGUES, WHICH HAD ALWAYS BEEN MORE ABOUT PITCHING, DEFENSE, AND BASERUNNING.

YET ANOTHER SIGN OF THE PASSING GOLDEN AGE CAME IN THE FORM OF THE *DEMOLITION OF THE POLO GROUNDS*, WHICH HAD STOOD SINCE 1890.

THE METS, ITS FINAL TENANTS, WERE OFF TO *SHEA STADIUM*, THEIR NEW HOME IN QUEENS.

THE NEXT YEAR, THE *LAST* NEGRO LEAGUE TEAM*--AND ARGUABLY THE *GREATEST*--PLAYED ITS FINAL SEASON.

FOUNDED THE YEAR RUBE FOSTER CREATED THE FIRST NEGRO NATIONAL LEAGUE, THE *KANSAS CITY MONARCHS* LASTED FORTY-FIVE YEARS, DOMINATED THE NEGRO LEAGUES, AND *SENT MORE PLAYERS* TO THE MAJOR LEAGUES THAN ANY OTHER NEGRO LEAGUE FRANCHISE--STARTING WITH JACKIE ROBINSON.

NEGRO NATIONAL LEAGUE PENNANTS: 1923, '24, '25, '29

NEGRO AMERICAN LEAGUE PENNANTS: '37, '39, '40, '41, '42, '46, '50, '53, '55

KANSAS CITY MONARCHS

THEIR OWNER, J. L. WILKINSON, PUT THE TEAM TOGETHER FROM HIS *MULTIRACIAL ALL-NATIONS* BARNSTORMING SQUAD AND THE BEST PLAYERS FROM THE *25TH INFANTRY WRECKERS*, A BLACK ARMY TEAM HE LEARNED ABOUT COURTESY OF A TIP FROM CASEY STENGEL AFTER WORLD WAR I.

*IT SHOULD BE NOTED THAT THE INDIANAPOLIS CLOWNS CONTINUED TO BARNSTORM UNTIL THE 1980S, BUT PRIMARILY AS A CIRCUS ACT THAT HAPPENED TO TAKE PLACE ON A BASEBALL FIELD.

AMONG THE STARS OF THE EARLY MONARCHS SQUADS WAS CUBAN PITCHER *JOSÉ MÉNDEZ*. HE WAS ALSO THE TEAM'S FIRST MANAGER, WHICH UNDOUBTEDLY MAKES HIM THE *FIRST LATINO MANAGER* OF A PROFESSIONAL AMERICAN BASEBALL TEAM.

IT WAS PERHAPS FITTING THAT ON SEPTEMBER 25, IN THE SAME YEAR AS THE MONARCHS' DEMISE, *SATCHEL PAIGE* WAS BROUGHT BACK FOR A *SINGLE APPEARANCE* WITH THE A'S IN KANSAS CITY, WHERE HE HAD PITCHED SO BRILLIANTLY FROM 1939 TO 1947.

PAIGE THREW *THREE SCORELESS INNINGS* AT THE AGE OF FIFTY-NINE.

Charley Pride

Born to Mississippi sharecroppers in 1934, *Charley Pride* pitched for the Negro League Memphis Red Sox in 1952 and then briefly with the Yankees' Class C Boise affiliate. Back in the Negro Leagues with the Louisville Clippers, Pride was traded to the Birmingham Black Barons *for a team bus*. The collapse of the Negro Leagues led to him bouncing around the minors until he joined the Army in the late 1950s. Pride returned to minor league ball with the Reds' affiliate the *Missoula Timberjacks*, and had tryouts with the California Angels and New York Mets. Neither paid off, so he returned to Montana and ended up working at a *smelter* in Helena that kept a number of jobs open specifically for baseball players.

It was about that time that his musical career started to take off and ten years later, Charley Pride was an *established country music star*. One of the few African Americans to make a mark in that musical genre, he has always kept in touch with baseball, singing the *national anthem* at two World Series games and becoming a part of the *Texas Rangers* ownership group in 2010.

BASEBALL AND THE COUNTERCULTURE

1966 SAW THE END OF THE DODGERS' TWENTY-YEAR RUN OF EXCELLENCE, AS THEY WERE **SWEPT** IN THE WORLD SERIES BY THE BALTIMORE ORIOLES.

1967 WAS KNOWN FOR THE **SUMMER OF LOVE,** BUT IN MANY AMERICAN CITIES IT WAS A SUMMER OF RIOTING, AS THE **CIVIL RIGHTS MOVEMENT** COLLIDED WITH **ENTRENCHED RACISM.**

CIVIL DISTURBANCES ERUPTED IN MORE THAN ONE HUNDRED AMERICAN CITIES THAT YEAR.

THE SPECTER OF THE **VIETNAM WAR** ALSO HUNG OVER EVERYTHING. UNLIKE WORLD WAR II, THIS TIME BASEBALL PLAYERS WEREN'T LINING UP OUTSIDE ENLISTMENT OFFICES.

THE SLUGGING DUO OF **BROOKS** AND **FRANK ROBINSON** LED THE BIRDS.

FRANK, TRADED TO BALTIMORE FROM CINCINNATI IN THE OFF-SEASON, BECAME THE FIRST MAN TO WIN **MVP AWARDS IN BOTH LEAGUES** WHEN HE TOOK HOME THE 1966 AWARD.

BROOKS FINISHED SECOND, AND WON THE SEVENTH OF HIS SIXTEEN CONSECUTIVE **GOLD GLOVES**-- THE AWARD GIVEN TO THE BEST FIELDER AT EACH POSITION.

IT WAS THE ORIOLES' FIRST TITLE.

DETROIT WAS THE SCENE OF THE MOST WIDESPREAD DISTURBANCES. AS THE RIOTING SPREAD, TIGERS SLUGGER *WILLIE HORTON* TOOK TO THE STREETS IN HIS JERSEY TO TRY TO RESTORE CALM.

THE DIVIDED COUNTRY COULDN'T AGREE ON *MUCH,* BUT IT COULD STILL AGREE ON ITS LOVE OF BASEBALL.

THE TIGERS MISSED OUT ON THE AMERICAN LEAGUE PENNANT BY ONE GAME, AS THE RED SOX RODE *CARL YASTRZEMSKI'S* TRIPLE CROWN SEASON ALL THE WAY TO THE WORLD SERIES.

BUT THE *OVERACHIEVING* SOX COULDN'T MATCH THE *CARDINALS.* BOB GIBSON WON THREE GAMES AND HIT A HOME RUN IN THE DECISIVE GAME 7.

IN 1968, THE NATION REELED FROM THE ASSASSINATIONS OF *ROBERT KENNEDY* AND *MARTIN LUTHER KING JR.*, AND DETROIT WAS STILL A WOUNDED CITY.

THE *TIGERS* BECAME THE ONE THING DETROITERS COULD RALLY AROUND. THE TEAM WON *103 GAMES* AND CHARGED INTO THE WORLD SERIES AGAINST THE RETURNING CARDINALS.

THE MATCHUP EVERYONE WANTED TO SEE WAS THE TIGERS' THIRTY-ONE-GAME WINNER *DENNY MCLAIN* AGAINST THE CARDS' DOMINANT *BOB GIBSON*.

GIBSON BEAT MCLAIN TWICE IN GAMES 1 AND 4, BUT THE TIGERS' *MICKEY LOLICH* TURNED THE TABLES, BEATING GIBSON IN GAME 7.

LOLICH IS THE LAST MAN TO WIN *THREE COMPLETE GAMES* IN A WORLD SERIES.

THE TIGERS' WIN WAS THE ONLY WORLD SERIES APPEARANCE FOR ONE OF BASEBALL'S QUIETEST LEGENDS: *AL KALINE.*

THE *YOUNGEST* MAN EVER TO WIN A BATTING TITLE (AT TWENTY), KALINE WAS IN HIS SIXTEENTH SEASON WHEN THE TIGERS TOOK THE FIELD AGAINST THE CARDINALS.

KALINE TOOK FULL ADVANTAGE, HITTING .379 AND PLAYING A FLAWLESS OUTFIELD.

AT HIS RETIREMENT IN 1974, HE WAS THE *TWELFTH* PLAYER WITH 3,000 HITS, AND HE WALKED AWAY FROM THE GAME WITH 399 HOME RUNS.

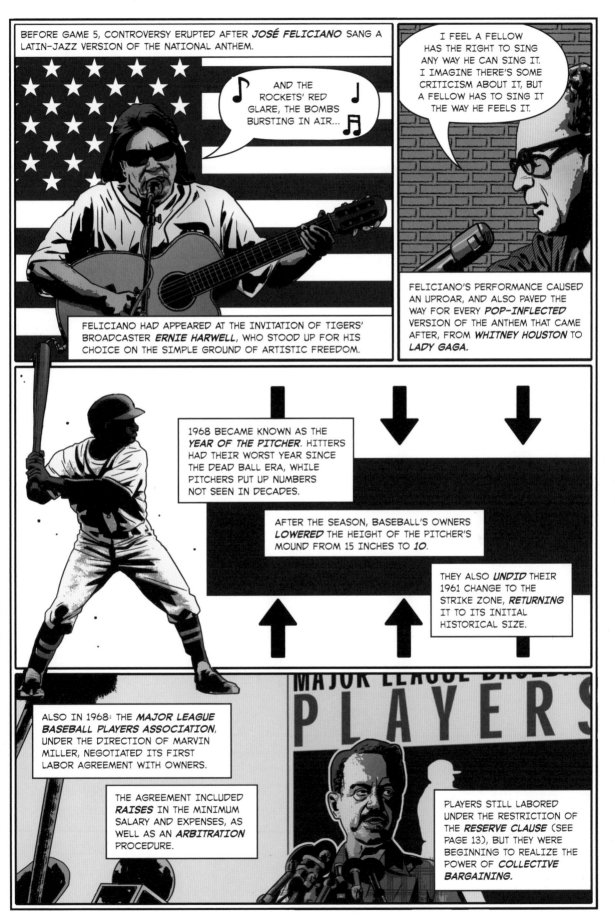

BEFORE GAME 5, CONTROVERSY ERUPTED AFTER *JOSÉ FELICIANO* SANG A LATIN-JAZZ VERSION OF THE NATIONAL ANTHEM.

AND THE ROCKETS' RED GLARE, THE BOMBS BURSTING IN AIR...

I FEEL A FELLOW HAS THE RIGHT TO SING ANY WAY HE CAN SING IT. I IMAGINE THERE'S SOME CRITICISM ABOUT IT, BUT A FELLOW HAS TO SING IT THE WAY HE FEELS IT.

FELICIANO HAD APPEARED AT THE INVITATION OF TIGERS' BROADCASTER *ERNIE HARWELL*, WHO STOOD UP FOR HIS CHOICE ON THE SIMPLE GROUND OF ARTISTIC FREEDOM.

FELICIANO'S PERFORMANCE CAUSED AN UPROAR, AND ALSO PAVED THE WAY FOR EVERY *POP-INFLECTED* VERSION OF THE ANTHEM THAT CAME AFTER, FROM *WHITNEY HOUSTON* TO *LADY GAGA*.

1968 BECAME KNOWN AS THE *YEAR OF THE PITCHER*. HITTERS HAD THEIR WORST YEAR SINCE THE DEAD BALL ERA, WHILE PITCHERS PUT UP NUMBERS NOT SEEN IN DECADES.

AFTER THE SEASON, BASEBALL'S OWNERS *LOWERED* THE HEIGHT OF THE PITCHER'S MOUND FROM 15 INCHES TO *10*.

THEY ALSO *UNDID* THEIR 1961 CHANGE TO THE STRIKE ZONE, *RETURNING* IT TO ITS INITIAL HISTORICAL SIZE.

ALSO IN 1968: THE *MAJOR LEAGUE BASEBALL PLAYERS ASSOCIATION*, UNDER THE DIRECTION OF MARVIN MILLER, NEGOTIATED ITS FIRST LABOR AGREEMENT WITH OWNERS.

THE AGREEMENT INCLUDED *RAISES* IN THE MINIMUM SALARY AND EXPENSES, AS WELL AS AN *ARBITRATION* PROCEDURE.

PLAYERS STILL LABORED UNDER THE RESTRICTION OF THE *RESERVE CLAUSE* (SEE PAGE 13), BUT THEY WERE BEGINNING TO REALIZE THE POWER OF *COLLECTIVE BARGAINING*.

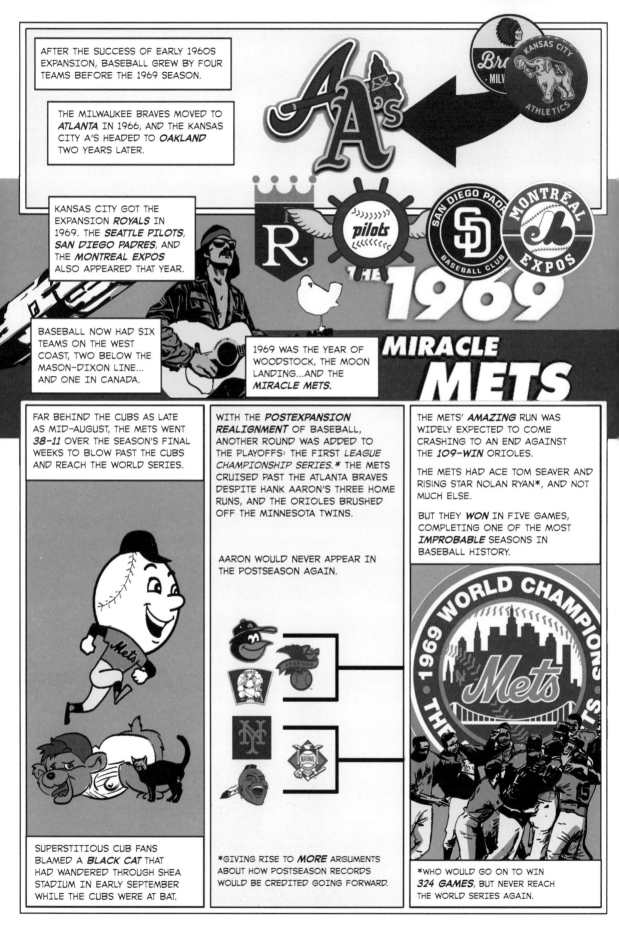

AFTER THE SUCCESS OF EARLY 1960S EXPANSION, BASEBALL GREW BY FOUR TEAMS BEFORE THE 1969 SEASON.

THE MILWAUKEE BRAVES MOVED TO *ATLANTA* IN 1966, AND THE KANSAS CITY A'S HEADED TO *OAKLAND* TWO YEARS LATER.

KANSAS CITY GOT THE EXPANSION *ROYALS* IN 1969. THE *SEATTLE PILOTS*, *SAN DIEGO PADRES*, AND THE *MONTREAL EXPOS* ALSO APPEARED THAT YEAR.

BASEBALL NOW HAD SIX TEAMS ON THE WEST COAST, TWO BELOW THE MASON-DIXON LINE... AND ONE IN CANADA.

1969 WAS THE YEAR OF WOODSTOCK, THE MOON LANDING...AND THE *MIRACLE METS.*

THE 1969 MIRACLE METS

FAR BEHIND THE CUBS AS LATE AS MID-AUGUST, THE METS WENT *38-11* OVER THE SEASON'S FINAL WEEKS TO BLOW PAST THE CUBS AND REACH THE WORLD SERIES.

WITH THE *POSTEXPANSION REALIGNMENT* OF BASEBALL, ANOTHER ROUND WAS ADDED TO THE PLAYOFFS: THE FIRST *LEAGUE CHAMPIONSHIP SERIES.* * THE METS CRUISED PAST THE ATLANTA BRAVES DESPITE HANK AARON'S THREE HOME RUNS, AND THE ORIOLES BRUSHED OFF THE MINNESOTA TWINS.

AARON WOULD NEVER APPEAR IN THE POSTSEASON AGAIN.

THE METS' *AMAZING* RUN WAS WIDELY EXPECTED TO COME CRASHING TO AN END AGAINST THE *109-WIN* ORIOLES.

THE METS HAD ACE TOM SEAVER AND RISING STAR NOLAN RYAN*, AND NOT MUCH ELSE.

BUT THEY *WON* IN FIVE GAMES, COMPLETING ONE OF THE MOST *IMPROBABLE* SEASONS IN BASEBALL HISTORY.

SUPERSTITIOUS CUB FANS BLAMED A *BLACK CAT* THAT HAD WANDERED THROUGH SHEA STADIUM IN EARLY SEPTEMBER WHILE THE CUBS WERE AT BAT.

*GIVING RISE TO *MORE* ARGUMENTS ABOUT HOW POSTSEASON RECORDS WOULD BE CREDITED GOING FORWARD.

*WHO WOULD GO ON TO WIN *324 GAMES*, BUT NEVER REACH THE WORLD SERIES AGAIN.

Let's Play Two

Breaking into the big leagues along with Willie Mays and Hank Aaron, Ernie Banks--*"Mr. Cub"*--became one of the most beloved Cubs in that franchise's long and (until just recently) miserable history. Part of the reason for his adulation was his unquenchable love for the game, exemplified by his famous (and probably exaggerated) habit of saying, *"Let's play two"* when he got to the park and only one game was scheduled.

He sandwiched two stints with the Kansas City Monarchs around *Korean War* service before joining the Cubs for the 1954 season as their *first black player*. For the rest of the 1950s, Banks was without question the *best hitting shortstop* in the game, winning back-to-back National League MVP awards in 1958 and '59.

Unfortunately, the Cubs were never better than average when Banks was at his best. Later in his career, Leo Durocher returned to baseball as the Cubs' manager, and spurred them to better years--though never quite good enough. Banks holds the major league record for most games played without a postseason appearance: *2,528.* He was the ninth man to reach 500 home runs, finishing with 512.

Dear Mr. Kuhn:

After twelve years in the Major Leagues, I do not feel
that I am a piece of property to be bought and sold
irrespective of my wishes. I believe that any system

AFTER THE 1969 SEASON, THE ST. LOUIS CARDINALS
AND OUTFIELDER *CURT FLOOD* ENGAGED IN A
BITTER ARGUMENT OVER HIS SALARY.

a ~~~~~~~~~~~~~~~~~~~~~~~~~~ th the laws of the
United States and of the several States.

It is my desire to play baseball in 1970, and I am
capabl~~~~~~~~~~~~~~~~~~ receive

AFTER THE TEAM TRADED HIM TO THE
PHILLIES, FLOOD HAD HAD ENOUGH.

HE *REFUSED* THE TRADE AND WENT
TO MLBPA DIRECTOR MARVIN MILLER
WITH A SIMPLE QUESTION: COULD
HE FIGHT THE DECISION?

right to consider offers from other
any decisions. I, therefore, reque~~~
known to all the Major League Clubs my feelings in this
matter, and advise them of my availability for the

I TOLD HIM EVEN IF
HE *WON,* HE'D NEVER
GET ANYTHING OUT OF IT.
HE'D NEVER GET A JOB
IN *BASEBALL* AGAIN.

BUT FLOOD KNEW HIS STAND COULD HELP FUTURE PLAYERS,
SO HE REFUSED TO BACK DOWN. HE *SUED COMMISSIONER
BOWIE KUHN* FOR THE RIGHT TO FREE AGENCY.

MARVIN MILLER WAS RIGHT: BASEBALL, BY
AND LARGE, *TURNED ITS BACK* ON FLOOD.

ON HIS DAY IN COURT, ONLY TWO
FORMER PLAYERS SHOWED UP TO
OFFER THEIR SUPPORT: *JACKIE
ROBINSON* AND *HANK GREENBERG.*
NO ACTIVE PLAYERS WERE PRESENT.

IN 1970, THE METS WERE BACK TO MEDIOCRITY
AND A *NEW FORCE* APPEARED ON THE SCENE:
THE CINCINNATI REDS, WHO WOULD COME TO
BE KNOWN AS THE *BIG RED MACHINE.*

I'M BEGINNING TO SEE BROOKS IN
MY SLEEP. IF I DROPPED THIS *PAPER
PLATE,* HE'D PICK IT UP ON ONE HOP
AND *THROW ME OUT* AT FIRST.

Ball Four

Jim *Bouton*, who began his career with the Yankees, wrote one of the funniest baseball books you'll ever read with his memoir *Ball Four*, focusing on his 1969 season with the expansion Seattle Pilots. The book *blew the lid off* baseball's long-held tradition of clubhouse omertà, especially in its portrayal of widespread drug use and Mickey Mantle's various excesses. Bouton was *ostracized* for years after its publication. He did not attend an official major league function until 1998.

Bouton also invented *Big League Chew,* bubble gum shredded to replicate the experience of chewing tobacco—only without the troublesome spitting and cancer.

The O-N Cannon

Major league baseball had Ruth and Gehrig, Aaron and Mathews, Mays and McCovey—and Japanese baseball had the *O-N Cannon.*

Sadaharu Oh and *Shigeo Nagashima* were teammates on the Yomiuri Giants for sixteen years. For most of that time, Oh batted third and Nagashima fourth. Known as the O-N Cannon, the two players combined for an astonishing *1,049* home runs as teammates, with Oh contributing *634.*

Oh would hit *868 home runs* during the course of his career, and along the way earn the respect of every major leaguer he ever played against. On the day he hit #756, *eclipsing* Hank Aaron's professional record, Aaron called in to the stadium and *congratulated* Oh over the loudspeaker system.

Nagashima was as legendary for his *flashy fielding* as for his bat, and retired as one of Japanese baseball's more flamboyant characters. Along with Oh, he was considered one of the Japanese players who could have been a *star* in the majors. Neither of them ever chose to leave Japan, despite the efforts of big-league teams to sign them in the 1970s.

THE 1960S AND '70S ALSO SAW THE BIRTH OF THE BASEBALL *MEMORA-BILIA INDUSTRY*. BALLPLAYERS STARTED MAKING EXTRA MONEY NOT BY TAKING OFF-SEASON JOBS, BUT THROUGH *PERSONAL SIGNING APPEARANCES*.

CIGARETTE CARDS WENT OUT OF FASHION IN THE EARLY TWENTIETH CENTURY, BUT THE *BOWMAN* BUBBLE GUM COMPANY PICKED UP THE SLACK.

BY THE 1950S, BOWMAN IN TURN YIELDED THE MARKET TO TOPPS, AND BY THE '60S *TOPPS* HAD CONSOLIDATED A *MONOPOLY*.

THIS SUCCESS COINCIDED WITH EXPLOSIVE GROWTH IN BASEBALL MEMORABILIA AND COLLECTING, WITH *MICKEY MANTLE* ITEMS LEADING THE WAY.

MANTLE'S 1952 TOPPS CARD IS CONSIDERED THE *MOST EXPENSIVE* POSTWAR CARD.

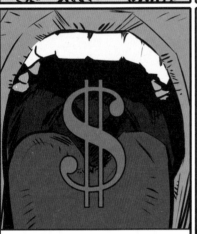

SO OVERHEATED WAS THE MANTLE COLLECTOR MANIA THAT A FAN EVEN TRIED TO *BUY MANTLE'S TONSILS* AFTER HE HAD THEM REMOVED IN 1956.

ON THE FIELD, THE 1971 ORIOLES MADE THEIR THIRD STRAIGHT WORLD SERIES, LOSING THIS TIME TO THE PITTSBURGH PIRATES AND *ROBERTO CLEMENTE*. CLEMENTE AND THE HERO OF THE 1960 SEASON, *BILL MAZEROSKI*, WERE THE ONLY PIRATES LEFT FROM THE BUCS' LAST CHAMPIONSHIP TEAM.

AFTER THE 1972 SEASON, CLEMENTE WOULD DIE IN A *PLANE CRASH* WHILE DELIVERING RELIEF SUPPLIES TO THE EARTHQUAKE-STRICKEN POPULATION OF MANAGUA, NICARAGUA.

HE HAD JUST GOTTEN HIS THREE THOUSANDTH HIT IN THE *FINAL AT-BAT* OF HIS MAJOR LEAGUE CAREER.

1971 ALSO SAW THE FIRST BLACK PLAYER ELECTED TO THE *HALL OF FAME*. HE WAS, OF COURSE, *SATCHEL PAIGE*.

THE HALL HAD ORIGINALLY PROPOSED A *SEPARATE WING* FOR FORMER NEGRO LEAGUERS, BUT THAT PROPOSAL CAUSED AN *UPROAR*-- NOT LEAST FROM PAIGE HIMSELF.

I WAS JUST AS GOOD AS THE WHITE BOYS. I AIN'T GOING IN THE *BACK DOOR* OF THE HALL OF FAME.

SO THERE WAS A FULL INDUCTION, AND THE HALL HAS SINCE TRIED TO *MAKE AMENDS* FOR THE LONG-TIME EXCLUSION OF NEGRO LEAGUERS FROM BASEBALL'S HALL OF IMMORTALS.

The First All-Black Lineup

APART FROM WINNING THE WORLD SERIES, THE PIRATES ALSO FIELDED THE *FIRST ALL-BLACK LINEUP* IN MAJOR LEAGUE HISTORY THAT YEAR.

Ellis, D.

The counterculture percolated into baseball the same way it did every other walk of American life, and perhaps no example is more renowned than Pittsburgh Pirate pitcher *Dock Ellis's* June 1970 no-hitter, which he claimed to have pitched while *tripping on LSD.*

During the 1971 All-Star Game at Tiger Stadium, Ellis played a role in another bit of baseball history. The A's *Reggie Jackson* hit a *legendary home run* off him that evening, an all-time tape-measure clout that reached the light tower on the roof in right-center field.

Ellis was so angry about it that the next time he faced Jackson, in 1976, he *beaned* him with a high fastball.

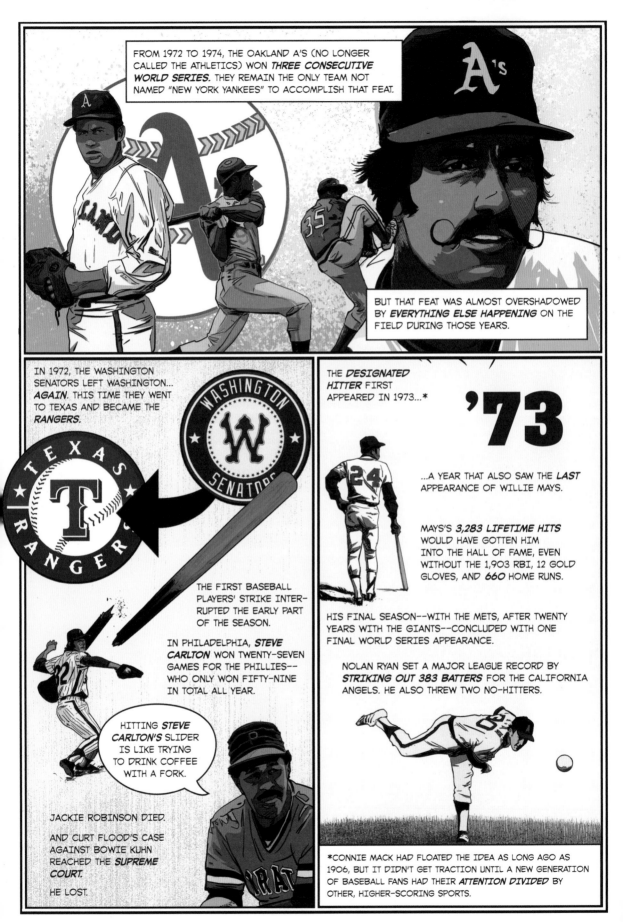

FROM 1972 TO 1974, THE OAKLAND A'S (NO LONGER CALLED THE ATHLETICS) WON *THREE CONSECUTIVE WORLD SERIES.* THEY REMAIN THE ONLY TEAM NOT NAMED "NEW YORK YANKEES" TO ACCOMPLISH THAT FEAT.

BUT THAT FEAT WAS ALMOST OVERSHADOWED BY *EVERYTHING ELSE HAPPENING* ON THE FIELD DURING THOSE YEARS.

IN 1972, THE WASHINGTON SENATORS LEFT WASHINGTON... *AGAIN.* THIS TIME THEY WENT TO TEXAS AND BECAME THE *RANGERS.*

THE FIRST BASEBALL PLAYERS' STRIKE INTERRUPTED THE EARLY PART OF THE SEASON.

IN PHILADELPHIA, *STEVE CARLTON* WON TWENTY-SEVEN GAMES FOR THE PHILLIES—WHO ONLY WON FIFTY-NINE IN TOTAL ALL YEAR.

HITTING *STEVE CARLTON'S* SLIDER IS LIKE TRYING TO DRINK COFFEE WITH A FORK.

JACKIE ROBINSON DIED.

AND CURT FLOOD'S CASE AGAINST BOWIE KUHN REACHED THE *SUPREME COURT.*

HE LOST.

THE *DESIGNATED HITTER* FIRST APPEARED IN 1973...*

'73

...A YEAR THAT ALSO SAW THE *LAST* APPEARANCE OF WILLIE MAYS.

MAYS'S *3,283 LIFETIME HITS* WOULD HAVE GOTTEN HIM INTO THE HALL OF FAME, EVEN WITHOUT THE 1,903 RBI, 12 GOLD GLOVES, AND *660* HOME RUNS.

HIS FINAL SEASON—WITH THE METS, AFTER TWENTY YEARS WITH THE GIANTS—CONCLUDED WITH ONE FINAL WORLD SERIES APPEARANCE.

NOLAN RYAN SET A MAJOR LEAGUE RECORD BY *STRIKING OUT 383 BATTERS* FOR THE CALIFORNIA ANGELS. HE ALSO THREW TWO NO-HITTERS.

*CONNIE MACK HAD FLOATED THE IDEA AS LONG AGO AS 1906, BUT IT DIDN'T GET TRACTION UNTIL A NEW GENERATION OF BASEBALL FANS HAD THEIR *ATTENTION DIVIDED* BY OTHER, HIGHER-SCORING SPORTS.

1974 SAW THE NAMING OF FRANK ROBINSON AS MAJOR LEAGUE BASEBALL'S *FIRST BLACK MANAGER.*

IF I HAD ONE WISH IN THE WORLD TODAY, IT WOULD BE THAT *JACKIE ROBINSON* COULD BE HERE TO SEE THIS HAPPEN.

'74

IN THE OFFSEASON, CATFISH HUNTER BECAME THE FIRST PLAYER TO SIGN A FREE-AGENT CONTRACT.*

ON THE FIELD, BOB GIBSON REACHED THREE THOUSAND STRIKEOUTS--*THE FIRST PITCHER* TO HIT THAT MILE-STONE SINCE WALTER JOHNSON.

THE CARDINALS AND METS PLAYED THE LONGEST GAME IN HISTORY ON SEPTEMBER 11: *TWENTY-FIVE INNINGS.*

*A FREE AGENT IS A PLAYER WHO CAN NEGOTIATE A CONTRACT WITH ANY TEAM HE CHOOSES.

PITCHER *TOMMY JOHN* UNDERWENT THE TENDON REPLACEMENT SURGERY THAT NOW BEARS HIS NAME.

BUT NONE OF THAT COULD HOLD A CANDLE TO ONE OF BASEBALL'S GREAT DRAMAS, WHICH UNFOLDED THROUGHOUT THE 1973 SEASON AND THROUGH THE EARLY PART OF 1974. THAT, OF COURSE, WAS THE *COUNTDOWN* TO... (SEE NEXT PAGE.)

The Lip

Leo "the Lip" Durocher played his first major league game in 1925 and managed his last game in 1973. In between, he saw the integration of the game, the West Coast relocations, expansion, and the first big-money ballplayers.

As a manager, he won more than *two thousand* games, welcomed Jackie Robinson to the big leagues, and was *ejected* more than any other manager except for John McGraw. He was also suspended for the 1947 season due to his associations with gamblers and mobsters. Known for his mouth as much as his managerial acumen, he was famously misquoted as saying (about Mel Ott), *"Nice guys finish last."*

133

715

...APRIL 8, 1975. THAT WAS WHEN *HANK AARON BROKE BABE RUTH'S HOME RUN RECORD*--PROBABLY THE MOST CHERISHED RECORD IN AMERICAN SPORTS.

ALL THE PREVIOUS YEAR, AARON HAD BEEN SUBJECTED TO TORRENTS OF *RACIAL ABUSE AND HATE MAIL.*

ATLANTA JOURNAL SPORTS EDITOR LEWIS GRIZZARD EVEN *PREPARED AN OBITUARY* FOR AARON, FEARING HE WOULD BE MURDERED BY A RACIST FAN.

AARON WAS THE LAST REMAINING VETERAN OF THE *NEGRO LEAGUES* WHEN HE HIT NUMBER 715.

HE WOULD RETIRE THE NEXT YEAR, WITH AN ALL-TIME HOME-RUN TOTAL OF *755.* HE ALSO HELD MAJOR LEAGUE RECORDS FOR *RBIS* AND TOTAL BASES, AND STOOD AT #2 IN *CAREER HITS* BEHIND TY COBB.

THERE'S A DRIVE INTO LEFT-CENTER FIELD. THAT BALL IS GONNA BE... *OUTTA HERE!* IT'S GONE! IT'S *715!* THERE'S A *NEW HOME-RUN CHAMPION* OF ALL TIME, AND IT'S HENRY AARON!

WHAT A MARVELOUS MOMENT FOR BASEBALL; WHAT A *MARVELOUS MOMENT* FOR ATLANTA AND THE STATE OF GEORGIA; WHAT A MARVELOUS MOMENT FOR THE COUNTRY AND THE WORLD. *A BLACK MAN IS GETTING A STANDING OVATION IN THE DEEP SOUTH* FOR BREAKING A RECORD OF AN ALL-TIME BASEBALL IDOL. AND IT IS A GREAT MOMENT FOR ALL OF US, AND PARTICULARLY FOR HENRY AARON.

1975 WAS ALSO THE YEAR THAT THE BIG RED MACHINE CLAIMED THE FIRST OF THEIR *BACK-TO-BACK* WORLD SERIES WINS.

POWERED BY THREE FUTURE HALL OF FAMERS IN *JOHNNY BENCH, JOE MORGAN, AND TONY PÉREZ,* THE REDS DOMINATED THE NATIONAL LEAGUE FROM 1970 TO 1976.

*AND A FOURTH PLAYER, PETE ROSE, WHO WOULD BE IN THE HALL IF HE HADN'T BEEN BANNED FOR GAMBLING.

BOSTON CATCHER *CARLTON FISK* HIT A DRAMATIC HOME RUN TO WIN GAME 6...

BUT AFTER TAKING A 3-0 LEAD IN GAME 7, THE SOX SAW IT ALL SLIP AWAY.

THREE STRAIGHT *HEARTBREAKING* WORLD SERIES LOSSES HAD RED SOX NATION FEELING CURSED, AND THE IDEA OF THE *CURSE OF THE BAMBINO* REALLY TOOK HOLD. MAYBE THE TEAM WAS DOOMED BY THE ILL-FATED DECISION TO SELL BABE RUTH ALL THE WAY BACK IN 1919...

Charlie Hustle

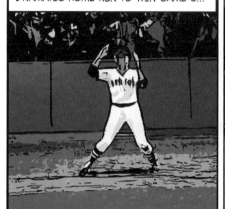

An unheralded prospect signed by the Reds as a *favor to his uncle,* Pete Rose broke into the big leagues in 1963. He proceeded to carve out a twenty-four-year career in which he made the All-Star team at five different positions and collected an *all-time record 4,256 base hits.*

He acquired the nickname *"Charlie Hustle,"* courtesy of Whitey Ford-- who meant it as an insult after Rose sprinted to first following a walk. Rose adopted the moniker as a badge of honor, and was known throughout his career as a player who would do *anything* to win.

This reputation led to some unfortunate situations. During the 1970 All-Star Game, he ran over catcher *Ray Fosse,* permanently injuring Fosse's shoulder. Rose also caused more than one on-field fracas for *hard slides* into second base.

Rose was plagued by a *gambling problem* and banned from induction into the Hall of Fame after it emerged that he had *bet on the Reds* while managing them in the 1980s.

AS THE 1977 SEASON BEGAN, THE GAME WAS VERY DIFFERENT THAN IT HAD BEEN ONLY TEN YEARS PREVIOUS.

AND THE YANKEES, *DORMANT* FOR THE PREVIOUS DECADE, HAD JUST *SURGED BACK INTO CONTENTION* WITH A RUN TO THE '76 WORLD SERIES.

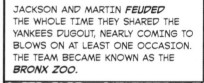

RUTH'S RECORDS HAD FALLEN. WILLIE, MICKEY, AND THE DUKE WERE ALL RETIRED. *EXPANSION AND EXPANDED* PLAYOFFS HAD CHANGED BASEBALL'S TRADITIONAL PENNANT RACES.

THEY WOULD WIN *BACK-TO-BACK* SERIES IN 1977 AND '78 UNDER THE FIERY LEADERSHIP OF *BILLY MARTIN*, ANNOUNCING THEIR RETURN TO BASEBALL'S ELITE.

NO PLAYER HAD MORE TO DO WITH THIS RESURGENCE THAN *REGINALD MARTINEZ JACKSON.*

THERE'S *NOT ENOUGH MUSTARD IN THE WORLD* TO COVER REGGIE JACKSON.

JACKSON AND MARTIN *FEUDED* THE WHOLE TIME THEY SHARED THE YANKEES DUGOUT, NEARLY COMING TO BLOWS ON AT LEAST ONE OCCASION. THE TEAM BECAME KNOWN AS THE *BRONX ZOO.*

AN UNAPOLOGETIC HOT DOG, WITH A BAT TO BACK IT UP, JACKSON WAS A *POLARIZING FIGURE* FOR FANS AND TEAMMATES ALIKE.

IN GAME 6 OF THE 1977 WORLD SERIES, JACKSON HIT *THREE HOME RUNS* ON THREE *CONSECUTIVE PITCHES,* CEMENTING HIS REPUTATION AS *MR. OCTOBER.* *

AT THAT TIME, BABE RUTH WAS THE ONLY OTHER PLAYER WITH THREE HOMERS IN A WORLD SERIES GAME.

*THIS MONIKER WAS ORIGINALLY APPLIED BY HIS TEAMMATE THURMAN MUNSON.

JACKSON BARELY MADE IT THROUGH THE THRONGS OF FANS AFTER THE LAST OUT OF THE SERIES. EARLIER IN THE GAME, THEY WERE THROWING *FIRECRACKERS* AT HIM. NOW HE WAS THE *TOAST* OF BASEBALL.

THE YANKEES WERE BACK. FITTINGLY, BOTH THEIR 1977 AND '78 WINS CAME AGAINST THE DODGERS.

George Foster

I WANTED TO *INTEGRATE* THE BAT RACK.

One of the underappreciated members of the Big Red Machine, George Foster was a key member of their two championship teams, providing home-run power and a strong arm in left field. In 1977, he was the tenth man to record *fifty home runs in a season*--and the *only* one to do so between 1965 and 1990.

TM

He also caused a bit of a stir when he began using a *black bat* in the mid-'70s, when few players used bats with painted finishes. Injuries slowed him in the '80s and prevented him from reaching the level of the all-time greats.

The Bird

When he burst on the scene in 1976, Tigers rookie pitcher Mark Fidrych--nicknamed *"The Bird"* for his resemblance to Big Bird--was an immediate sensation. Part of it was his skill, but much of his appeal came from his *eccentricities.* He groomed the mound on hands and knees before innings and sometimes between plays. He *talked to the ball* before throwing pitches. He sometimes threw balls back to the umpires if he thought they were going to be hit. And fans, in Detroit and all over baseball, ate it up.

Such was Fidrych-mania that he became the only baseball player ever to appear on the cover of *Rolling Stone.* But his decline had already set in. A spring-training injury in 1977 led to shoulder problems, and by 1980 he was out of the league.

FOUR DIFFERENT TEAMS MADE AT LEAST THREE WORLD SERIES APPEARANCES IN THE 1970S.

THE EXPANSION OF THE PLAYOFFS MEANT **MORE TEAMS HAD A CHANCE** TO GET TO THE SERIES. THE GAME HAD MORE AND BETTER RIVALRIES THAN EVER BEFORE.

IN 1979, THE PITTSBURGH PIRATES **BOOKENDED** THE DECADE WITH ANOTHER SERIES WIN. RALLYING BEHIND THE DISCO ANTHEM **"WE ARE FAMILY,"** THE PIRATES MET THE ORIOLES IN A REMATCH OF THE 1971 SERIES.

AND JUST LIKE IN 1971, **WILLIE "POPS" STARGELL** SCORED THE WINNING RUN IN GAME 7.

DISCO SUCKS

DISCO ALSO PLAYED A ROLE IN THE MOST INFAMOUS BASEBALL INCIDENT OF 1979, THE **"DISCO DEMOLITION"** RIOT AT COMISKEY PARK.

THE POPULARITY OF DISCO--WITH ITS ROOTS IN **MINORITY AND GAY CULTURES**--PROVOKED A SNEERING BACKLASH FROM ROCK-AND-ROLL FANS.

THE WHITE SOX STAGED AN EVENT IN WHICH A CRATE FULL OF DISCO RECORDS WOULD BE **BLOWN UP** ON THE FIELD BETWEEN GAMES OF A DOUBLEHEADER.

COMISKEY PARK WAS PACKED OVER CAPACITY, WITH PEOPLE **JUMPING TURNSTILES** AND **CRAMMING THE CONCOURSES.**

ROWDY FANS THREW RECORDS **ONTO THE FIELD** DURING THE FIRST GAME. THE RECORDS SLICED THROUGH THE AIR AND STUCK INTO THE GROUND.

GOD ALMIGHTY, I'VE NEVER SEEN ANYTHING SO **DANGEROUS** IN MY LIFE.

THE EXPLOSION LEFT A *CRATER* IN THE OUTFIELD AND SPARKED A *FIELD INVASION.* FANS STOLE THE BASES AND TORE UP PATCHES OF GRASS BEFORE *RIOT POLICE* DISPERSED THEM. THE WHITE SOX HAD TO FORFEIT THE SECOND GAME.

BEER AND BASEBALL GO TOGETHER, HAVE FOR YEARS. BUT I THINK THOSE KIDS WERE DOING THINGS *OTHER* THAN BEER.

AS WITH JOSÉ FELICIANO'S *NATIONAL ANTHEM* PERFORMANCE, DISCO DEMOLITION WAS ONE OF SEVERAL TIMES *CULTURAL TENSIONS* WOULD PLAY OUT ON THE BASEBALL FIELD DURING THE 1960S AND '70S.

SHOW ME THE MONEY

AS THE AMOUNT OF **MONEY** POURING INTO THE GAME INCREASED, SO DID **TENSIONS** OVER WHO SHOULD GET IT.

PROFIT   SALARIES

SHORT STRIKES AND LOCKOUTS IN THE 1970S HAD NOT AFFECTED THE REGULAR SEASON--EXCEPT IN 1972, WHEN THE START OF THE SEASON WAS DELAYED UNTIL APRIL 13.

IN **1981**, TENSIONS BETWEEN PLAYERS AND MANAGEMENT CAME TO A HEAD.

ON JUNE 12 OF THAT YEAR, PLAYERS **WENT ON STRIKE** AND STAYED OUT UNTIL THE OWNERS CAVED ON JULY 31.

SEVEN HUNDRED THIRTEEN GAMES WERE LOST. THE 1981 SEASON WAS DIVIDED INTO HALVES, WITH FIRST- AND SECOND-HALF DIVISION WINNERS PLAYING IN BASEBALL'S FIRST **DIVISION SERIES.**

THERE WOULD NOT BE **ANOTHER** DIVISION SERIES UNTIL 1995--AFTER ANOTHER PAINFUL STRIKE AND LEAGUE-WIDE **REALIGNMENT** OF TEAMS. (SEE PAGES 146-147.)

SHOW ME THE MONEY: BASEBALL'S HIGHEST-PAID PLAYERS

1913: FIRST $10,000 PLAYER -- TY COBB

1949: FIRST $100,000 PLAYER -- JOE DIMAGGIO

1980: FIRST $1,000,000 PLAYER -- NOLAN RYAN

1997: FIRST $10,000,000 PLAYER -- ALBERT BELLE

2001: FIRST $20,000,000 PLAYER -- ALEX RODRÍGUEZ

FRESH OFF THIS VICTORY, PLAYERS SAW THE STRENGTH OF THEIR UNION INCREASE, AND THEIR SALARIES BEGAN TO **SKYROCKET.** (SO DID TICKET PRICES.)

A **MILLION.** FOR PLAYING **BASEBALL?**

THESE HUGE INVESTMENTS LED TO CHANGES IN THE WAY THE GAME WAS PLAYED.

THERE WAS LESS **HEADHUNTING**, FEWER HARD SLIDES, AND A NOTABLE DECREASE IN PLAYERS **STEALING HOME.**

Average Salaries

Baseball first had a *minimum salary* in 1967. Since then, the average salary of a major league baseball player has risen more than *22,000 percent.* Curt Flood's courage and Marvin Miller's tenacity produced results they never would have imagined.

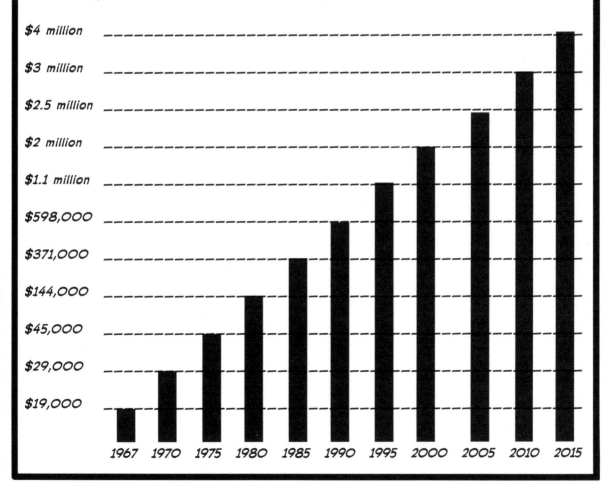

THE URGE TO *SIMULATE* BASEBALL GAMES AND LEAGUES GOES BACK AS FAR AS THE FIRST *FAN ARGUMENTS* ABOUT WHICH FAVORITE PLAYER WAS BETTER.

A FAMOUS EXAMPLE IS SEEN AMONG *JACK KEROUAC'S* PAPERS. BEFORE HE BECAME THE FAMOUS WRITER OF *ON THE ROAD*, KEROUAC CREATED AN ENTIRE *FICTIONAL BASEBALL LEAGUE* AND KEPT METICULOUS TRACK OF ITS STATS AND RECORDS.*

*FOR THE RECORD, SO DID THE WRITER OF THIS BOOK.

BY THE 1970S AND '80S, COMPUTER PROGRAMMERS WERE PUTTING THE POWER OF COMPUTERS TO WORK SIMULATING BASEBALL GAMES AND SEASONS.

ORIOLES THIRD-BASEMAN *DAVEY JOHNSON* WROTE COMPUTER PROGRAMS TO SIMULATE BASEBALL GAMES IN THE 1970S. LATER, AS MANAGER OF THE METS IN THE 1980S, HE *PIONEERED* THE USE OF *COMPUTER-GENERATED STATISTICS* TO GUIDE STRATEGY.

FANTASY BASEBALL DEVELOPED IN PARALLEL WITH THESE MORE SOPHISTICATED SIMULATIONS.

SO-CALLED *ROTISSERIE LEAGUE* GROUPS SPRANG UP IN THE EARLY '80S--AND, IT'S SAID, BUOYED *USA TODAY'S* CIRCULATION NUMBERS BECAUSE ITS BOX SCORES WERE MORE DETAILED THAN THOSE OF LOCAL PAPERS.

ONE OF THE FIRST PUBLIC FANTASY LEAGUES WAS *DUGOUT DERBY*, PLAYABLE VIA NEWSPAPER ADS.

WITH THE SPREAD OF PERSONAL COMPUTERS AND THE *INTERNET*, FANTASY BASEBALL WENT *ONLINE*, AND NOW MILLIONS OF PEOPLE PLAY.

ALL OF THIS WOULD LEAD INEXORABLY TO ADVANCED STATISTICS KNOWN AS *SABERMETRICS.*

ANOTHER FORM OF FANTASY WAS AND IS THE *FANTASY CAMP.* MEN WHO DREAM OF BEING BALLPLAYERS CAN GO TO AN *ERSATZ SPRING TRAINING* ALONGSIDE FORMER BIG-LEAGUE PLAYERS--FOR A *HEFTY FEE.*

LIKE OTHER FORMS OF *MONETIZED NOSTALGIA,* THIS ONE FOCUSED FIRST ON MICKEY MANTLE, WHO RAN FANTASY CAMPS THROUGHOUT THE 1980S.

MICKEY MANTLE FANTASY BASEBALL CAMP WHITEY FORD

THAT TERM, DERIVED FROM *SABR, THE SOCIETY FOR AMERICAN BASEBALL RESEARCH,* ENTERED THE SPORT IN THE 1980S AND HAS PLAGUED OLD-FASHIONED BASEBALL GURUS AND FANS EVER SINCE.

ITS LEADING ADVOCATE, *BILL JAMES,* HAS DONE MORE TO ADVANCE (SOME WOULD SAY *COMPLICATE*) BASEBALL STATISTICS THAN ANYONE ELSE.

ALL MAJOR LEAGUE TEAMS NOW CONDUCT THEM, BRINGING IN FAMOUS EX-PLAYERS TO *HOBNOB* WITH FANS WHO CAN *AFFORD* THE EXPERIENCE.

The Universal Baseball Association

The Universal Baseball Association Inc. Robert Coover

Robert Coover's 1968 novel *The Universal Baseball Association, Inc., J. Henry Waugh, Prop.* imagined the creation of a fantasy league that has unexpected effects on the creator's real life. A *black comedy masterpiece,* it belongs on the shelf of any baseball lover.

EXPANSION AND FREE AGENCY DISINTEGRATED BASEBALL'S TRADITIONAL POWER CYCLES.

NINE DIFFERENT TEAMS WON SERIES IN THE '80S. (INCLUDING THE *PHILLIES* WINNING THE *FIRST* IN THEIR NINETY-EIGHT-YEAR HISTORY!)

THE *ROYALS, BREWERS, AND PADRES* MADE THEIR FIRST APPEARANCES IN THE WORLD SERIES DURING THOSE YEARS.

THE INCREASING USE OF *SPECIALIZED RELIEF PITCHERS* WAS ANOTHER EQUALIZING FORCE.

MOST WORLD SERIES WINNERS IN THE '80S RELIED ON A DOMINANT *CLOSER,* A PATTERN THAT CONTINUES TO THE PRESENT DAY.

THE ON-FIELD PRODUCT IN THE 1980S IS OFTEN COMPARED *UNFAVORABLY* TO THE DECADES BEFORE AND AFTER, BUT IT WAS IN FACT A DECADE OF *LANDMARKS.*

IN 1982, RICKEY HENDERSON SET A MAJOR LEAGUE RECORD WITH *130 STOLEN BASES.*

IN 1983, WALTER JOHNSON'S STRIKEOUT RECORD OF 3,509 WAS BROKEN NOT ONCE, BUT *THREE TIMES*: BY *NOLAN RYAN, STEVE CARLTON, AND GAYLORD PERRY.*

IN 1985, PETE ROSE *BROKE TY COBB'S ALL-TIME HITS RECORD.* IN A *RARE* MOMENT OF HUMILITY, HE REFLECTED ON HIS PLACE IN THE GAME.

WHEN I GET THE RECORD, ALL IT WILL MAKE ME IS THE PLAYER WITH THE MOST HITS. I'M ALSO THE PLAYER WITH THE MOST *AT-BATS* AND THE MOST *OUTS.* I NEVER SAID I WAS A BETTER PLAYER THAN COBB.

SPARKY ANDERSON WAS THE FIRST MANAGER TO **WIN WORLD SERIES IN BOTH LEAGUES** WHEN HIS TIGERS BEAT THE PADRES IN 1984.

I'VE GOT MY FAULTS, BUT LIVING IN THE *PAST* ISN'T ONE OF THEM. THERE'S NO *FUTURE* IN IT.

ROGER CLEMENS BECAME THE FIRST PITCHER WITH *TWENTY STRIKEOUTS* IN A GAME IN 1986.

20K

AND IN 1988, JOSÉ CANSECO BECAME THE FIRST PLAYER IN BIG-LEAGUE HISTORY TO *HIT FORTY HOME RUNS AND STEAL FORTY BASES* IN THE SAME SEASON.

300/3000

Twenty-four pitchers have recorded three hundred or more wins, but only nine have *three hundred wins and three thousand strikeouts.* Thirty hitters have more than three thousand hits, but only eleven have *three thousand hits and three hundred home runs.*

The hitters: Hank Aaron, Stan Musial, Carl Yastrzemski, Willie Mays, Al Kaline, Rafael Palmeiro, Dave Winfield, George Brett, Cal Ripken Jr., Eddie Murray, Álex Rodríguez

The pitchers: Nolan Ryan, Roger Clemens, Steve Carlton, Tom Seaver, Don Sutton, Gaylord Perry, Walter Johnson, Phil Niekro, Greg Maddux.

IN 1982, *GAYLORD PERRY*--THE MAJORS' LAST UNREPENTANT *SPITBALLER*--BECAME THE FIRST MEMBER OF THE 300/3000 CLUB SINCE WALTER JOHNSON CREATED IT IN 1923.

300 WINS IS NOTHING TO TO SPIT AT

Three hundred wins and three thousand hits are considered *sure-fire tickets to the Hall of Fame.* The only exceptions to this rule are Pete Rose, Roger Clemens, and Rafael Palmeiro: two doomed by steroids (see page 154) and one by gambling. Rodríguez's status will be clearer when he becomes eligible for the Hall in 2021.

THE 1980S WERE ALSO A GREAT ERA FOR *SHORTSTOPS:* THE ACROBATICS OF *OZZIE SMITH,* THE STEADY EXCELLENCE OF *ALAN TRAMMELL,* AND THE DURABLE POWER OF *CAL RIPKEN JR.*

TRAMMELL AND LOU WHITAKER PLAYED *NINETEEN YEARS* TOGETHER WITH THE TIGERS, A RECORD FOR A SHORTSTOP—SECOND BASEMAN PAIRING.

ON THE DARKER SIDE, THE '80S ALSO SAW AN EPISODE OF *COLLUSION* AMONG OWNERS, IN WHICH THEY AGREED NOT TO SIGN PROMINENT FREE AGENTS AS A WAY TO KEEP SALARIES DOWN...

...CASTING A SHADOW OVER A NUMBER OF *HUGE INVESTMENTS* IN NEW BASEBALL STADIUMS.

CAMDEN YARDS IN BALTIMORE WAS THE FIRST OF THE NEW *RETRO-STYLED* PARKS, WHICH REPUDIATED THE *MULTIFUNCTIONAL DRABNESS* OF 1970S AND EARLY-'80S STADIUMS IN FAVOR OF A MORE NOSTALGIC BALLPARK FEEL.

BY *1994,* WHEN NEW STADIUMS WERE UNDERWAY IN DENVER, TEXAS, AND CLEVELAND, THE LABOR SITUATION WAS *RAPIDLY WORSENING.*

BEFORE THE SEASON, BASEBALL HAD *REALIGNED ITS DIVISIONS,* CREATING THREE IN EACH LEAGUE INSTEAD OF TWO AND ADDING A *WILD-CARD ROUND* TO THE PLAYOFFS.

OWNERS ALSO PROPOSED A NEW COLLECTIVE BARGAINING AGREEMENT THAT INCLUDED A *SALARY CAP* AND THAT *ELIMINATED* SALARY ARBITRATION.

AFTER MONTHS OF ARGUING, PLAYERS *WENT ON STRIKE* IN AUGUST 1994.

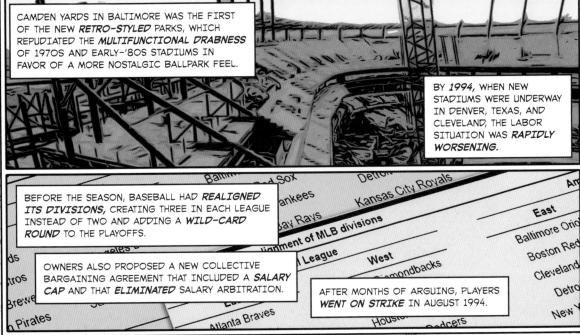

FOR THE FIRST TIME SINCE 1904, *NO WORLD SERIES WAS PLAYED.*

THE STRIKE WAS RESOLVED IN TIME FOR A 144-GAME 1995 SEASON...AND FOR CONSTRUCTION ON MORE NEW BALLPARKS--WITH LUXURY BOXES AND $10 BEERS.

TABERNAC!

AND TONY GWYNN SR., BATTING *.394* AT THE TIME OF THE STRIKE, NEVER GOT A CHANCE TO FIND OUT IF HE COULD MATCH TED WILLIAMS.

BUT THE *MONTREAL EXPOS,* ON THE CUSP OF MAKING THE PLAYOFFS FOR THE FIRST TIME IN FRANCHISE HISTORY, NEARLY COLLAPSED. THEY WERE *RELOCATED* TO WASHINGTON, D.C. TEN YEARS LATER AND RENAMED THE *WASHINGTON NATIONALS.* (NOBODY HAD THE HEART TO TRY SENATORS FOR A THIRD TIME.)

The Negro League Baseball Museum

Founded in 1990 by a group of former Negro League stars, including Hall of Famer *Buck O'Neil,* the *Negro Leagues Baseball Museum* established a permanent home by 1997. It's located in the historic *Eighteenth and Vine* section of Kansas City, the epicenter of African American cultural life there and formerly the site of *Blues Park,* where the Monarchs played for thirty years.

THE NEGRO LEAGUES BASEBALL MUSEUM

One of the centerpieces of the museum's collection is the *Field of Legends,* a game scene featuring twelve of the greatest figures from Negro League history.

BEGINNING WITH THE OPENING OF *CAMDEN YARDS* IN 1992, BASEBALL'S NOSTALGIA IMPULSE SPREAD TO BALLPARK CONSTRUCTION.

IN THE NEXT TEN YEARS, *ELEVEN* TEAMS BUILT NEW PARKS, OFTEN PROPOSING THEM AS PART OF *REDEVELOPMENT SCHEMES* FOR STRUGGLING DOWNTOWN AREAS.

THE ECONOMICS OF THIS ARGUMENT REMAIN *QUESTIONABLE,* BUT THE RESULTS FOR THE TEAMS WERE CLEAR.

NEW STADIUMS MEANT *MORE MONEY* AND IN MOST CASES A BETTER *FAN EXPERIENCE.* BOTH WERE CRITICAL IN THE AFTERMATH OF THE 1994 STRIKE.

BY 2000, THE ONLY TWO BALLPARKS LEFT FROM THE FIRST ERA OF CONSTRUCTION WERE *WRIGLEY* AND *FENWAY,* BOTH OF WHICH OPENED IN 1912.

Japanese Imports

Change came to baseball on a number of different fronts in the 1990s. Among them was the arrival of *Hideo Nomo* with the Dodgers in 1995.

Nomo was the first Japanese player in the majors since *Masanori Murakami* in 1964.

The Art Of The Steal

939

I AM THE *GREATEST.*

When Ty Cobb *stole 96 bases* in 1915, it would be forty-seven years before Maury Wills broke his record, stealing 104 in 1962.

In St. Louis, a young Lou Brock was watching and learning. He would break Wills's record in 1974, with *118* steals. Wills was not happy.

YOU DON'T THINK *HEMINGWAY* OR *MICHELANGELO* WOULD HAVE BEEN DELIGHTED TO SEE THEIR ACCOMPLISHMENTS SURPASSED, DO YOU?

Only eight years after that, Rickey Henderson topped Brock's record with *130 steals* in 1982. He would break Brock's career steals record nine years later, in 1991--and on the way become *Nolan Ryan's five-thousandth strikeout victim*, to which he had a typically Rickey-esque response.

IF YOU HAVEN'T BEEN STRUCK OUT BY NOLAN RYAN, YOU'RE *NOBODY.*

Rickey Henderson is the *only* modern player to record one hundred walks, one hundred steals, and one hundred runs in a season--and he did it *three times.* He also collected three thousand hits and transformed the game's ideal of what a *leadoff hitter* could do, hitting *eighty-eight* leadoff home runs over the course of his career. Flashy, outspoken, and a *certifiable weirdo*, he is one of the game's true greats.

THE 1995 ALL-STAR GAME, AT THE TEXAS RANGERS' BRAND-NEW BALLPARK AT ARLINGTON, FEATURED PLAYERS FROM *SIX DIFFERENT COUNTRIES*. A DEMOGRAPHIC SHIFT WAS UNDERWAY ON THE FIELD.

IN 1975, *27 PERCENT* OF BIG-LEAGUERS WERE AFRICAN AMERICAN.

BY 2015, THAT NUMBER WOULD DROP TO 10 *PERCENT* WHILE 28 PERCENT OF PLAYERS WOULD BE *HISPANIC*.

NEW IDEAS ALSO PERCOLATED INTO THE *FRONT OFFICES*. A YOUNGER GENERATION OF EXECUTIVES TRUSTED *DATA* THE WAY THAT OLD SCOUTS AND MANAGERS ONLY TRUSTED THEIR *EYES*. THE RESULT? *MONEYBALL*.

THE IDEA WAS SIMPLE USE THE POWER OF COMPUTING TO FIND *HIDDEN VALUE*.

FORMER PLAYER *BILLY BEANE* JOINED THE OAKLAND A'S AND LEARNED THE PRINCIPLES OF MONEYBALL FROM A'S GENERAL MANAGER *SANDY ALDERSON*.

THE RESULTS, ONCE BEANE TOOK OVER AS A'S GENERAL MANAGER IN 1997, WERE *DRAMATIC*. THE A'S WERE WINNING THEIR DIVISION AGAIN BY 2000.

OTHER TEAMS TOOK NOTICE AND *SABERMETRIC PRINCIPLES* BEGAN TO TAKE ROOT IN BASE-BALL. (YOU LAST SAW THIS WORD ON PAGE 143.)

IN PARALLEL, SCOUTING NETWORKS GOT MORE SOPHIS-TICATED, DATA-DRIVEN--AND *INTERNATIONAL*.

TEAMS STARTED SETTING UP *ACADEMIES* IN BASEBALL-CRAZY COUNTRIES THROUGHOUT LATIN AMERICA.

THE MOST FAMOUS OF THESE IS IN THE CITY OF *SAN PEDRO DE MACORÍS* IN THE DOMINICAN REPUBLIC.

A CITY ABOUT THE SIZE OF WORCESTER, MASSACHUSETTS, SAN PEDRO DE MACORÍS HAS PRODUCED *SEVENTY-SIX* MAJOR LEAGUE PLAYERS OVER THE PAST FORTY YEARS.

VENEZUELA AND PANAMA ALSO BECAME RICH SOURCES OF TALENT.

ONE PART OF BASEBALL CULTURE THAT *HASN'T* MADE MUCH RACIAL PROGRESS IS THE *UMPIRING CORPS.*

IN 1966, *EMMETT ASHFORD* BECAME THE FIRST AFRICAN AMERICAN UMPIRE TO CALL A MAJOR LEAGUE GAME.

BASEBALL HAS NEVER HAD MORE THAN A *HANDFUL* OF BLACK OR HISPANIC UMPIRES.

IN 1988, *PAM POSTEMA* BECAME THE FIRST WOMAN UMPIRE TO CALL A MAJOR LEAGUE SPRING TRAINING GAME. AFTER THE 1989 SEASON HER CONTRACT WAS TERMINATED. SHE FILED A *SEX-DISCRIMINATION LAWSUIT,* WHICH WAS EVENTUALLY SETTLED.

POSTEMA PUSHED A FRONTIER FIRST EXPLORED IN THE 1970S BY *BERNICE GERA*, WHO CALLED A SINGLE MINOR LEAGUE GAME BEFORE RESIGNING DUE TO *ABUSE* AND *DEATH THREATS.*

EVEN AFTER THE TURN OF THE CENTURY, NOTHING HAD CHANGED. *RIA CORTESIO,* AFTER PROGRESSING AS FAR AS MAJOR LEAGUE SPRING TRAINING, FOUND HER UMPIRING CAREER STALLED. SHE LEFT THE GAME IN 2007.

Bull Durham

The best baseball movie ever made isn't even about the major leagues. It's *Bull Durham*, which follows the story of a career minor leaguer mentoring a young, headstrong pitcher ticketed for the big leagues. They also compete for the affections of a team groupie, of course named *Annie.*

The film's character of Nuke LaLoosh is loosely based on real-life phenom *Steve Dalkowski*, who entered baseball legend when he pitched to a *recently retired Ted Williams* in a spring training game. Williams said he'd never seen anyone throw harder.

But Dalkowski's control problems and hard-living lifestyle doomed him. He *flamed out* before ever reaching the big leagues...unlike Nuke LaLoosh, who makes it to The Show at the end of *Bull Durham.*

THE STEROID ERA

ONE REASON FOR MONEYBALL'S POPULARITY WAS THAT BASEBALL'S *TV REVENUES AND ATTENDANCE* WERE DOWN. THERE WAS TALK OF *CONTRACTING* THE LEAGUE AND CONCERN THAT THE RECENT EXPANSION HAD *DILUTED* TALENT.

THE *REAL* PROBLEM, OF COURSE, WAS LINGERING *FAN ANGER* OVER THE STRIKE.

WHAT THE GAME NEEDED WAS *A DRAMATIC* STORY, AND FROM 1996 TO 1998 THEY GOT ONE--CENTERED AROUND *MARK "BIG MAC" MCGWIRE*, NEWLY MOVED FROM OAKLAND TO THE ST. LOUIS CARDINALS.

THE HOME-RUN RACES OF THE LATE 1990S *INVIGORATED* A GAME BADLY IN NEED OF A SHOT IN THE ARM.*

*UNFORTUNATELY, THERE HAD BEEN A FEW *TOO MANY* SHOTS IN DIFFERENT PLAYERS' BODIES. BUT NOBODY (EXCEPT THE PLAYERS INVOLVED) KNEW THAT YET.

OVER THE PREVIOUS *THIRTY YEARS,* ONLY *FOUR* PLAYERS HAD RECORDED FIFTY-HOME-RUN SEASONS.

BUT IN 1996, MCGWIRE HIT FIFTY-TWO AND *BRADY ANDERSON* OF THE ORIOLES HIT AN IMPROBABLE FIFTY.

IN 1997, MCGWIRE AND *KEN GRIFFEY JR.* RACED TOWARD SIXTY-ONE. MCGWIRE BEAT GRIFFEY FIFTY-EIGHT TO FIFTY-SIX.

THEN CAME 1998. MCGWIRE AND *SAMMY SOSA* WERE TIED WITH *FIFTY-FIVE HOMERS* EACH AT THE END OF AUGUST.

MCGWIRE HIT SIXTY-ONE AND SIXTY-TWO AGAINST SOSA'S CUBS, *BREAKING MARIS'S RECORD.*

SOSA HIT HIS OWN *#62* A WEEK LATER.

MCGWIRE ENDED THE SEASON WITH SEVENTY TO SOSA'S SIXTY-SIX. BASEBALL HAD NEVER SEEN ANYTHING LIKE IT.

62!

ATTENDANCE NUMBERS CAME BACK UP, AND THE GAME STARTED TO *HEAL THE WOUNDS* FROM THE STRIKE.

Grand Slam Flukes

The *grand slam* might not be the most exciting play in baseball, but it is certainly the most remarkable *single* thing a batter can do. And there are some remarkable quirks in the history of the grand slam.

On April 23, 1999, *Fernando Tatís* became the first player to hit *two grand slams in one inning.* His victim for both was the Los Angeles Dodgers' *Chan Ho Park.*

The first player to hit two grand slams in one season was Brooklyn's *Jimmy Sheckard*, who did it on consecutive days in 1901 against Cincinnati...and *both were inside-the-park* home runs!

The only other pitcher to give up two grand slams in a game is *Tex Shirley* of the St. Louis Browns, who had his memorably bad day against Boston's *Rudy York* in 1946.

The Yankees' Don Mattingly hit a single-season record *six grand slams* in 1987. He had never hit one *before* that season, and never hit one *again.*

IN 2001, THREE YEARS AFTER THE SUMMER OF MAC AND SAMMY, **BARRY BONDS** WOULD BREAK MCGWIRE'S RECORD WITH A **SEVENTY-THREE-HOMER** SEASON.

BONDS WOULD ALSO BREAK HANK AARON'S CAREER RECORD, RETIRING WITH **762 HOME RUNS** AFTER THE 2007 SEASON...

73

THAT SAME YEAR THE **MITCHELL REPORT**, AN INVESTIGATIVE STUDY OF PLAYER DRUG USE, REVEALED FOR THE FIRST TIME JUST HOW PERVASIVE BASEBALL'S **STEROID PROBLEM** WAS.

BONDS, MCGWIRE, SOSA, ROGER CLEMENS, ALEX RODRÍGUEZ, RAFAEL PALMEIRO...MANY OF THE GAME'S BIGGEST STARS HAD THEIR RECORDS AND REPUTATIONS **TARNISHED.**

BASEBALL SAW **FOUR** FIFTY-HOMER SEASONS FROM 1965 TO 1995, AND **TWENTY-FOUR** FROM 1996 TO 2007.

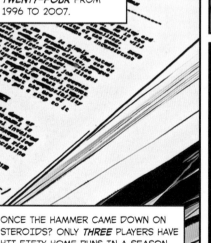

ONCE THE HAMMER CAME DOWN ON STEROIDS? ONLY **THREE** PLAYERS HAVE HIT FIFTY HOME RUNS IN A SEASON SINCE 2007: **JOSÉ BAUTISTA** IN 2010, **CHRIS DAVIS** IN 2013, AND **GIANCARLO STANTON** IN 2017.

DRUGS HAVE **ALWAYS** BEEN PART OF BASEBALL. IN THE 1890S, PITCHER **PUD GALVIN**--BASEBALL'S FIRST THREE-HUNDRED-GAME WINNER--USED AN ELIXIR CONTAINING **MONKEY TESTOSTERONE** AND FLUIDS FROM THE **TESTICLES OF DOGS.**

"**GREENIES,**" OR AMPHETAMINES, WERE IN CONSTANT USE FROM THE 1950S THROUGH THE '70S.

IF THERE WAS A PILL THAT COULD GUARANTEE YOU WOULD WIN TWENTY GAMES BUT WOULD TAKE **FIVE YEARS OFF YOUR LIFE,** PLAYERS WOULD TAKE IT.

SEVERAL PLAYERS WERE JAILED AND/OR SUSPENDED IN A SERIES OF *COCAINE SCANDALS* DURING THE 1980S.

SOMEONE HAS TO SAY *ENOUGH IS ENOUGH* AGAINST DRUGS. BASEBALL'S GOING TO ACCOMPLISH THIS. WE'RE GOING TO *REMOVE DRUGS* AND BE AN EXAMPLE.

AS THE MITCHELL REPORT WOULD DEMONSTRATE, THEN-COMMISSIONER UEBERROTH'S STATEMENT WAS NAIVE.

STEROIDS WERE DIFFERENT.

IT'S WORTH POINTING OUT THAT SOME OF THE GAME'S GREATS PLAYED IN THIS ERA AND ARE *UNFAIRLY TAINTED* BY ASSOCIATION WITH IT.

THEY MADE PLAYERS *STRONGER*, LET THEM TRAIN *HARDER* AND HEAL *FASTER*...IN SHORT, THEY GAVE THE PLAYERS AN *UNFAIR ADVANTAGE* OVER THOSE WHO STAYED CLEAN.

THOMAS 521

THOME 612

GRIFFEY JR. 630

FRANK THOMAS, JIM THOME, AND *KEN GRIFFEY JR.* ALL HIT FIVE HUNDRED OR MORE HOME RUNS PRIMARILY DURING THE STEROID ERA, AND NEVER ATTRACTED THE SLIGHTEST SUSPICION.

RANDY JOHNSON 4,875 K'S

PEDRO MARTÍNEZ 3,154 K'S

THE SAME HOLDS TRUE FOR *MOST* OF THE ERA'S BEST PITCHERS. (THE MOST NOTABLE *EXCEPTION* BEING ROGER CLEMENS.)

GREG MADDUX 355 WINS

AS THE STEROID PROBLEM FORCED ITS WAY INTO BASEBALL'S CONSCIOUSNESS IN THE YEARS BEFORE THE RELEASE OF THE MITCHELL REPORT, FANS COULD TAKE COMFORT IN SOME OF THE GAME'S *TRADITIONS* REASSERTING THEMSELVES.

CHIEF AMONG THESE WAS THE YANKEES' *RETURN TO DOMINANCE.* THEY APPEARED IN SIX OF EIGHT WORLD SERIES FROM 1996 TO 2003, WINNING FOUR.

AS IN PAST TIMES OF CRISIS, BASEBALL GAVE PEOPLE SOMETHING TO *UNIFY AROUND* IN THE AFTERMATH OF THE *SEPTEMBER 11* TERRORIST ATTACKS.

GAMES WERE CANCELED FOR A WEEK AND THEN BASEBALL RESUMED, CONSCIOUS OF ITS *INTEGRAL PART* IN AMERICAN CULTURE.

THE GAME'S CYCLICAL HISTORY THEN RETURNED THE *RED SOX* AND *GIANTS* TO THE TOP OF THE BASEBALL WORLD IN THE FIRST YEARS OF THE TWENTY-FIRST CENTURY, JUST AS THEY HAD BEEN IN THE FIRST YEARS OF THE TWENTIETH.

IF THE FIRST PART OF THE TWENTY-FIRST CENTURY HAS BEEN KNOWN FOR ANYTHING, IT IS THE *ENDINGS* OF SOME OF BASEBALL'S LONGEST-RUNNING *DRAMAS.*

IN 2005, THE WHITE SOX, INSPIRED PERHAPS BY THEIR SCARLET BRETHREN, TOOK HOME THE FIRST WORLD SERIES THE SOUTH SIDE HAD SEEN SINCE *1917.*

AFTER 86 YEARS OF *HEARTBREAK*, THE RED SOX FINALLY WON A WORLD SERIES IN 2004--AGAINST THE CARDINALS, WHO HAD BEAT THEM IN 1946 AND '67.

FITTINGLY FOR SUCH AN INSPIRING MOMENT, THE RED SOX BEGAN IT BY COMING BACK IN THE AMERICAN LEAGUE CHAMPIONSHIP SERIES (ALCS) AFTER BEING DOWN *THREE GAMES TO NONE*...AGAINST THE YANKEES.

THERE HAS NEVER BEEN A GREATER COMEBACK IN BASEBALL HISTORY. THE *CURSE OF THE BAMBINO* WAS FINALLY BROKEN.

CHICAGO'S SERIES DROUGHT WAS TWO YEARS *LONGER* THAN BOSTON'S, THOUGH MUCH LESS *OPERATIC.* SUCH IS THE INFLUENCE OF BABE RUTH EVEN DECADES AFTER HIS DEATH.

The Only Woman In The Hall Of Fame

Effa Manley got involved in baseball after her marriage to *Newark Eagles* owner Abe Manley, and quickly took over the marketing and day-to-day operations of the team. She improved conditions for her players, which spurred other Negro League teams to make changes as well. Manley was also a *civil rights pioneer*, leading boycotts of New York businesses that refused to employ blacks and funding construction of the Booker T. Washington Community Hospital for training black doctors and nurses.

When the major leagues were *integrated*-- the year after the Newark Eagles won the Negro League World Series--Manley argued that Negro League teams should be entitled to *compensation for lost players*. For her, those players included Larry Doby, Don Newcombe, and Monte Irvin, all of whom are in the Hall of Fame.

Elected to the Hall of Fame herself in 2006, twenty-five years after her death, Manley remains the *only woman* in the Hall.

SINCE THE *UPHEAVALS* OF THE STEROID ERA, BASEBALL SEEMS TO HAVE FOUND ITS *EQUILIBRIUM* AGAIN. IT'S A LITTLE MORE MATHEMATICAL THAN IT USED TO BE, A LITTLE MORE CAUTIOUS.

BUT BASEBALL IS ALWAYS MAKING ROOM FOR *NEW IMMORTALS.*

ICHIRO SUZUKI SET A SINGLE-SEASON RECORD FOR HITS IN 2004, WITH 262, AND REACHED 3,000 HITS IN 2016. *MORE JAPANESE PLAYERS* WERE ENTERING THE GAME, ALONG WITH A TRICKLE OF *KOREANS.*

YANKEES RELIEVER *MARIANO RIVERA* SET THE CAREER-SAVES RECORD WITH 652.

HIS FELLOW YANKEE *DEREK JETER* RETIRED IN 2014 WITH 3,465 HITS, SIXTH-MOST OF ALL TIME.

IN 2012, *MIGUEL CABRERA,* ONE OF THE BEST RIGHT-HANDED HITTERS THE GAME HAS SEEN, WON THE FIRST *TRIPLE CROWN* BASEBALL HAD SEEN SINCE 1967.*

*ACCORDING TO THE SABERMETRICIANS, IT WASN'T EVEN THE BEST SEASON OF HIS CAREER.

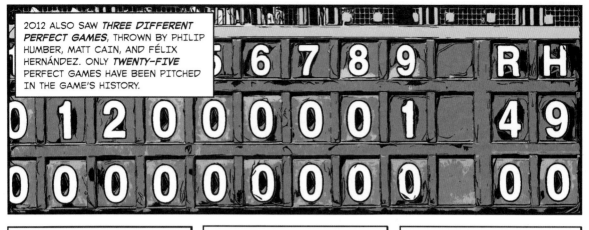

2012 ALSO SAW *THREE DIFFERENT PERFECT GAMES*, THROWN BY PHILIP HUMBER, MATT CAIN, AND FÉLIX HERNÁNDEZ. ONLY *TWENTY-FIVE* PERFECT GAMES HAVE BEEN PITCHED IN THE GAME'S HISTORY.

IN 2017, *ALBERT PUJOLS* BECAME THE NINTH MEMBER OF THE *600 HOME-RUN CLUB*.

GREG MADDUX AND *ROGER CLEMENS* RETIRED WITH *355* AND *354* WINS RESPECTIVELY.

BOSTON'S *DAVID ORTIZ* RETIRED IN 2016 WITH *541* HOME RUNS, STARTING A CONVERSATION ABOUT WHETHER *DESIGNATED HITTERS* BELONG IN THE HALL OF FAME.

NEW STADIUM CONSTRUCTION CONTINUED AS CROWDS GREW ONCE AGAIN. ONLY THREE OF BASEBALL'S CURRENT THIRTY-TWO TEAMS STILL PLAY IN MULTIPURPOSE STADIUMS.

AND ONLY TWO OF BASEBALL'S OLD *JEWEL BOX PARKS* STILL EXIST. ONE OF THEM IS FENWAY PARK, AND THE OTHER...

...WRIGLEY FIELD.

IN BASEBALL, *NO RECORD IS FOREVER* (EXCEPT MAYBE 511).

NO STREAK IS FOREVER (EXCEPT MAYBE 56).

AND *NO DROUGHT IS FOREVER*. IN 2016, AFTER 108 YEARS, *THE CHICAGO CUBS WON THE WORLD SERIES.*

IT WAS A SEVEN-GAME *THRILLER,* WITH THE CUBS COMING BACK FROM A 3-1 DEFICIT AND TAKING GAME 7 IN EXTRA INNINGS.

THEIR OPPONENT? THE TEAM WITH THE *SECOND-LONGEST DROUGHT,* THE CLEVELAND INDIANS.

MORE THAN *170 YEARS* AFTER ALEXANDER CARTWRIGHT WROTE DOWN THE KNICKER-BOCKER RULES, IT MAY SEEM LIKE THE LAST OF BASEBALL'S *SIGNATURE STORYLINES* HAS FINALLY WRAPPED UP.

BUT LIKE A LOSING TEAM'S FANS ALWAYS SAY: *WAIT 'TIL NEXT YEAR.* THE GAME ALWAYS HAS SURPRISES IN STORE.

UMPIRES

2ND

Glossary

ACE: The best starting pitcher on a team.

BALL: A pitch thrown outside the *strike zone*. (See "strike zone.")

BARNSTORMING: The practice of teams touring small towns to play against either local teams or other barnstorming squads. Some teams barnstormed full-time, while others were put together for specific tours.

BASE HIT: A batted ball that can't be fielded before the batter *reaches base* safely. Typically a single.

BASERUNNER: A player on base trying to make it around to score a run.

BATTING AVERAGE: The percentage of time a player gets a base hit. Calculated by dividing the number of hits by the number of plate appearances.

BOX SCORE: A concise listing of the events in a baseball game.

BRUSHBACK: A pitch deliberately thrown close to the batter, to keep him from getting too close to home plate.

BULLPEN: The area reserved for relief pitchers. Also a collective term for a team's relief pitching.

BUNT: A batting tactic in which the batter holds the bat horizontally in both hands and lets the ball hit it instead of swinging. Results in the ball going only a few feet.

CHANGEUP: A pitch thrown with the same arm motion as a fastball, but that travels much more slowly and disrupts a batter's timing.

CLOSER: Pitcher brought in to pitch the last few outs of a game. Closers typically have one dominant pitch but can't pitch more than two innings. Usually they are kept to one.

CURVEBALL: A ball thrown with spin that causes it to *curve* sharply downward at an angle as it approaches the plate.

CUTTER: A ball thrown so it moves sharply to the side as it approaches the plate.

DEAD BALL ERA: The years from 1901 to approximately 1920, when few home runs were hit due to the different composition of the baseball. Players also did not try to hit home runs, believing that defense and baserunning were key to winning games.

DESIGNATED HITTER: A player who *does not play in the field* but only hits, almost always in place of the pitcher. Only used in the American League.

DOUBLE: A hit that lets the runner advance as far as second base. A *ground-rule double* is a ball that bounces over the outfield fence (or, rarely, hits another obstruction in the stadium), causing the hitter to be awarded second base.

DOUBLE PLAY: A single play in which *two outs* are recorded.

DOUBLE SWITCH: A two-player substitution of a *pitcher and a position player*, done to delay the pitcher's next at-bat.

EARNED RUN AVERAGE (ERA): A pitching statistic computed by averaging how many earned runs a pitcher gives up in each nine innings of work. An *earned run* is scored as a result of hits, walks, and/or sacrifices; an *unearned run* is scored if the baserunner crosses the plate as a result of an error. (*See* "inning.")

EXTRA BASE HIT: Any hit other than a single: a double, triple, or home run. (*See* "base hit," "double," "triple," "home run.")

ERROR: A player is charged with an error when the official scorer judges he has failed to make a play he should have made—either fielding, throwing, or missing a catch. (*See* "official scorer.")

FASTBALL: A ball thrown at high velocity, designed to be too fast for the batter to hit rather than to deceive the hitter by curving.

FIELDER'S CHOICE: A scorer's decision made when an infielder has a choice of two different plays to make.

FOUL BALL: A batted ball that hits the ground in foul territory before a fielder can catch it.

GRAND SLAM: A home run hit with runners already on all three bases. (This is known as having the *bases loaded*.)

GROUND BALL: A ball hit so it bounces on the ground instead of being driven through the air.

HIT: A play in which the batter puts the ball in play and makes it to a base before the fielders can throw him out.

HOME RUN: A ball hit over the outfield fence, allowing the batter to circle the bases and score a run. Also called four-bagger, homer, tater, dinger, big fly. An *inside-the-park home run* occurs when the batter is able to circle the bases and score before the outfielders can retrieve the ball and throw it to home plate.

INFIELD FLY RULE: A rule that prevents an infielder from *deliberately* dropping a pop fly (see "popup") with runners on base to set up a double or triple play.

INNING: One full inning is completed when each team has come to bat and recorded three outs. The visiting team bats first, in the *top* of the inning; the home team bats last, in the *bottom*.

INTERFERENCE: A play in which one player's actions prevent another player from hitting, running, or fielding. Can result in the umpire awarding extra bases or calling a batter or runner out.

JOURNEYMAN: A player who carves out a major league career without ever becoming a star.

KNUCKLEBALL: A pitch gripped with the knuckles instead of the fingertips. When thrown, the ball approaches the plate with almost *no spin*, causing it to move erratically.

LINE DRIVE: A ball hit hard at a low angle.

MANAGER: The coach of a team, responsible for in-game strategy. Baseball managers, unlike those in other sports, wear team uniforms.

MIDDLE RELIEVER: A pitcher brought in when the starting pitcher struggles, to keep the game close until the closer can be called in from the bullpen. (*See* "bullpen.")

NO-DECISION: When a pitcher does not get a win or a loss, his outing is said to be a no-decision.

NO-HITTER: A game in which a pitcher does not give up a hit. Baserunners may reach base on walks or errors without costing the pitcher a no-hitter. (*See* "perfect game.")

OFFICIAL SCORER: The observer given the responsibility of keeping game statistics and deciding whether a particular play should be judged a hit or an error.

PASSED BALL: A pitch that gets away from the catcher, judged by the official scorer to be the *catcher's* fault. (*See* "official scorer.")

PERFECT GAME: A game in which a pitcher faces only *twenty-seven batters* and gets them all out without letting any of them reach base.

PEPPER: A pregame exercise in which a batter hits sharp ground balls to a group of fielders. One of them fields and quickly throws the ball to the batter, who has to hit it again.

PICKOFF: A play in which the pitcher throws to a base and tries to catch the runner off the base so he can be *tagged out*.

PINCH HITTER: A player substituted in to *hit* for another player. In the National League, often done in the pitcher's spot in the batting order.

PINCH RUNNER: A player substituted in after another player has gotten a hit, usually because he is faster and the team is in need of a run.

PITCH COUNT: The number of pitches a pitcher has thrown in a game. Managers now typically remove a pitcher when he gets to a certain number no matter how well he is doing, decreasing the number of games pitchers can win.

PLATOON: An arrangement in which two players *share a position* depending on the opposing team's pitcher.

POPUP: A ball hit nearly straight up and caught by an infielder. A *pop fly* is a pop up that reaches the outfield.

RECORD: The number of wins and losses for a team or a pitcher. A team that has won and lost the same number of games is said to have a .500 record.

RELIEF PITCHER: A pitcher who does not start the game. Also known as a *reliever*.

RUNS BATTED IN (RBI): A player is credited with an RBI when a run scores as a result of what he did at the plate. (The exception is hitting into a double play.)

RUNDOWN: A situation in which a baserunner is *caught between two bases* and infielders throw the ball back and forth as they close in on him.

SABERMETRICS: Advanced statistics that attempt to give a more accurate picture of a player's value than that provided by old-fashioned statistics.

SACRIFICE: A batted ball that results in the *runner* being out but *baserunners* advancing or scoring.

SAVE: A statistic kept to measure the effectiveness of a relief pitcher in preserving his team's lead.

SCREWBALL: A pitch that *curves in the opposite direction* from the traditional curveball or slider. (See "curveball" and "slider.")

SINGLE: See "base hit."

SINKER: A pitch that drops as it approaches the plate.

SITUATIONAL RELIEVER: A relief pitcher generally used only in specific situations in a game, most often to get a specific left-handed hitter out. (See "relief pitcher.")

SLIDER: A pitch that breaks sideways (slides) as it approaches the plate.

SETUP MAN: A pitcher brought in to get a few outs and preserve a lead before a team brings in its closer.

SPITBALL: A ball *doctored* with saliva or some other substance to make its motion unpredictable or to sharpen its curve. Also known as a *spitter*.

SPLIT-FINGER FASTBALL: A fastball thrown with the index and middle fingers forked around the ball. If thrown properly, it *drops sharply* as it approaches the batter.

SQUEEZE PLAY: The execution of a bunt as a runner takes off from third, trying to score before the ball can be fielded and thrown home. (See "bunt.")

STOLEN BASE: When a baserunner runs from one base to the next *without* the batter putting the ball in play. (See "baserunner.")

STRIKE: A pitch that passes through the strike zone is a strike whether the batter swings or not. If the batter swings and misses a pitch, it is recorded as a strike whether it passed through the strike zone or not.

STRIKE ZONE: The area defined laterally by the edges of home plate and vertically by the batter's knees and the letters on his jersey.

STRIKEOUT: When a hitter, by some combination of swings, foul balls, and/or called strikes, reaches three strikes. Traditionally represented by a K in scorecards.

TAG: When a fielder touches a baserunner with the ball, or with the glove holding the ball. (*See* "baserunner.")

TAGGING UP: When a ball is hit in the air, a baserunner must *tag up*, meaning he must wait on the base until the ball is caught before trying to advance. (*See* "baserunner.")

TRIPLE: A three-base hit.

TRIPLE PLAY: A single play in which *three outs* are recorded. The rarest play in baseball.

UMPIRE: One of the officials responsible for calling balls and strikes, determining whether batted balls are fair or foul, and determining whether runners are safe or out.

UTILITY MAN: A player who can play a number of different positions.

VALUE OVER REPLACEMENT PLAYER (VORP): A sabermetric assessment of a player's value *relative to the average* (replacement) player.

WALK: Also known as a *base on balls*. The result of a pitcher throwing four balls is the batter being awarded first base. (*See* "ball.")

WALKOFF: A hit or sacrifice that drives in the *winning run* in the bottom of the ninth or later inning. (*See* "inning.")

WHIP: A newer method for calculating a pitcher's success, measured by *adding* walks plus hits and *dividing* the sum by the number of innings pitched.

WINS ABOVE REPLACEMENT (WAR): A method of calculating how many *wins* a player is worth compared to the *average* (replacement) player.

WILD PITCH: A pitch that gets past the catcher, judged by the official scorer to be the *pitcher's responsibility*. (*See* "official scorer.")

Index

A

Aaron, Henry "Hank," 91, 102, 110, 126, 129, 134, 145, 154
Adams, Charles Benjamin "Babe," 26
African American players, 7, 15, 30, 34, 42, 45, 48, 54–55, 64–65, 68, 83, 84–85, 87–95, 100, 110, 112, 119–20, 130–31, 147, 150
Alderson, Sandy, 150
Alexander, Grover Cleveland, 36, 41, 43, 57, 67
All-American Girls Professional Baseball League (AAGPBL), 82, 105
Allen, Lee, 21
All-Star Game, 66, 131, 135, 150
Almeida, Rafael, 113
American Association, 10, 12, 15, 18
American League, 15, 18–20
American Tobacco Company, 28
Anderson, Brady, 152
Anderson, Sparky, 145
Angell, Roger, 59
Anson, Adrian Constantine "Cap," 14, 15, 28
Ashford, Emmett, 151
Atlanta Braves, 11, 16, 126
Avila, Bobby, 112

B

Bagby, Jim, Sr., 51
Baker, Frank "Home Run," 29
Ball, Neal, 26
Ball Four, 129
balls, 51, 52, 80
Baltimore Orioles, 18, 19, 63, 102, 122, 126, 130, 138

Banks, Ernie, 35, 91, 127
Barrow, Ed, 53
baseball
    myths of, 1
    origin of, 1–5, 21–23, 41
    standardization of rules for, 3–5, 17
    unique nature of, 1
baseball cards, 28, 130
batting averages, 27, 73, 77, 117
Bautista, José, 154
Beane, Billy, 150
Bell, James Thomas "Cool Papa," 55
Bellán, Esteban, 113
Belle, Albert, 140
Bench, Johnny, 134
Bender, "Chief," 33, 34, 37, 67
Berg, Morris J., 81
Berra, Lawrence Peter "Yogi," 96, 109, 118
Birmingham Black Barons, 121
Black Sox scandal, 46–50, 53, 70
Blackwell, Ewell, 84
Blues Park, 147
Bonds, Barry, 154
Bonner, James, 45, 68
Boston Americans, 18, 19, 21
Boston Beaneaters, 16
Boston Braves, 11, 16, 33, 36, 37, 41, 92
Boston Red Sox, 1, 19, 33, 35, 36, 37, 38, 42, 50, 51, 52, 53, 81, 86, 87, 112, 123, 135, 153, 156, 157
Boston Red Stockings, 10, 11
Boudreau, Lou, 92
Bouton, Jim, 129
Brett, George, 27, 77, 145
Briggs, William, 64

Brock, Lou, 119, 149
Brooklyn Dodgers, 11, 45, 51, 65, 68, 74, 76, 83, 85, 86, 88–90, 93, 96, 100, 106, 110
Brooklyn Excelsiors, 7
Brooklyn Grays, 11
Brooklyn Stars, 7
Brown, Mordecai "Three Finger," 24, 34, 35, 67
Brown, Willard, 84
Brush, John, 21
Bull Durham, 99, 151
Bush, Leslie Ambrose "Bullet Joe," 38

C

Cabrera, Miguel, 158
Cain, Matt, 159
Caldwell, Ray, 44
California Angels, 118, 121, 132
Camden Yards, 146, 148
Campanella, Roy, 96, 110
Canseco, José, 145
Carew, Rod, 77
Carlton, Steve, 132, 144
Cartwright, Alexander, 3, 4, 102
Cash, Norm, 116
Castro, Fidel, 112
Catto, Octavius V., 7
Chadwick, Henry, 7, 22, 23, 59
Chance, Frank Leroy, 24
Chapman, Ben, 88
Chapman, Ray, 50
Charleston, Oscar, 55
Chesbro, Jack, 27
Chicago American Giants, 30, 54
Chicago Cubs, 1, 11, 24–25, 35, 50, 66, 70–71, 82, 84, 91, 98, 109, 126, 127, 160

Chicago Giants, 54
Chicago Whales, 35
Chicago White Sox (White Stockings), 10, 11, 12, 15, 19, 25, 30, 32, 41, 46–50, 93, 138–39, 157
Cicotte, Eddie, 46
Cincinnati Reds (Red Stockings), 8, 9, 10, 11, 29, 46, 56, 74, 78, 113, 128, 134, 135, 137
Clark, Stephen Carlton, 72
Clarke, Fred, 26
Clemens, Roger, 145, 154, 155, 159
Clemente, Roberto, 105, 130
Cleveland, Grover, 71
Cleveland Bluebirds, 19
Cleveland Broncos, 19
Cleveland Indians, 19, 37, 39, 51, 90, 91, 92, 93, 95, 104, 112, 160
Cleveland Naps, 19, 26, 33, 37
Cleveland Spiders, 37
Cobb, Ty, 25, 26, 36, 39, 42, 49, 56, 57, 61, 71, 73, 87, 116, 119, 140, 144, 149
Cochrane, Mickey, 45, 62, 68
Collins, Eddie, Jr., 41
Comiskey, Charles, 46
Comiskey Park, 30, 138
Cooperstown, New York, 1, 3, 15, 23, 36, 41, 72
Coover, Robert, 143
Cortesio, Ria, 151
Cox, Bill, 83
Crane, Sam, 41
Crawford, Sam, 39
Crosby, Bing, 98
Cuban Giants, 30
Cuban Stars, 54, 113
Cummings, William Arthur "Candy," 7
Curtiss Candy Company, 71
curveball, invention of, 7

D
Dalkowski, Steve, 151
Daniels, Daniel M., 74
Davis, Chris, 154
Day, Leon, 64, 84
Dayton Marcos, 54
Dead Ball Era, 26, 27, 37, 50, 51, 117
Dean, Jay Hanna "Dizzy," 64, 66, 67
Dean, Paul, 66
Detroit Stars, 54
Detroit Tigers, 19, 25, 26, 39, 61, 64, 66, 84, 91, 123, 124, 137, 145, 146
Dihigo, Martín, 112, 113
DiMaggio, Joe, 64, 77, 96, 101, 106, 115, 140
"Disco Demolition" riot, 138–39
Doak, Bill, 13
Doby, Larry, 90, 91, 92, 93, 104, 157
Doolittle, Jimmy, 81
Doubleday, Abner, 1–2, 6, 23, 36, 41, 102
Doubleday Field, 41
double plays, 24
Dreyfuss, Bernhard "Barney," 28
Drysdale, Don, 119
Duffy, Hugh, 16, 87, 117
Durocher, Leo, 48, 66, 88, 104, 127, 133

E
Eastern Colored League, 54
Ellis, Dock, 131
Ellsbury, Jacoby, 37
Evers, John (Johnny) Joseph, 24

F
fantasy baseball, 142
fantasy camps, 143
Federal League, 33, 34–35, 48
Feliciano, José, 125
Feller, Bob, 92, 108
Fenway Park, 32, 148, 159
Fidrych, Mark, 137

Fisk, Carlton, 135
Flood, Curt, 13, 128, 132, 141
Forbes Field, 26, 27, 65
Ford, Whitey, 108, 135
Fort Wayne Daisies, 105
Fosse, Ray, 135
Foster, George, 137
Foster, Rube, 29, 30, 42, 54, 55
Fowler, Bud, 15
Foxx, Jimmie, 62, 69, 97
Frazee, Harry, 52
free agency, 13, 128, 133, 144, 146
Frick, Ford, 83, 90, 116
Frisch, Frankie, 66
Fullerton, Hugh, 47

G
Gaffney, James, 35
Galvin, Pud, 117
Garciaparra, Nomar, 77
Gehrig, Lou, 45, 56, 58, 68, 69, 75, 76
Gera, Bernice, 151
Gibson, Bob, 39, 119, 123, 124, 133
Gibson, Josh, 64, 87
Glenn, John, 87
gloves, 12, 13
Goldsmith, Fred, 7
González, Miguel Angel, 112
Gould, Chester, 37
Gowdy, Hank, 41
grand slams, 44, 51, 153
Graves, Abner, 23
Gray, Pete, 84
Green, Pumpsie, 112
Greenberg, Hank, 66, 84, 91, 128
Greenlee, Gus, 64, 65
Greenlee Field, 65
Griffey, Ken, Jr., 152, 155
Griffiths Stadium, 103
Grizzard, Lewis, 134
Gromek, Steve, 92
Grove, Lefty, 45, 62, 68
Gwynn, Tony, Sr., 27, 77, 147

H

Habana Baseball Club, 113
Hartford Dark Blues, 10
Harwell, Ernie, 125
Heilmann, Harry, 41
Heisenberg, Werner, 81
Helton, Todd, 77
Henderson, Rickey, 144, 149
Hernández, Félix, 159
Hicks, Nat, 7
Hillerich & Bradsby, 17
Hogsett, Elon Chester "Chief," 37
home runs, 38, 53, 58, 62, 70, 93, 103,
    116–17, 129, 134, 152–54
Homestead Grays, 55, 64, 65
Hoover, Herbert, 63
Hornsby, Rogers, 16, 49, 57, 73,
    87, 116
Horton, Willie, 123
House of David barnstorming team,
    24, 57, 67, 79
Houston, Whitney, 125
Houston Colt .45s, 118
Hoyt, Waite, 58
Huggins, Miller, 53
Hulbert, William, 10, 12
Humber, Philip, 159
Hunter, Catfish, 133
Hunter, Herb, 45, 68

I

Indianapolis ABCs, 54
Indianapolis Clowns, 105, 120
International League, 15
Irvin, Monte, 96, 157

J

Jackson, Joseph "Shoeless Joe,"
    42, 49, 53, 61
Jackson, Reggie, 131, 136
James, Bill, 143
Japanese baseball, 45, 68–69, 85,
    129, 148, 158
Jeter, Derek, 158
Jewish players, 91
John, Tommy, 133
Johnson, Byron Bancroft "Ban," 18

Johnson, Davey, 142
Johnson, Mamie "Peanut," 105
Johnson, Randy, 155
Johnson, Walter, 27, 34, 36, 38–39, 56,
    92, 119, 133, 144
Johnson, William Julius "Judy," 55
Judge, Joe, 58

K

Kalamazoo Lassies, 105
Kaline, Al, 124, 145
Kansas City Athletics, 19, 102,
    120, 126
Kansas City Monarchs, 54, 55, 79,
    83, 120, 127, 147
Kansas City Royals, 126, 144
Keeler, Wee Willie, 77
Kelly, Gene, 33
Kelly, Michael Joseph "King," 13
Kerouac, Jack, 142
Kiner, Ralph, 98
Klem, Bill, 31
Knickerbocker Base Ball Club, 3
Koufax, Sandy, 21, 118, 119
Kuhn, Bowie, 128, 132

L

Lady Gaga, 125
Lajoie, Nap, 27, 28, 37
Landis, Kenesaw Mountain, 35, 48,
    56, 83
Lardner, Ring, 59
Latin players, 112–13, 120, 150–51
Leonard, Buck, 64
Leonard, Hubert "Dutch," 33
Lloyd, John Henry "Pop," 55
Lolich, Mickey, 124
López, Al, 31
Los Angeles Dodgers, 11, 114–15, 119,
    122, 136, 148, 153
Los Angeles Nippons, 68
Louisville Clippers, 121
Louisville Grays, 10
Louisville Slugger, 17, 28
Luque, Adolfo, 112

M

Mack, Connie, 33, 38, 62, 69, 97, 132
Maddux, Greg, 155, 159
Maglie, Sal "The Barber," 96
Major League Baseball Players
    Association, 125
Malamud, Bernard, 99
Manley, Effa, 157
Mantle, Mickey, 96, 101, 103, 106–8,
    116, 118, 129, 130, 143
Maris, Roger, 116, 117, 153
Marquard, Rube, 29
Marsans, Armando, 113
Martin, Billy, 108, 136
Martin, Jonny Leonard Roosevelt
    "Pepper," 37
Mathews, Eddie, 102
Mathewson, Christy, 29, 30, 42,
    57, 118
Mattingly, Don, 153
Mays, Carl, 50
Mays, Willie, 61, 62, 91, 93, 96, 100,
    104, 106–7, 132, 145
Mazeroski, Bill, 130
McGraw, John, 30, 63, 97, 133
McGwire, Mark, 152–53, 154
McLain, Denny, 124
McLish, Cal, 37
Memphis Red Sox, 121
Méndez, José, 120
Meusel, Bob, 58
Miller, Marvin, 125, 128, 141
Mills, Abraham G., 10, 12, 22
Milwaukee Braves, 11, 102, 110, 126
Milwaukee Brewers, 19, 144
Minnesota Twins, 118, 126
Miñoso, Minnie, 112
Missoula Timberjacks, 121
Mitchell Report, 154–55
Monroe, Marilyn, 77
Montreal Expos, 126, 147
Montreal Royals, 85, 86, 88
Morgan, Connie, 105
Morgan, Joe, 134
Mulcahy, Hugh, 76
Munson, Thurman, 136
Murakami, Mansanori, 148

Murray, Eddie, 145
Murray, John Joseph "Red," 33
Musial, Stan, 77, 82, 119, 145

N

Nagashima, Shigeo, 129
Nahem, Sam, 84
National Anthem, 42, 125
National Baseball Hall of Fame, 3, 15, 23, 29, 36, 41, 72, 74, 87, 113, 130, 157
National League, 10–12, 15, 16, 18
Native Americans, 37
Navin, Frank, 66
Negro Leagues, 30, 42, 48, 54–55, 64–65, 87, 91, 100, 120, 157
Negro Leagues Baseball Museum, 147
Newark Eagles, 157
Newark Little Stars, 15
Newcombe, Don, 157
New York Giants, 11, 20, 21, 29, 30, 32, 33, 41, 63, 93, 96, 100, 104, 106, 110
New York Gothams, 11
New York Highlanders, 18, 19
New York Mets, 56, 98, 101, 109, 111, 118, 120, 121, 126, 128, 133
New York Mutuals, 10
New York Yankees, 18, 19, 36, 37, 40, 51, 52–53, 56, 58–60, 62, 63, 70–71, 74, 75, 76, 82, 90, 96, 100, 101, 102, 105, 106, 108, 110, 115, 118, 119, 136, 153, 156, 157, 158
night games, 78–79
Nihon Undo Kyokai, 45, 68
Nomo, Hideo, 148
Northwestern League, 10, 12

O

Oakland A's (Athletics), 19, 126, 132, 150
Oh, Sadaharu, 129
O'Laughlin, Francis H. "Silk," 31, 43
O'Neil, Buck, 147

Ortiz, David, 159
Ott, Mel, 93, 133
Owens, Clarence Bernard "Brick," 40

P

Paige, Leroy "Satchel," 64, 67, 87, 92, 94–95, 120, 130
Palmeiro, Rafael, 145, 154
Park, Chan Ho, 153
Patterson, Red, 103
Patton, George, 84
Pérez, Tony, 134
perfect games, 20, 40, 159
Perry, Gaylord, 144, 145
Pesky, Johnny, 86
Philadelphia Athletics, 10, 19, 21, 26, 29, 36, 38, 62–63, 66, 83, 97, 102
Philadelphia Cuban X-Giants, 30
Philadelphia Olympics, 7
Philadelphia Phillies, 11, 36, 48, 76, 88, 128, 132, 144
Philadelphia Pythians, 7
Philadelphia Quakers, 11
Phinney, Elihu, 1–2, 41
Pipp, Wally, 56
Pittsburgh Alleghenys, 11
Pittsburgh Crawfords, 55, 64, 65
Pittsburgh Pirates, 11, 26, 27, 59, 74, 91, 98, 105, 130, 131, 138
Plank, Eddie, 33, 34
Polo Grounds, 20, 53, 93, 120
Posey, Cumberland, 65
Postema, Pam, 151
Powers, John, 34
Pride, Charley, 121
Pujols, Albert, 159

R

racism, 15, 37, 48, 61, 88–90, 92, 122–23, 130, 134
Rath, Morrie, 46
Red Circles, 84
Reese, Pee Wee, 88, 96, 111
Reitz, Henry Peter "Heinie," 27
reserve clause, 12, 13, 34, 35, 125
Reynolds, Allie, 37

Rice, Grantland, 59
Richard, Rocket, 86
Richardson, Hardy, 41
Rickey, Branch, 83, 85, 88, 90, 95, 98
Ripken, Cal, Jr., 145, 146
Rivera, Mariano, 158
Rizzuto, Phil, 96
Robinson, Brooks, 122
Robinson, Frank, 122, 133
Robinson, Jackie, 45, 68, 83, 85, 86, 88–90, 91, 93, 95, 96, 109, 110, 120, 128, 132, 133
Rodríguez, Alex, 140, 145, 154
Roosevelt, Franklin Delano, 78
Rose, Pete, 77, 119, 134, 135, 144, 145
Rosen, Al, 104
Rothstein, Arnold, 46, 47
Roush, Edd, 34
Ruppert, Jacob, Jr., 52
Ruth, Babe, 1, 28, 33, 36, 40, 42, 44, 48, 51, 52–53, 55, 56, 58, 61, 62, 63, 64, 66, 69–71, 75, 93, 98, 103, 116, 117, 134, 135, 136
Ryan, Nolan, 126, 132, 140, 144, 149

S

sabermetrics, 143, 150
salaries, 140, 141
San Diego Padres, 126, 144, 145
San Francisco Giants, 11, 114–15, 156
Sarandon, Susan, 99
Sawamura, Eiji, 69
Schaefer, William Herman "Germany," 33
Schang, Walter Henry "Wally," 38
Schmidt, Charles "Boss," 25
Schroeder, Dottie, 82
screwball, 29, 30
Seattle Mariners, 24
Seattle Pilots, 126, 129
Seaver, Tom, 126
Sharman, Bill, 65
Shea Stadium, 120

Sheckard, Jimmy, 153
Shibe, Ben, 97
Shirley, Tex, 153
Shore, Ernie, 40, 41
Sianis, Billy, 25, 84
Simmons, Al, 62
Sinatra, Frank, 33
Sisler, George, 42
Slaughter, Enos, 86
Smith, Elmer, 51
Smith, Ozzie, 146
Snider, Duke, 96, 106, 110
Sockalexis, Louis, 19, 37
softball, 17, 105
Sosa, Sammy, 153, 154
Southern Negro League, 54
Spahn, Warren, 110–11, 117
Spalding, Albert G., 10, 12, 13, 22, 32, 36
Spalding Sporting Goods, 12, 52
spitball, 50, 145
Stanky, Eddie, 88, 96
Stanton, Giancarlo, 154
Stargell, Willie "Pops," 138
Stearnesa, Turkey, 64
Steinhagen, Ruth Ann, 98–99
Stengel, Charles Dillon "Casey," 101, 111, 120
steroids, 117, 145, 154–56
Stevens, John Paul, 71
St. Louis Brown Stockings, 10, 11
St. Louis Browns, 19, 35, 82, 84, 90, 93, 102, 153
St. Louis Cardinals, 11, 56, 66, 82, 86, 90, 91, 119, 123, 124, 128, 133, 152, 157
St. Louis Giants, 54
St. Louis Perfectos, 11
St. Louis Terriers, 34
stolen bases, 33, 144, 149
Stone, Toni, 105
Stoneham, Horace, 114
Stump, Al, 61
Sullivan, Joseph J. "Sport," 46
Suzuki, Ichiro, 27, 77, 158
Syracuse Stars, 15

T
Take Me Out to the Ball Game, 33
Tatís, Fernando, 153
Terry, Bill, 77, 87
Texas Rangers, 121, 132, 150
Thomas, Frank, 155
Thome, Jim, 155
Thompson, Hank, 90
Thorpe, Jim, 37
Tinker, Joseph (Joe) Bert, 24
Tokyo Kyojin, 69
Toledo Blue Stockings, 15
Topps, 130
Trammell, Alan, 146
Traynor, Pie, 59
triple play, unassisted, 26, 51

U
umpires, 4, 18, 31, 43, 151
The Universal Baseball Association, Inc., 143
Updike, John, 59, 87

V
Veeck, Bill, 48, 83, 92, 93

W
Waddell, George Edward "Rube," 20, 21, 30
Wagner, Honus, 20, 26, 28, 55, 63
Waitkus, Eddie, 98
Walker, Dixie, 88
Walker, Harry "The Hat," 84, 86
Walker, Larry, 77
Walker, Moses Fleetwood, 15
Wambsganss, Bill, 51
Waner, Lloyd "Little Poison," 59
Waner, Paul "Big Poison," 59
Ward, Arch, 66
Warhop, Jack, 36
Washington, George, 39
Washington Nationals, 97, 147
Washington Senators, 33, 34, 39, 40, 56, 58, 87, 118, 132

Weeghman, Charles, 35
Weeghman Field, 35
Wheat, Zack, 37
Whitaker, Lou, 146
White, George Frederick "Deke," 41
Whitman, Walt, 5
Wilkinson, J. L., 120
Williams, Claude Preston "Lefty," 47
Williams, Ted, 27, 77, 87, 117, 151
Wills, Maury, 118, 149
Wilson, John Owen "Chief," 27
Wilson, Woodrow, 40
Winfield, Dave, 145
women, 7, 16, 17, 82, 105, 151, 157
Wood, Howard Ellsworth "Smokey Joe," 16
Woolf, Virginia, 59, 64
World Series, creation of, 18
Wrigley, Philip K., 82
Wrigley, William, Jr., 35
Wrigley Field, 32, 35, 70, 71, 79, 84, 93, 148, 160
Wynn, Early, 119

Y
Yankee Stadium, 53, 71
Yastrzemski, Carl, 123, 145
Yellow Horse, Moses J., 37
Yomiuri Giants, 129
York, Rudy, 37, 153
Young, Cy, 16, 18, 20, 27, 39, 56, 77

Z
Zaharias, Babe Didrikson, 67

Check out alexirvine.blogspot.com/baseball for detailed chapter notes, additional material, news, recommendations for further reading, and more.

Published in the United States by Ten Speed Press, an imprint of the
Crown Publishing Group, a division of Penguin Random House LLC, New York.
www.crownpublishing.com
www.tenspeed.com

Ten Speed Press and the Ten Speed Press colophon are registered trademarks
of Penguin Random House LLC.

Library of Congress Cataloging-in-Publication Data
Names: Irvine, Alexander (Alexander C.), author. | Coker, Tomm, author. |
    Smith, C.P., illustrator.
Title: The comic book story of baseball : the heroes, hustlers, and
    history-making swings (and misses) of America's national pastime /
    Alex Irvine ; art by Tomm Coker and C.P. Smith.
Description: First edition. | New York : Ten Speed Press, 2018. | Includes
    bibliographical references and index.
Identifiers: LCCN 2017009796 (print) | LCCN 2017039323 (ebook)
Subjects: LCSH: Baseball—United States—History—Comic books, strips, etc. |
    Graphic novels. | BISAC: COMICS & GRAPHIC NOVELS / Manga / Sports.
    | COMICS & GRAPHIC NOVELS / Nonfiction. | SPORTS & RECREATION /
    Baseball /History.
Classification: LCC GV867.4 (ebook) | LCC GV867.4 .I78 2018 (print) |
    DDC 796.357022/2—dc23
LC record available at https://lccn.loc.gov/2017009796

Trade Paperback ISBN: 978-0-399-57894-6
eBook ISBN: 978-0-399-57895-3

Printed in China

Design by Chloe Rawlins

10 9 8 7 6 5 4 3 2 1

First Edition